SEDUCTIVE SPIRITS

SP SPIRITUAL PHENOMENA

TANYA LUHRMANN and ANN TAVES, Editors

SEDUCTIVE SPIRITS

Deliverance, Demons,
and Sexual Worldmaking
in Ghanaian Pentecostalism

NATHANAEL J. HOMEWOOD

Stanford University Press • Stanford, California

Stanford University Press
Stanford, California

Printed in the United States of America on acid-free, archival-quality paper

Library of Congress Cataloging-in-Publication Data available on request.

Library of Congress Control Number: 2023020624

ISBN 9781503637931 (cloth)
ISBN 9781503638068 (paper)
ISBN 9781503638075 (ebook)

Cover design: Michele Wetherbee
Cover art: Atta Kwami, *Indece*, 2020, oil on linen, 65x100 cm, Beardsmore Gallery, London, England

CONTENTS

ACKNOWLEDGMENTS

My deepest gratitude to:

The Wagoner Foreign Study Scholarship Program and the Center for the Study of Women, Gender, and Sexuality, both at Rice University, for helping to fund this research.

My colleagues at Rice, especially Justine Bakker, Elliot Berger, Jessica Davenport, Enoch Olugide Gbadegesin, Biko Gray, David Kline, Cleve Tinsley, and Rachel Vlachos Schneider. To my colleagues at DePauw who were so encouraging, Justin Glessner, Sujung Kim, Leslie James, and Jeff Kenney. And especially to Pascal Lafontant and his extraordinary writing group!

Adriaan van Klinken and Phil Yoo whose friendship alone would be enough but who both read every word and whose careful and thoughtful engagement has made this a much better work. And to Meghan Drury whose wise advice made this a much more readable text.

The team at Stanford, including Erica Wetter, Dylan Kyung-lim White, and Sarah Rodriguez. To the series editors Tanya Marie Luhrmann and Ann Taves. And to the anonymous reviewers whose suggestions significantly improved this book.

My mentors who carefully guided me through successes, failures, ideas, dissertating, and beyond: Anthony Pinn, Elias Bongmba, Jeffrey Kripal, and Cymene Howe.

The interlocutors whose stories fill these pages. Thank you for sharing your religious communities, life stories, and kindness with me. And especially to Kwabena Asamoah-Gyadu, Sandra Talata, and Mary for guiding me through the Ghanaian world of Pentecostalism.

My family, especially my mother who, occasionally to her chagrin, read every word of this book. To Avondale who lovingly watched me write most of this book. To my most amazing wife who not only tolerated the time I was spending with sex demons, but who encourages me and loves me despite my own demons. And to my son who arrived between the dissertation and revisions and whose love makes all things possible.

SEDUCTIVE SPIRITS

INTRODUCTION

The Ghanaian Pentecostal prophet Emmanuel, a prophet who figures prominently in this book, is a difficult prophet to write about in that, despite all the public over-the-top caricatures, he is immensely human, prone to mood swings, sweet in private, and occasionally violent and raging in public.[1] When I first arrived in Accra, a long, winding, and tumultuous yearslong journey, people were hesitant to recommend his church as a research site. Both scholars and practitioners of Pentecostalism would start the sentence, "But if you really want to know what is going on . . ." and then the sentence would die off before even mentioning Emmanuel's name or church and replacing it with some variation of "it's too much." But I ended up there anyway, in part due to its proximity to my flat in Adjiriganor, in part due to Emmanuel and his church's charismatic magnetism, and mostly due to my interest in "what was really going on" within the excessive elements of Pentecostalism. I found myself there every Wednesday for nine months for his dramatic deliverance services. I ended up there most Sundays for the slightly more sedate church services. I spent weeks in his television station editing studio pouring over video and watching the employees create content for Emmanuel's exclusive television channel. And I spent incalculable time sitting and chatting just inside the gate of the ostentatious compound watching the hustle and bustle of a spiritual empire.

While Emmanuel's ministry is only one of four highlighted throughout this book, I inaugurate the introduction with the retelling of a deliverance I attended at his church on a temperate Sunday because it is both instructive and relatively banal in the world of deliverance. Deliverance, for Pentecostals, is the exorcistic ritual of evacuating demons from human bodies. As one prophet said, demons "have to be dealt with in a concrete way," and that concrete response is through the physical interactions of deliverance.[2] In the words of another prophet, "Whenever a demon is invited in, he must be kicked out!" Deliverance promises to expel the demons and their attendant problems from the human body. Whether or not deliverance delivers on its promises will unfold throughout this book.

It would be difficult, however, to overstate just how vital deliverance is in Ghanaian Pentecostalism. As far back as 1998 Paul Gifford saw deliverance as "perhaps Ghanaian Christianity's most pressing issue."[3] Deliverance is especially prominent in the Ghanaian religious sensescape. It makes up a key part of the ever-audible Pentecostal soundscape that dominates the Ghanaian ear. Late into the night, you can hear the shrieks of those being delivered. In the middle of the day, you might find a crowd outside a local church awaiting deliverance to start, slowing traffic to a halt as they congregate outside the church's doors. At the very least, you will be able to spot a poster or billboard promising miraculous deliverance. It does not matter where you are or when, you are likely to be close enough to sense deliverance.

This particular deliverance did not start any differently than the many scenes that fill these pages. Esther, a first time attendee at Emmanuel's church, fell out, her body spasming as she went from her chair onto the floor. Emmanuel quickly had his ushers stand her up and bring her forward. A woman quickly wrapped her body in an orange creamsicle-colored piece of material.[4] Her chest heaved heavily so that her body appeared to move in a wave. Somehow, in their limited interaction, Emmanuel identified the demon possessing Esther as the spirit of masturbation.[5]

In deliverance, once the offending demon is named, in this case the spirit of masturbation, the afflicted person is prayed for. That prayer is embodied, often accompanied by the laying on of hands or a physical enactment of spiritual warfare. The spirit must then be slain or removed through a combination of prayers and physical rituals that might involve hitting the person, rubbing the person's stomach, smearing oil, or pouring consecrated water on the person.[6] These physical rituals are often impromptu, extemporaneous, and creative, which will become evident from the scenes throughout this book.[7] At the first touch from a pastor, spirits often manifest with cursing, vulgar remarks, or remarkable physical feats. At times manifestations can be extremely violent with bodily shaking, jumping, spinning, or the thrashing of limbs. Audible signs of demonic oppression can include screaming, crying, sobbing, belching, laughing, and screeching.[8] Sudden outbursts are interpreted as the demon reacting to the presence of the Holy Spirit. These are physical attempts to find spirits and not merely symbolic battles. When Emmanuel thrust his hand toward Esther and yelled perhaps the most common phrase of charismatic deliverance, "Holy Ghost, FIRE!" Esther squirmed out of the grasp of the ushers and again fell to the floor. Esther propelled herself around the floor by moving her knees, waist, and neck, and sliding toward the congregation to evade Emmanuel and his spiritual invectives.

As soon as Esther slid across the floor, Emmanuel altered his diagnosis, or at least expanded upon it, and loudly and definitively yelled: "Spiritual marriage." Spiritual marriage is a popular possession diagnosis in West African Pentecostalism and refers to a covenanted relationship between a human and at least one demon. Despite its relatively innocuous or ambivalent name, it is considered a serious condition and one that plagues all of humanity. The relationship is wide-ranging in its effects, from the most quotidian to fantastic. It is, though, primarily defined by sexual relations between a human and demon. The simple mention of spiritual marriage by Emmanuel immediately alerted the thousands in attendance that Esther was engaged in some sort of sexual relationship with the demonic. Prior to fieldwork in Ghana, I was largely unaware of spiritual marriage despite performing ethnographic research of Pentecostalism elsewhere. There are, of course, the world over many practices that involve ghostly and human paramours. Nonetheless, the prominence of spiritual marriage is one component of Ghanaian Pentecostalism that led me to write *Seductive Spirits*.

Emmanuel continued to expand on the details of Esther's relationship with the demonic by asking, "Have you seen the snake married to this lady?" The question was revealing in multiple ways. First, by addressing the audience with the question Emmanuel demonstrates how all deliverance is a communal performance. Secondly, by invoking the word *marriage* the logic of spiritual marriage dictated that Esther was in a sexual relationships with a spirit who manifested as a snake. Almost on cue, Esther slid across the floor, screaming loudly, persistently, and angrily. She tried all sorts of bodily movements to move her body across the floor, eventually relying on a slithering action. When her body looked most snakelike in its movements, Emmanuel interjected: "It's a snake spirit, and sometimes it turns into a lion." He had seen the snake and the lion, but his statements of fact toward the congregation indicated that he did not expect everyone else to see what he was seeing.

Sometimes deliverance is relatively sedate, but other times it is wild and fierce. The stage of spirit removal marks the frenzied climax of deliverance. The amount of frenzy is said to correlate with the depth of demonization. Esther's deliverance was middle-of-the-road in terms of frenzy. She struggled to stand. She tried to foist herself up in slow, unsure movements. She eventually staggered to her feet. When a group of pastors approached her, she swung her arms in a wild front stroke; her eyes were wide open, and her mouth was gaping. She took quick and short backward steps away from the encroaching pastors, all the while still screaming. She stopped just before the front row of the congregation and bent up and down at the waist so that she moved quickly between standing erect and the top of her head pointing toward her toes. Esther then started rolling at the waist instead of moving up and down so that her torso drew large circles into the charged air.

Emmanuel interjected again, "Holy Ghost," and the crowd joined him as he yelled, "Fire!" Emmanuel then threw a flurry of questions toward the spirit: "How has the girl wronged you? What is she to you?"

Esther continued to struggle, but her resistance was mostly futile against the tight grip the ushers had hooked around her wrists and armpits. A third pastor held the microphone up to her face augmenting a loud sigh that descended in pitch. She dramatically shook her head no and took deep, heaving breaths. The orange cloth wrapped around her waist shook loose and fell to the ground, no longer clashing with her purple shirt emblazoned with 01, revealing her black and white leggings.[9]

Emmanuel and Esther partook in the standard dialogue that outlined the basic parameters of spiritual marriage. Esther said, "She's my wife." Emmanuel repeated it back in the form of a question. And Esther, more forcefully this time, repeated, "She's my wife!" With Esther trying very weakly to pull away from her captors, not so much creating a scene of resistance but a gentle sway, Emmanuel observed, "You demons always prefer the beautiful and handsome ones." Something about Emmanuel's observation provoked Esther, and she began to struggle in earnest, moving quickly and fervently, twisting rapidly until two ushers could no longer control her body. Emmanuel urgently called for more pastors. A pastor in purple yelled at an usher whose smile made it seem as if he enjoyed the physicality of the confrontation. In the commotion, Esther broke free and began slapping and biting the ushers. Emmanuel yelled, "She is biting them, so help hold her, hold her in numbers." A slew of pastors emerged, running toward Esther, and in no time six people were restraining her. The sonic volume of the congregation rose in a crescendo as she struggled with the ushers in the same way that crowd noise swells during the more vicious parts of a prizefight.

Emmanuel, confident that Esther was once more restrained, asked, "Who again did you say you are?" and then followed up the question with an observation, "Oh, so you've made yourself a tiger." At the remark, she flashed her teeth and growled. For a moment, she kept her lips separated in an effort to make all her teeth visible. Her eyes bulged. She was performing the role of a tiger with polymorphous dexterity—now having been a tiger, a lion, and a snake. The conversation went in multiple directions until Emmanuel brought it back to the crux of the deliverance: spiritual marriage, or sex with demonic spirit animals, in this case, a snake, tiger, and lion. Emmanuel asked, even though their dialogue had already established the fact, "You are her spiritual husband?"

With a look of disgust and a roll of her eyes, Esther responded, "Yes! I don't even know who directed her here."

Emmanuel pushed the issue, "Who blessed her marriage to you?"

Esther pursed her lips, "No one gave her to me. I love her."

The conversation rambled on as Emmanuel posed more questions, received answers, and then implied that he already knew the answer. For example, he asked, "Is it right what you've done to her?" To which Esther responded, "Ask her, I've given her sickness." She was suggesting that these animal spirits had sickened her through their sexual liaisons. Emmanuel countered with, "Do you need to tell me? I'm aware of the virus you've injected into her blood; I didn't want to say."

Esther laughed, spat, and yelled, "Wooooo!" Emmanuel kept talking: "Do you know that the virus will be taken out of her today?"[10]

The charade continued with Esther threatening Emmanuel, "I want to fight you. If you think you are man enough, let them free me."

Incredulous, Emmanuel shot back, "You want to fight me?"

Esther responded with a question and a demand, "But can you fight me? Let them free me."

Increasingly confident, Emmanuel asked, "Do you know the Bishop you talk to?" He turned to his ushers and said, "Bring her here."

The soundscape grew tense. There was an errant cymbal crash, and the murmurs of anticipation pulsed through the crowd. Emmanuel, with his hand raised and fingers outstretched, yelled into his microphone, "Today, any spirit married to this girl! Fire! Leave her!"

Esther screamed and ran backward away from the prophet. When she had moved a safe distance away, she stopped running and started jumping up and down like a boxer skipping rope, bouncing on one foot and then the other.

Emmanuel goaded her by stating, "But you said you wanted to fight me?" This angered Esther. She flipped the orange material, which an usher had deftly reapplied, over her head and let out a desperate scream. She strolled confidently right up into the prophet's face so that they were eye to eye until Esther stumbled backward. Emmanuel continued to mock her with cries of "Won't you hit me? Hit me!"

Mocking shenanigans aside, Emmanuel returned to the serious business of deliverance. He yelled, "Holy Ghost!" and the crowd enthusiastically responded with, "Fire!" This call and response played out a few times, and ended when Emmanuel screamed "In the name of Jesus!"

Esther growled a deep, guttural growl. She moved her head back and forth. In between growls she got down on all fours and bared her teeth. Emmanuel combatted this manifestation, presumably the tiger spirit previously named, by spitting "pfft" into the microphone and shooting his hand in her direction. She collapsed. The crowd applauded and cheered the animal spirit's apparent death.

When Esther stood up, she immediately started vomiting. People will often vomit during deliverance, so deliverers usually carry toilet paper with them or something to wipe away the detritus.[11] Esther vomited a stream of white foam that dangled off her lips before falling to the ground. She said while pointing at Emmanuel, "Because of you, I'm going to leave her." She added, "I'm a snake, so I want to leave." As with much of deliverance, performances often end with many fragments unresolved. Was Ether's claiming to be a snake a challenge to Emmanuel's characterization of her as a snake, lion, and tiger? Or was she now a snake, the feline spirits having been dispensed with? The fragments, unbeholden to a particular order, are part of what makes deliverance and the demonic so rich for analysis. There are copious details often seemingly left vague and unsettled. But to those present, be it prophets, deliverees, or congregational members, little underdeveloped details can mean everything.

Emmanuel encouraged Esther, "Vomit and bring out the sickness. If you do not vomit, I shall hit at you again. Vomit out all your evil sicknesses injected into her." Esther retched a couple of times, heaved deeply, and vomited some more. Emmanuel added with an air of braggadocio, "You snake who turns into lions and tigers cannot scare me." Esther went to all fours, growled more meekly than before, and continued to vomit.

Emmanuel continued to make demands of the animal spirit, "Take out your sicknesses. Take out your virus. You mad spirit!" Esther tried to stand but slipped this way and that way as if she were running on ice. Emmanuel continued to instruct the spirit, "Take your sickness and break your spiritual marriage to her." The instructions to the spirit also served as a reminder to the watching audience that at the core of this whole performance was a sexual relationship between Esther and the demonic in the form of animalistic spirits.

Emmanuel suddenly and purposefully swung his arm toward Esther at eye level, not making contact but coming uncomfortably close. Esther's eyes rolled back and then bulged in anger. She started slithering like a snake in Emmanuel's direction. "Snake!" Emmanuel yelled. He launched into a deliverance prayer, "In the name of Jesus Christ our Lord! This is why Jesus called Emmanuel, to free the children of the living God! Marine spirits and animal spirits, take out your sickness and spiritual marriage." With that, Esther rolled onto her back, sat up, and performed a lengthy and melodramatic scene of death, which ended with her lying still and docile on her back.

To experience deliverance is to experience the removal of invading spirits from one's body and to be brought fully under the control of the Holy Spirit.

Ultimately, the only evidence that the evil spirits have indeed departed is the docile body. Until the moving body becomes still and quiet, deliverance will continue.[12] Up until that moment of calm passivity, deliverance is a loud, messy, noisy experience. Deliverance ends when the body falls to the ground, unmoving. This docile ending is the norm in deliverance and is sometimes referred to as resting in the spirit. Resting in the spirit is the experience of falling and lying still on the ground. Thomas J. Csordas calls it a "sacred swoon" as it is the moment when the power of the divine completely overwhelms the evil spirits. The body reacts to this overwhelming divine power by ceasing to move.[13]

While theoretically docility is crucial, for without it there are no accompanying signs that the evil spirits have departed, it is more accurate to think of docility as deliverance's denouement. That is, if docility occurs, because as some scenes in this book will illustrate, docility does not always materialize. When it does, it creates space for the prophet to add a few details to the possession story. Usually though, once docility is procured the service moves with surprising rapidity to another scene, completely ignoring the actionless, unmoving body for it offers nothing; the primary interest and preoccupation is exclusively with the possessed, exuberant body.

As Esther lay docile, the crowd erupted with cheers. After a few moments of docility, Esther stood up. She was confused about why she was at the front and what had just occurred. As Emmanuel gave her a shortened version of the events, she continued vomiting. Emmanuel informed the congregation, "You see her vomiting out the snake's venom that caused her sickness. God has saved her from every sickness."

There is much to analyze about Esther's story. However, I share the story here at the onset of *Seductive Spirits* to demonstrate how central sex is to deliverance-dominant Pentecostalism. This entire drama renders real and public a sexual relationship between Esther and a demon or demons. But such sexual experiences and storytelling (or sextifying) have been mostly left unexplored in academic analysis of Pentecostalism.[14] Such ignorance is a mistake. There is too much at stake to ignore sex with demons.

While the sexual components of Esther's deliverance story may shock the reader, I must warn that this book is filled with materials that may discomfit. If these materials shock, though, I'd like to point out that wherever you find yourself, similar materials have been hiding in plain sight. Pentecostal ideas about sex with demons have increasingly been part of the public discourse. For example, as I write this in my office in Houston, Texas, I am only miles away from experts in deliverance from spiritual marriage. More prominently, though, in July of 2020 the sitting American president promoted a video of Cameroonian and Houstonian Dr. Stella Immanuel as she hawked hydroxychloroquine. Quickly, Immanuel's fondness for hydroxychloroquine was a mere footnote as the media and late-night comedians honed in on her beliefs about sexual relations between demons and humans, exotic fodder for joke writers. Immanuel was derisively given the moniker Dr. Demon Sperm. However, the kind of spiritual-material demonic sexualities described by Dr. Stella Immanuel are not that unique in a growing segment of Pentecostalism.

And yet, demonic sexualities are unique in what they offer to the study of religion and sexuality, the focus of this text. To frame it more accurately, sex with spirits is not an exotic or new religious phenomenon within and beyond Christianity, but its fruitfulness for thinking about religion and sexuality has been limited hitherto. *Seductive Spirits* aims to change this limitation and think through the many theoretical possibilities and potentialities that sex with demons offer.

Scholars, in different contexts and epochs, have examined the significance of erotic demons. Walter Stephens, in his book *Demon Lovers,* argues that confessions of diabolic copulation in early modern Europe were primarily pertinent to theologians and clergy to assuage their lack of certainty in the reality of the supernatural.[15] Testimonies about the sexual combinations of women's bodies and demons were not for the benefit of those testifying but were actually for those prompting the testimonies, the early modern theologians wracked with spiritual doubts. Erotic demons were a means to an end. The embodied experience of sex with demons was treated as irrefutable, truer than any other claims about the supernatural; if demons existed, then angels existed, and most importantly, God existed. In many ways, Stephens is building on a long Christian tradition where "knowing" was conflated with sexual intercourse. To have sex was to know deeply, intimately, and indisputably.

While rich and generative, Stephens's argument falls short in the Ghanaian Pentecostal context in two crucial ways. First, sex with demons is not archaic but a flourishing tool of meaning-making. Stephens's tying sex with

demons to a specific contextual and historical epoch is laudable but not necessarily translatable. It is necessary to reevaluate sex with demons, in this case,
in the context and historical moment of Ghana. Further, Stephens's interpretation limits the utility of sex with demons to epistemological and ontological
realms. I am not arguing that these are not useful lenses for Ghanaian Pentecostals' obsession with demonic sex. But for Ghanaian Pentecostals, sex with
demons is not only about shaping theological and cosmological visions, but it
impinges on all sorts of practical problems in the quotidian, political possibilities, and social frameworks. The idea that Ghanaian Pentecostals need sex
to assuage a lack of certainty about the supernatural is not borne out by the
evidence. Pentecostals assume the world in the here and now is teeming with
a broad diversity of spiritual forces waiting to impose their sensual prowess
on human bodies.

The fundamental shortcoming in most texts about demonic sex, though,
is the speed with which each book moves away from the sex, from the bodies,
from the multisensory elements of sex with demons. Each text is missing, in the
words of L. H. Stallings, the "funk" of coitus.[16] These books reduce demons to
something else—a tool for knowledge, meaningless rhetoric, merely simile—
and assume that if demons are something else, then so is the sex in which they
allegedly participate. The sex then fades into the background, even when it
is that around which arguments pivot. At some point while listening to my
interlocutors emphasize the extreme pleasure of sex with demons, I realized
that many of the academic models and tools for identifying and analyzing
demonic erotic experiences ignored the funk, the bodily sensations, and the
primacy of pleasure in sex. In the case of Stephens, for example, knowledge
through sex is fundamental to the argument, but there is no exploration of the
various sexual expressions described. Sex is simultaneously overdetermined
as truth and undetermined in almost every other facet.

Many studies of Pentecostalism similarly discipline, sanitize, and bowd-
lerize the rituals, fantasies, practices, and desires of Pentecostals. In each
case, the authors uncritically accept Pentecostal self-representations and their
rhetorical claims of sexual discipline. For example, Jessica Moberg writes that
"neocharismatic groups are particularly intriguing from a 'body perspective'
since they combine extensive physical interaction during worship and emphasis on physical (and mental) wellbeing with strict bodily discipline in other

areas, including sexuality."[17] Her first claim about the richness of Pentecostals from a body perspective is undoubtedly valid, evidenced by the many sources that have articulated just that. The declaration of strict bodily discipline in sexuality, though, is dubious. And Moberg is not alone. Nimi Wariboko writes, "One of the goals of [pneumatic] spiritual practice is to produce the clean, proper, divine law-abiding body."[18] Pentecostal sexual discipline is only valid if we take preachers, prophets, and teachers at their words; however, in interpreting Pentecostal sexualities, one must probe and interrogate their idealized self-representations.[19] Pentecostals preach and teach strict sexual discipline within the bounds of marriage, but ritual and practice effectively eviscerate such discipline.

In practice, the Pentecostals I spent time with are not particularly disciplined sexually. That is not to say they are prodigiously sexual, but many shared with me stories of affairs, desires, and fantasies. Sometimes these stories were sextified, that is shared in sexual testimony: I once was addicted to this type of sinful sex, and now I am delivered. But most often, they were shared unremorsefully as a matter of fact, whether or not the particular sexual relationships had been discontinued or continued into the present. And the prophets I worked with were not disciplined either; their oblique acknowledgments, the rumors, and the explicit information of congregants illustrated a significant divorce between their words and sexual experiences. While I have no desire to reveal their specific sexual experiences except when directly relevant to the arguments of this book, none of the prophets herein were as disciplined as their speech indicated. And none of this is to say Pentecostals are more sexually active in practice than anyone else; I simply wish to push against the move to accept Pentecostal idealized self-representations of sexual discipline as sexual evidence.

More so than their personal proclivities, it is in ritual that it becomes most obvious that sexual discipline is not the point. In my research I did not experience deliverance ministries as being particularly interested in sexual discipline. The regularity with which deliverance ministries visit and revisit, cite and recite, iterate and reiterate a wide variety of sexualities leaves me convinced that, in Wariboko's terms, Pentecostals find meaning in the anti-holy element of their "holy–anti-holy ambiguity."[20] Instead of sexual discipline, the emphasis here on bodily sensations and sexual obsessions in ritual does the opposite by opening up a libertine space. Instead of rushing past the cunnilingus, the spilled semen, and public masturbation, this book will tarry with the sex, much the same way deliverance ministries do.

THINKING WITH PENTECOSTALISM

Increasingly, academics are embracing Pentecostalism as a rich theoretical source to think with. James K. A. Smith has called Pentecostalism "a kind of theoretical provocateur."[21] No longer is Pentecostalism merely an interesting ethnographic topic but plentiful in its ability to reorder and rethink the world and the place of humans in that world. *Seductive Spirits* melds both approaches with abundant thick ethnographic description combined with theoretical musings about the possibilities therein. The theory flows from watching and participating in deliverance-dominant Pentecostalism; it engages with Pentecostalism as an embodied set of practices and rituals "that implicitly carry a worldview."[22] Pentecostalism happens in spontaneous ways where one often experiences before explication is provided, if it ever is. And so, I started with the bodies and senses, the stories and testimonies, the interruptions and surprises in order to then theorize. Because the theoretical reflections followed the ethnography, an intense interdisciplinarity was required. As such, queer theory, sense studies, animal studies, philosophy, theology, and black studies are just some of the fields utilized to better understand the theoretical richness of Pentecostalism.

Ashon Crawley, perhaps more than anyone else, has captured the theoretical richness of Pentecostalism. Crawley argues that central to philosophy and theology is a subjectivity that rests on the categorical distinction of thought. The blackness and Pentecostalism constitutive of one another in Crawley's portmanteau *Blackpentecostalism* provide the tools to think and be without the restrictions of subjectivity so central to philosophy and theology.[23] As such, Blackpentecostalism finds itself in the world but not of it, acting for the hope of something new, something different.[24] In particular, Crawley captures this in Blackpentecostalism's commitment to "Otherwise possibilities."[25] That is to say that Pentecostalism creates the possibility of thinking about the world in new ways—especially sensually in the celebration of black flesh—and can be an alternative approach for organizing, performing, and producing thought.[26] In the words of Crawley, "Blackpentecostalism is the capaciousness of otherwise resistance that rises to, while emerging from, the occasion of its genesis."[27] Not to get too far ahead, but in the conclusion of this book I will argue, in particular agreement with Crawley, that in performances typically deemed excessive Ghanaian Pentecostalism is a decolonial project.

THINKING WITH DEMONS

A significant element of thinking with Pentecostalism is thinking with demons. Thinking with demons has also gained popularity recently.[28] Bruce Lincoln notes that while discourse around demons was thoroughly discredited during the Enlightenment, demons should be given the same scholarly attention as any other component of religion.[29] Using the case of ancient Mazdaean demonology, Lincoln demonstrates that thinking with demons is a project with wide-ranging implications, challenging "our most fundamental ideas about the nature of being itself."[30] Meanwhile, David Gordon White articulates perhaps the most important distinction of thinking with demons when he writes, "Daemons have always traveled more lightly than gods."[31] That is to say in their indeterminacy, their ambiguity, and their ability to morph between forms, demons challenge us to think in more loose and flexible ways, challenging the certainty of Enlightenment thought.

In Pentecostalism, thinking with demons is primarily done not through theological prose but through the performance of demons in deliverance. Deliverance is the most consequential of the many embodied and experiential charismata among a large swath of Pentecostal Christians in Ghana.[32] In the early twentieth century, the teachings of Charles Parham and William Seymour spread the belief that the marker of a spiritually attuned life for Pentecostals was the gift of tongues. The tongue moving in particular ways and producing various sounds was the initial evidence of the baptism of the Holy Spirit. But as Pentecostalism, especially in non-Western settings, has shifted to a deliverance-dominant model, the spirits and senses are different. No longer is the movement mostly about sensing the Holy Spirit but in sensing the demonic, often sexually. No longer is the relationship between spirit and human primarily about the verbal, in either glossolalic or xenolalic form, but about the activation of a host of senses that stretch and expand the human sensorium in various directions. The performance of the demonic in deliverance has emerged as the primary embodied ritual.[33]

Deliverance is central to Pentecostalism in the same way that conversion or confession may be for many other Christians. It is its own form of conversion, its own confessional practice. In the same way that Evangelicals seek conversion, being born-again again and again, deliverance-dominant Pentecostals are ever engaged with the demonic. In the same way that confession reveals, deliverance exposes. And like the repetition of both practices, the experiences of the demonic are recursive, and so deliverance is continuously sought and resought, shaping and reshaping many along the way. Pentecostal ministries make their case for the centrality and necessity of deliverance in many ways, the foremost of which is the placement of deliverance within their church services. As Catholic masses build toward the climax of the Eucharist, or Evangelical services move toward the apogee of the altar call, Pentecostal deliverances services ensure that deliverance occupies the climactic portion of the church service.

The centrality of deliverance in Ghana extends far beyond the somewhat porous boundaries of Pentecostalism. Opoku Onyinah admits, "At present, almost all churches in Ghana include exorcistic activities, referred to as 'deliverance' in their programmes, since failure to do so amounts to losing members to churches that include such activities."[34] In the West African context, the emphasis on an individual gift from a singular spirit simply does not cohere with a religious worldview that sees spirits, many, as a real presence in all aspects of life. Deliverance responds specifically to such a world, where human beings are invariably and inevitably susceptible to the influence of numerous demons or evil spirits.

There are many ways to interpret this exorcistic boom and its shifting of the senses from heavenly utterings to demonic embodiments. *Seductive Spirits* will do much interpreting of this shift, but for now it is important to note how significant the change is. The demonic in deliverance Pentecostalism is all-consuming, casting a shadow over every element of Pentecostal life, from the most mundane and quotidian to unique bursts of the fantastic. According to Birgit Meyer, "In Accra the Devil is omnipresent," as are the Devil's spirited minions.[35] As Kwabena Asamoah-Gyadu writes of deliverance hermeneutics, "The devil and demons seem to wield so much power and their influence is so diffuse that it is impossible to be conscious of their presence and live a life devoid of fear and insecurity."[36] It is worth emphasizing just how all-consuming this worldview is. Asamoah-Gyadu adds, in reference to the probing questions of deliverance, "In view of the detailed nature of the questions, it is unlikely if all were to answer truthfully as requested, that anyone could escape being delivered from a demon of some sort."[37] In this worldview, everyone encounters the demonic always and everywhere. Unsurprisingly, the prophets I researched saw the need for deliverance as universal. Kwofie emphasized that all African Christians needed to go through deliverance, while Nikoi was adamant that all Christians needed to be set free from demons.[38] The uniqueness of deliverance-dominant Pentecostalism is not so much the ability to combat the demonic but the commitment to perform the demonic publicly, to draw close to demons. This is not, though, an entirely new approach for Christianity. Dayna Kalleres has noted in late antiquity urban Christianization that instead of fleeing the terrifying demons that filled the world, figures such as the Christian bishop John Chrysostom advocated close proximity to the demonic.[39]

On the surface, the primary import of demons for Pentecostals is revealing the supernatural. As Jonathon O'Donnell has pointed out, demons may hierarchically be the lowest of the supernatural beings, with God being found at the apex of that hierarchy. However, their existence points toward the apex, provides hints and signposts of the divine.[40] Meyer reached a similar conclusion after conducting research among Ewe Christians. She found that without the belief in the existence of the Devil and evil spirit-beings, the people's faith in God "would be devoid of any basis."[41] Similarly, Wariboko has argued that Pentecostalism radically appropriates the demonic to access the supernatural, "noumenally exposed in its naked, unmediated presence for the phenomenal gaze."[42] In this framework I myself have argued elsewhere, "Bad is to good as demon is to angel as devil is to god. Knowing one side of the ledger exists is to know that the other exists. In this world, for pneumatic Christians, there may be no better way to know God than to know God through the contrary, through the evil window into what lay beyond material existence."[43]

The weight given the demonic is evident in the concerns of Ghanaian scholar Abamfa Atiemo, who writes that "in most cases they [deliverance Pentecostals] are guilty of a terrible dualism. A dualism which creates a Devil

who seems to be equal in power and majesty with God himself."[44] Atiemo
worries that the fascination with evil has superseded Christian teachings in
deliverance ministries and obliterated themes such as salvation, repentance,
holiness, and consecration.[45] This is a genuine concern among some of the
faithful. I, however, hear Atiemo's complaint of manicheanism and demonic
obsession and recognize a need to reorient studies of deliverance-dominant
Pentecostalism to emphasize the demonic as powerful, majestic, and attractive. Academic adjudications which interpret demons in relation to God, including my own, underestimate the importance of demons. Demons are not
merely a window through which to see the good. In fact, I think the argument
that demons point to God or knowledge of God has been a limiting factor in
the understanding of Pentecostalism. Demons matter unto themselves.

Demons are a knowledge regime, one that shapes how Pentecostals think
about, engage with, and construct the cosmos.[46] In particular, in the spirit
of Michael Taussig who interpreted the devil as "he who resists the cosmic
process," I find demons to resist a great many structures, orders, and ideas.[47]
Indeed, this has been seen as constitutive of the demonic by many scholars.
The historian of religion Jonathan Z. Smith demonstrated that in Near East-
ern late antiquity, demonology had a subversive element.[48] Kalleres noted
that in late antiquity urban Christianization was a creative and competitive
ritual marketplace where demonology agitated political, socioeconomic, and
cultural realities.[49] Pentecostals, similarly, embrace the demonic and all its
attendant powers of political agitation.

It should already be clear that while Pentecostals deem the demonic re-
pulsive, there is a strong desire or attraction to the whole world of demonology. In their efforts to destroy the demonic, deliverance ministries end up
enacting the demonic in all its titillating glory. Pentecostals believe that deliverance is neither brought about instantly or permanently. Deliverance is a
continuous process; the demons abide! In the most intense, physical attempts
to banish evil, Pentecostals invite a certain kind of intimacy with evil and the
grotesque. Deliverance-dominant Pentecostalism, in its commitment to see
beyond physical reality, exuberantly embraces the nightmarish disorder of
bodily encounters between demons and humans. Pentecostalism's appeal is
not necessarily the power of the Holy Spirit but instead the enactment of the

forbidden, the power of the world teeming with demons. Meyer calls deliverance a kind of circular conversion whereby Pentecostals continuously revisit that which they cast out.[50] This recursivity will be demonstrated throughout the cases explored herein.

To be clear, in arguing that demons matter unto themselves I am not claiming that God or gods and Satan are wholly different. Undoubtedly, the demonic and heavenly parallel one another with significant similarities and powers. I simply contend that thinking about demons or with demons absent the rush to God or salvation offers much. The stories demons tell and people tell about demons are poignant and powerful. In order to clarify this, I invoke the idea of tarrying. Tarrying, traditionally, in Pentecostalism implies the active bodily work of waiting for, upon, with, and within the spirit of God in community. But deliverance-dominant Pentecostals tarry with the demonic. Tarrying is the act of staying longer than intended, to delay leaving a place, situation, milieu, or experience. In deliverance, Pentecostals stay with their demons.

If one pays attention to the practice of tarrying with the demonic, it becomes clear that deliverance is less about defeating demons and much more about embracing them. Think of Esther's story that inaugurated this chapter where much more time and effort were spent engaging and performing the demon(s) rather than tarrying in the presence of God. Though deliverance is ostensibly a ritual about defeating demons and being freed of their impositions, it is ultimately an exploration of what happens at those bodily sites of exchange between humans and demons. Deliverance ministries devote almost all of their ritual efforts to exploring specific details of how, when, and where demons possessed somebody. In these deliverance settings, "churches offer their members the opportunity to experience the satanic, i.e., the chance to experience possession which is simultaneously denounced as 'heathen.'"[51] Repeatedly, prophets mine the depths of that which is disallowed, making the central point of deliverance to experience the demonic rather than the freedom deliverance promises. Deliverance consists of the public embodied performances of that which is defined as sinful or evil, with minimal material or embodied evidence of that which is holy or good.

Primary among those disallowed elements in which deliverance intervenes is sex. Sexual demons, demonic sexualities, and possession by lustful demons are the central focus of this book because they are an overwhelming and overpowering recursive presence in the Ghanaian deliverance ministries I researched. While sexual possession requires its Pentecostal corollary, dramatic deliverance, Pentecostals use deliverance as a means to think with demons. In deliverance these sexual demons are tarried with, they are embraced, they are performed, they are rendered real and possible. In so doing, Pentecostals engage in a creative exercise of sexual worldmaking.

THINKING WITH DEMONS SENSUALLY

Nikoi, another prominent prophet in *Seductive Spirits*, led a small weekly deliverance service in a dilapidated tent behind the opulent church he pastored. One Saturday afternoon slumped in his office chairs, Nikoi and I wore our feebleness on our bodies. The morning deliverance session had been particularly intense, chaotic, and confusing and had ended abruptly when a possessed woman disrobed and ran down the street, prophets and ushers chasing her. Our exhausted bodies were in stark contrast to the previous six hours defined by bodies crying out, hands and fingers gesturing, feet stomping, and legs propelling people to and fro. But as Nikoi described deliverance something changed. It was as though his entire body reentered the deliverance milieu: his body tensed up, his face took on the tortured look of spiritual earnestness it carries during deliverance, he clenched his fist, and said with all the energy he had left, "The Holy Spirit will take over your senses and your whole body."

Nikoi's pronouncement about the senses echoed what I had read in the autobiography of yet another prominent prophet in *Seductive Spirits*, Kwofie. Only in Kwofie's case it was the evil corollary, "Demon entities use many different forms of control of humans, including having control over all the five senses."[52] Pentecostalism imagines the world, broadly speaking, in an epic struggle for control of the human sensorium. The senses—whether bound by the Enlightenment number of five, or not—are that over which spiritual warfare is waged. In a single sentence Nikoi sent my work spinning with the whirling intensity of a possessed body mid-deliverance. Deliverance is about the body, whatever that is bounded within or exceeding its fleshy material boundaries. Deliverance is a battle for control of the senses, however many they number in indecipherable combinations and permutations. Deliverance is felt, whatever that means.

This embodied reality should have dawned on me well before Nikoi's words fell on my ears. The evidence was all around me in the pandemonium of bodies moving in natural and unnatural ways at the behest of prophetic and demonic forces. As Sean McCloud acutely writes, "Demons, of course, have long been part of Christianity, and Pentecostals have been busy banishing demons from human bodies since the movement was born in the first decade of the twentieth century."[53] Or, as Jonathan R. Baer poignantly writes, "Pentecostalism originated in the body as much as the spirit."[54] The evidence was also embedded in every deliverance text, such as the popular *Pigs in the Parlor* by Frank and Ida Mae Hammond, which observes, "Demon spirits can invade and indwell human bodies. It is their objective to do so."[55] Or by the sensual chaos experienced by David in Malachi Martin's *Hostage to the Devil* when he screams, "If all my senses—sight, hearing, smell, taste, touch—are invaded like that, I'd be possessed. I'd be possessed. Jesus! I'd be possessed."[56] Demons enter and exit, move and shape, enhance and distort human bodies through the sensorium. *Seductive Spirits* is an effort to take the body seriously in all its permutations during the ritual of deliverance. This book traces the material body through its "sensuous potentiality."[57]

While demons can exist outside of embodiment, in Pentecostalism they only encounter the world through their ability to occupy the bodies of humans and animals, with human bodies always being the preferred avenue to invoke their powers. Demons wield power by problematizing the boundary between spirit and material in their relentless pursuit of the human body. In the words of the most renowned of all Pentecostal demonologists, Derek Prince, "disembodied spirit beings have an intense craving to occupy physical bodies."[58] Demons do not have bodies of their own so they prey on human embodiment, leaving humanity in a never-ending spiritual battle against these body-loving entities.[59]

When demons successfully invade, the human body becomes more than its material boundaries while also importantly becoming a tangible expression of the invading spirit. Possession is both a spiritual expansion of the body into the supernatural and a materialization of the spiritual. Wariboko poetically captures this when he writes,

Correlatively, we can state that the body of the human is the "idol" of the spirit, of the insubstantial self. It is the accomplice of the invisible. The body is the exposition of spirit. The body is the being-exposed of the spirit. That is to say, the body is how the spirit exposes itself, self-posits in existence. Yet the two can be "separated" into two different creatures, as they can follow different laws and trajectories of performance.[60]

The list of possible ways spirits self-posit in bodies is endless. There are seemingly infinite combinations and permutations of spirits and human bodies that come together and separate, self-posit, and disintegrate.

Multiple cultural scripts impinge on and shape the physical experiences of worshippers, including the global Pentecostal sensorium, an urban Ghanaian sensorium, the modern/colonial sensorium, and a decolonial sensorium. To understand these phenomena, I utilize Anthony Pinn's description of the discursive body and the material body as two distinct bodies inextricably linked: "Meaning is embodied. Human experience, then, involves an array of factors only some of which are discursive in nature. Bodies serve as a nonmaterial text to be read, but they are also material realities that shape information within the context of the world."[61] Theoretical consideration of one without the other is insufficient or incomplete.

In the ethnographic portions of this book I demonstrate a commitment to a robust consideration of the sensuous "stuff" of human beings: how human hands, vaginas, and penises encounter each other, demons, and the Holy Spirit. As such, the constitution of the body—its malleability, transformability, and porosity—is developed throughout this book, responding to how deliverance scenes shape and mold the body's protuberances and convexities. In the theoretical musings scattered throughout and amidst the ethnographic scenes I build on the discursive. It is, of course, entirely impossible to completely separate description and theory, material flesh and discursive bodies. They are co-constitutive with theory emerging from the bodies and bodies enacting theory. But with attention to both the stuff of bodies and their discursivity, this book is an invitation to think with the senses and in so doing think both about fleshy sensuousness and a new politics of bodily-being-in-the world.

This text borrows, mixes, matches, and rethinks the senses based on the erotic sensorium of a particular cultural community, Ghanaian Pentecostal deliverance ministries in and around the greater Accra area. In so doing it demonstrates how Ghanaian Pentecostalism constructs a unique sense-ability, pushing human senses, sensations, and sensuousness into new perceptual depths. The senses as traditionally described are, simply put, inadequate for describing sensuous sex with the supernatural. Pentecostals often describe spirited senses through redundant syntaxes, such as seeing eyes and hearing ears. In doing so, they mark their sensorium as unique, as capable of more than whatever senses Enlightenment thinkers defined. I have tried to enumerate some of the unique senses I saw operative in the performances of the demonic. In chapter 3, I explore an expansive version of touch. In chapter 4, I expand on Crawley's portmanteau *choreosonic* as a sense. In chapter 5, I elucidate the role of metakinesis. And in chapter 6, I challenge the occularcentric with *demonologeyes*. I illuminate these unique senses for a variety of reasons. The first is building on the foundational Pentecostal emphasis on the senses. Secondly, I try to capture a specific Ghanaian Pentecostal sensorium. And finally, I remain convinced that emphasizing these senses challenges the way in which modernity/coloniality has demanded we think, feel, and sense.[62]

The manner in which the Pentecostal sensorium pushes beyond the restrictive five senses is not an argument for the privileging of one sense over others or assuming that one carries truth more effectively than others. Still, it is a call to reimagine the senses as they reach beyond. The senses are not a zero-sum equation; the use of one sense does not atrophy all others, and the senses rarely operate singularly. For example, while the erotic senses of Pentecostalism certainly push against visual hegemony, Pentecostals are not inherently anti-occularcentric. As with all the other traditional senses, Pentecostals do not abandon sight; they reimagine it.

Attention to the body in Pentecostalism is still an emerging field. Candy Gunther Brown states that "Pentecostal ontologies and epistemologies of body and spirit have, nevertheless, remained largely opaque to non-Pentecostals."[63] The opaqueness stems largely from the radically different perspective of the body that Pentecostals have from traditional approaches to embodiment. Pentecostals are committed to the materiality of spirits and the experience of spirits—good and bad—in the body. Michael Wilkinson and Peter Althouse are correct when they state that Pentecostal embodiment "may look different and be particularized in specific ways."[64] Wariboko, writing about Pentecostalism in Nigeria writes, "The body is the context and condition through which the person is able to communicate not only with her world and environment but also with God and other forms of spirit."[65] Sensory aptitudes and experiences inflect everything in the Pentecostal worldview. The body always and everywhere is being interpreted for the signs it provides.

As Kristina Wirtz argues, understanding the relationship between humans and spirits can happen through two "orders": sensation and discourse.[66] For Pentecostals, the order is sensation. The commitment to the body as the primary locus of Pentecostal experience and knowledge gathering requires a "sense-ability" or sense-knowledge.[67] As Josh Brahinsky writes, "In the past century, Pentecostals expanded their vernacular ethos such that efforts to reach God no longer chiefly rely on stimulating the ability to speak in tongues or heal and instead are now rooted in generalized sensory experience . . . nearly any sensation makes the case."[68] The body's senses render material and comprehensible the noncorporeal and incomprehensible. The body's actions render visible the invisible.

As Wariboko writes so eloquently, the Pentecostal sensorium exists to "pierce any phenomenal (temporal) veil."[69] The Pentecostal sensorium is deeply embodied and pushes human bodily awareness beyond the bounds of the phenomenal realm into the spirited. In the words of Brahinsky describing American charismatics, it is sensorially "crossing the buffer."[70] The buffer or veil might be even thinner for Ghanaian Pentecostals who imagine everything from the mundane to the fantastic as enchanted. However, the buffer is still one that must be negotiated. The world is always teeming with demons and one is ever being moved and controlled by the demonic or divine, but one must pierce the veil to become aware of that reality. That piercing is always intensely sensual.

One way the senses break into deliverance-dominant Pentecostalism is that prophets seek to determine the identities of demons of oppression or possession by using their senses. Demonic identities might be revealed to prophets in what the spirits say or how they speak. But more often, it is in how the spirits make human bodies move. If a person slithers on the floor like a snake, then this is a serpentine spirit. If a person tries to remove imaginary wedding rings, then this is suggestive of a battle with a spiritual marriage. Loud and high-pitched screams are supposed to indicate possession by witchcraft.

And wriggling and flopping like a fish out of water means that Mami Wata, a water spirit, has taken possession of the body.[71] I found that this kind of prophetic interpretive work was standard across my various research sites. While often it is the experts, the prophets, who diagnose these situations, as Kwofie and Nikoi led me through the various embodied performances and their corresponding diagnoses, they admitted to me that it was not difficult and involved common sense or a common sense-ability.

Yet, each prophet has his personal sense-ability of diagnosing demonic problems. Some describe audible voices from both the Holy Spirit and evil spirits, while others describe physical impressions such as pain, heat, cold, etc. Some see pictures over people's heads that substantiate the presence of a demon, and still others associate colors with specific demons. Sometimes people only feel the demonic after laying hands on a person, whereby the demonic feeling is transferred through bodies. Stephen Hunt cites one long-time practitioner who could smell out demons: a smell similar to rotting flesh.[72] Similarly, there are ubiquitous descriptions of spiritual sight, which enables prophets to see the manifesting demon. While the particulars vary, demons are sensed by both those afflicted with them and those tasked with evacuating them through deliverance.

THINKING WITH THE A-THEOLOGY OF EMBODIED DEMONS

Ghanaian theologian Kwabena Asamoah-Gyadu offers the following definition of deliverance:

> the deployment of divine resources, that is, power and authority in the Name or Blood of Jesus—perceived in pneumatological terms as the intervention of the Holy Spirit—to provide release for demon-possessed, demon-oppressed, broken, disturbed and troubled persons, in order that victims may be restored to "proper functioning order," that is, to "health and wholeness"; and, being thus freed from demonic influence and curses, they may enjoy God's fullness of life understood to be available in Christ.[73]

Birgit Meyer similarly defines deliverance as "invoking the power of Jesus Christ to set a person free."[74] These definitions capture the theological underpinning of deliverance—liberation from demons who impinge equally on the mundane and fantastic elements of human existence. But deliverance is not strictly a theological construct. While invocations are certainly an element of deliverance, the process of eliminating the demonic and consenting to the indwelling of the Holy Spirit is much more than prayer. To define deliverance as Asamoah-Gyadu and Meyer have is to miss out on the facticity of the flesh that defines the ritual. To alter a popular scriptural phrase frequently and zealously invoked by Pentecostals: deliverance is wrestling against (spiritual) principalities and powers through flesh and blood.[75] Wrestling in this instance is not metaphorical but emphasizes the primacy of bodily movement in deliverance.

Deliverance is not merely a propositional belief; it is an experience felt in human bodies, an act that imprints its mark on bodies, a practice that reads bodies and that ultimately defines bodies. Pentecostals learn of the body and through the body in kinesthetic and tactile experiences. Their Christianity is not obsessed with right belief but about sensing and reading bodies in motion.[76] Non-embodied theological propositions are viewed with suspicion. As Simon Coleman importantly points out, not only do Pentecostals prefer the experience of the body over theological or cognitive propositions, but they also actually denigrate the theological as obscuring authentic experience which is found only in the body.[77]

Ghanaian Pentecostal's suspicion of formal theology is warranted as such theological thought is ordered by modernity/coloniality.[78] In particular, "theology produces a notion of heterosexual life that needs to be contained and controlled."[79] Instead, Ghanaian Pentecostals trust bodily, sensuous experiences. As Nikoi shared with me one day after we had consumed sufficient jollof and chicken, "Deliverance is more practical than theoretical or theological. Deliverance is more practical because these are the experiences of the people. It is more about people's experiences than theology." In this way, deliverance performances, and most especially the sexual worldings in these performances, fit the mode of a-theology. Crawley defines a-theology as "thought that exceeds normative theological figurations, found in performance of moving flesh."[80] It is this a-theology that *Seductive Spirits* is interested in exploring.

Josh Brahinsky calls this bodily way of thinking and knowing "body log-ics—or portable sensory dynamics." Pentecostal body logics are central to Pentecostal hermeneutics and epistemologies.[81] While the tripartite "portable sensory dynamics" expertly capture how the senses cultivated in Pentecostal-ism travel with believers everywhere they go and form a potent and creative force for Pentecostals, I wonder how portable these senses are. It would be an error to equate portability with universality.[82] If by portable we assume per-formances of moving in the body, then the body logics are portable.

The Pentecostal sensorium is also intensely public and co-creative, de-fined by relational complexity and intimacy on multiple levels. There are sen-suous exchanges between the possessed and their apparitional paramour; the expert (pastor or prophet) and their demonic adversary; the judge (pastor or prophet) and the sinfully possessed; the succor (pastor or prophet) and desper-ately possessed; the congregation and expert; and the participating congre-gation and the possessed. In this way, Pentecostalism represents a departure from a long Christian history of emphasizing inner assent or belief, perform-ing among moving bodies an a-theology that refuses limits and orders around relationality.

Focusing specifically on the sensorium of Pentecostal Ghanaians is an important a-theological move in part because it is rooted in the assumption that sensoria are not universal. To challenge the universality of theology as ordering everything from sensations to salvation is necessary. Sensations are subject to variation historically and cross-culturally: "Sight, hearing, smell, taste and touch: that the senses should be enumerated in this way is not self-evident. The number and order of the senses are fixed by custom and tradi-tion, not by nature."[83] Kathryn Geurts argues that "a culture's sensory order is one of the first and most basic elements of *making ourselves human.*"[84] This approach illuminates how "in a cultural community's sensorium we find re-fracted some of the values that they hold so dear that they literally make these themes or these motifs into 'body.'"[85]

And indeed, senses have made the human, in particular as a construct of modernity/coloniality. Accordingly, the senses as such come with a hierar-chical and racialized inheritance. Georg Wilhelm Friedrich Hegel as an ex-emplar of modernity/coloniality devalued the senses and dismissed Africans as being governed by and excessively beholden to the senses. Zakiyyah Iman Jackson has demonstrated that Hegel's conclusions from reports of African religions racialized Africans as sensuous and bestial which opposed his ideals of Spirit, reason, and self-governance.[86] Ashon Crawley has also demonstrated that the modern/colonial world privileged reason at the expense of sensual perception.[87] More particularly, some of the Enlightenment senses such as sound, smell, and touch were dismissed via racialization.[88] Other senses were merely shaped in particular ways so that there were, for example, correct ways to see or not see.[89] Modernity/coloniality shaped how people dressed, moved, spoke, ate, gave birth, expressed sexuality, and much more, all thinly veiled as common sense.[90] Modernity/coloniality is about control of how the world is sensed and perceived. The subjects of modernity/coloniality were those who sensed and perceived correctly, and it was dubious that Africans could ever fully embody subjectivity in part due to what was described as their sensory nature. The manichean nature of modernity/coloniality set Africa as sensuous and, in so being, evil.

Traditional forms of Protestant Christianity were very much obliged by these sensual restrictions. The embrace of the senses herein as an analytical tool is a dramatic departure from Protestant norms. John Wesley, for example, tied sensuality to Satan.[91] While this book explores the senses in relationship with the demonic, it is not a modern/colonial dismissal of sensory natures as primitive or sinful. Instead, the sensuous is embraced for the way it defies humanist imperialism. Even the elucidation of the senses herein (touch, choreosonicity, metakinesis, and demonologeyes) attempts to explode the way the five senses are deeply imbricated in the history of race, religion, gender, and sexuality in modernity/coloniality. This is why *Seductive Spirits* is so committed to exploring the sensorium of Ghanaian Pentecostals. And consistent with the overarching conclusion of decolonial demons, the senses offer significant decolonial possibilities. The sensual perception via experiences by Pentecostals is a "problem" for modernity/coloniality.[92] This "problem" is what makes the Ghanaian Pentecostal sensorium so interesting and brimming with discursive and decolonial possibilities.

The senses and sensuousness need not remain trapped by modernity/coloniality. Walter Mignolo and Rolando Vazquez argue that the decolonial process is about "sensing, knowing, and believing."[93] Sensing is expansive when embracing alternative sensorial affiliations. For example, Gayatri Gopinath demands a "retraining of our vision and a reattunement of our senses, and in so doing points to the limits of the entire apparatus of vision that is the inheritance of colonial modernity."[94] Senses other than those imposed by modernity/coloniality are needed, and in sex with demons Ghanaian Pentecostalism may provide such expansive senses. Sex with demons cultivates new worlds and alternate a-theological orders of knowledge through senses disconnected from modernity/coloniality. Attention to sensory ordering within Ghanaian Pentecostalism provides alternative possibilities about what constitutes the body and embodied ways of knowing. This follows the clarion call from L. H. Stallings that alternative approaches to the senses lead "us to other possibilities and configurations of bodies."[95]

THINKING WITH SPIRITS EROTICALLY

The Pentecostal sensorium relies heavily on sexual interactions. While not the only form of human-cum-spirit interaction, spirited or demonic sexualities provide the most productive encounters where the supernatural is unveiled, felt, and experienced as real in human bodies.

Sexual experiences with demons play an enormous and underanalyzed role in Pentecostalism. Nonetheless, I must admit that I never intended to write a book about the demonic nor deliverance. I set out to write about an implicit eroticism I witnessed in the rituals of glossolalia, prophecy, and faith healing within a prominent Pentecostal congregation in Zimbabwe. And yet, a series of events led me instead to the outskirts of Accra, Ghana, where I was (sometimes forcefully) initiated into the Pentecostal world of deliverance and all its dueling forces. The locale and rituals for the project changed dramatically as did the primary focus on eroticism.

I had initially intended to explore something like the argument Martyn Percy has made: that within Pentecostalism—in the mawkish worship lyrics, sighs and groans of pleasure, the pursuit of ecstatic desire—there is a latent ideology of sublimated eroticism.[96] I saw this unnamed and untaught but certainly cultivated and nurtured eroticism as deeply embodied in the Pentecostal rituals I was studying at the time—speaking in tongues, prophesying, and healings at the church I was researching. Others saw this eroticism too, for example, in an anecdote Harvey Cox provides in *Fire from Heaven* about his high school crush, Lois.[97] Cox said that within Pentecostalism *eros* was intertwined with *agape,* and it was "slightly seductive."[98] Percy went even further, claiming that Pentecostal experiences act as "sublimated masturbatory surrogates . . . for the otherwise arid diet of rational religion."[99]

As I turned my attention to deliverance ministry in Ghana, the implicit eroticism I had anticipated quickly became much more explicit; the sublimated masturbatory surrogates turned literal in scenes of public masturbation due to possession by the demon of masturbation. From my first Ghanaian deliverance service in early 2015, it became abundantly clear that this exorcistic ritual was explicitly sexual and sensual and that these characteristics underpinned how many Pentecostals understand everything from truth to deception, the body to the spiritual, wealth to poverty, and salvation to damnation. Instead of a theology of implicit eroticism, I was face-to face with a host of sexual demons as I encountered ubiquitous performances of and tales about Pentecostal believers having sensuous sexual partnerships with demons.

There are two distinct ways in which humans have sex with demons. The first revolves around those sexualities that Pentecostals consider sinful. Sexual sins lead to possession, and demons can be transferred between sexual partners, sometimes referred to as sexually transmitted demons.[100] In this worldview, there are innumerable sexual sins that can invite demons. Adewale Adelakun shares a sermon by Dr. Daniel K. Olukoya, a prominent Nigerian deliverance pastor whose ministry often revolves around sexual sins, in which Olukoya listed fifty sexual sins that bring about demons.[101] Various sexual sins, as identified in this earthly realm, including adultery, fornication, transvestitism, masturbation, incest, and bestiality, are all viewed as leading to intense possession. These are viewed as some of the most challenging spirits to be delivered from.[102] Illicit sex between humans is not the only activity that can lead to possession; one can eliminate the human mediator and have sex directly with demons. This occurs most prominently in spiritual marriage, as we have witnessed already in the case of Esther. In this framework, demons are capable of participating in human activities, especially but not limited to sex acts. In both sexual options deliverance-dominant Pentecostals spend a lot of time discussing, participating in, and ritually reenacting demonic sex that pushes beyond strictly material definitions of the body.[103] This expansive understanding and ubiquitous performance of the relationship between the demonic and human via sex demands scholarly attention.

Sex with demons and the Pentecostal response in deliverance performs sensual sympoiesis. Donna Haraway defines sympoiesis as "making with," that is to say that one does not make oneself.[104] Sex allows for all sorts of sympoiesis, the making and unmaking of the human in conjunction with demons and creating the potential for surprising change, blurred boundaries, and endless possibilities. Within this sympoiesis there is a kind of suspension of Pentecostal morals, a lack of censure. The possessed, the prophet, and the demon all speak with a frankness that can be described as "highly pornographic."[105] Discussion flows freely about sexual encounters, orgasms, violence, transgressive sexual acts, and pleasure.

Thinking erotically with spirits has been done in the past and necessitates a rethinking of some of the most standard academic categories. It requires pushing beyond sexual identities to rethink foundational categories such as normative and nonnormative, good and evil, human and nonhuman. Theologian Marcella Althaus-Reid used Soq'a Machu to think with and through sex with spirits. Soq'a Machu, a sexually mischievous Peruvian spirit who existed before humanity, haunts the night.[106] Althaus-Reid, though, is particularly adept at reading hauntings, dismissals, and negativity for their liberatory possibilities. And so, while Soq'a Machu is dismissed by many, Althaus-Reid instead notes the story of the widow Adela whose claiming that Soq'a Machu fathered her child alleviated some oppressive social consequences.[107] The liberation may remain constrained by social mores and cisheteropatriarchy, but it "provides a 'way out,' a means of normalizing a sexual transgression in society."[108] Others have made similar claims emphasizing the central role of spirits in African sexual theorizing, especially sexualities beyond heteronormativity. For example, academic and activist Stella Nyanzi, in her essay "Queering Queer Africa," makes the point that spirits are a vital category for indigenous African queer theorizing.[109] It is this kind of thinking that *Seductive Spirits* participates in, unwilling to simply reprise the obvious cisheteropatriarchal scripts and convinced that each sexual encounter with the demonic offers something more, a different worlding, and maybe even something liberatory.

The performance of sex with demons in deliverance rituals stretches and shatters normative definitions of sex. Each sexual encounter with spirits is an important addition to "erotic diversity," a category which Keguro Macharia uses to expand sexuality beyond post-sexological taxonomies (homosexual, heterosexual, bisexual, man, woman) in order to understand African sexualities of the past, present, and future.[110] Sexuality cannot encounter spirits and remain beholden to traditional theories of sexuality. Instead of effacing such experiences, adding sex with spirits to our understandings of erotic diversity will create potent ruptures in modernity/coloniality and its many sexual appendages.

The answer to the question "what is sex?" will develop throughout the scenes of this book, not linearly but with each new piece of information tugging and pulling definitional possibilities in new directions. Each tiny variation reshapes the act(s) at the core of this book. Combining intimacy and corporeality, the various experiences of sex with spirits begin to create a whole new sexual cosmos. So, while each chapter loosely correlates to a familiar sexual category (chapter 3 to masturbation, chapter 4 to homosexuality, chapter 5 to heteronormative marriage, and chapter 6 to bestiality), none of these categories are of much utility. The experiences described bear only a passing resemblance to the title ascribed. For example, in chapter 3, "Singular Scenes," the mechanics of the public performance surely match masturbation. The chapter is filled with people who are manually stimulating their genitals. But monosexuality or autoeroticism does not apply here because they are not acting alone; instead, demons are intimately implicated in every element of masturbation, from arousal to climax and thereafter. These sexual categories should be thought of merely as placeholders as we seek a language and grammar to describe the sexuality at hand. They are not in any way meant, like sexology, to maintain the means of cataloging or managing sexual difference. Especially because with demons none of these sexual categories are dichotomous; instead, each category bleeds and blends into the others. In many ways, as the deliverance episodes throughout demonstrate, the sexualities herein are uncapturable, flying in the face of the efforts of modernity/coloniality to limit, define, and hierarchize sexualities.[111] The only constant is the performative excess of deliverance-dominant Pentecostalism with its attendant writhing, flailing, whirling, obstreperous, languid, wanton, hot and bothered bodies.

SEDUCTIVE SPIRITS

This book is my ethnographic and theoretical attempt to explain and explore why sexual experiences with the demonic are so central to Pentecostal understandings of this world and beyond. In order to do so, I mine the polyvalent sensory experiences in bodily invasions by demons through sex and attempts to rid the body of these demons through deliverance. This book is an argument for the order of sensation, that is the perception of *pneuma* through various senses.[112] Through deep observation and thick description, we can begin to unwind the senses and their relationship to bodily modes of knowing. This book seeks to remain faithful to the materials of Pentecostalism, bodily feelings, and their centrality to religious rituals rather than propositional truths.

Seductive Spirits is made up primarily of ethnographic data I collected from four deliverance ministries in greater Accra, Ghana. I will describe each of these ministries in more detail in chapter 1. In 2015 and 2016, I spent nine months researching deliverance ministries in greater Accra, Ghana. As Joseph Quayesi-Amakye notes, "Accra is . . . the nerve centre of religious activities with the bustling presence of Pentecostal prophets."[113] Detailed phenomenological data were gathered at deliverance meetings I attended. At most of these places, I was a participant-observer who watched carefully as the various deliverance ministries went about their business of defeating the demons. At some of the sites, I had access to their recordings of various services, and at other places, I was able to capture some of the happenings on my camera. While I visited many different deliverance ministries, I visited the ministries of the four particular prophets at least weekly and often more frequently.[114]

I claim to have been a participant-observer at these sites, but I must admit that I carry with me a stubborn and cynical body. It wasn't always this way—I remember many an instance in my youth where bodily movements and sensations were chalked up to the Holy Spirit. In particular, I remember during one all-night prayer service being instructed by a charismatic pastor to pay attention to the spirit moving in my body. All it took was a shiver, and I became convinced that it was undoubtedly the Holy Spirit moving through my body. I do not know where this kind of certainty emerged. I disingenuously framed the experience with doubt despite being so self-assured. I had felt the spirit.

But things change, bodies change, and here I was in spaces familiar and unfamiliar, comfortable and uncomfortable, and my body did not move much, did not feel much. I found it extremely difficult to participate in all the embodied actions of deliverance. I would swing slightly to the music but without the out-and-out dancing that the congregation partook in. I would pray prayers that my interlocutors taught me but without the karate chops, fist pumps, and sweat-inducing physicality of my informants. I would clap along with the praying congregation, but my hands met absent the ferociousness with which my informants brought together their hands. And when prophets prayed over me, my body remained stuck, rigid, and unresponsive. But despite my own tepidness, I regularly experienced moments of sensory immersion where my senses were simply overloaded. There was so much to see, hear, and interpret, too much. Sometimes when things were particularly intense, I would find excuses to step outside of the intensity, pretending to take notes, playing with my camera, or usually sneaking out to snack on puff-puffs. Past experiences and the sensorial overload forced me to place this radical sensorium as knowledge at the center of this study.

In addition to participant observation, I conducted interviews with people who experienced sex with demons and/or sexual deliverance. I conducted over one hundred interviews that explored the sensations of deliverance. Interviews lasted between twenty-five minutes and two hours, depending upon the interest of the interviewees. Most of the interviews were conducted in English and tape-recorded. Where the interviewee did not allow tape recording—a rare occurrence—notes were taken. The bulk of the interviews were conducted with people from the ministries described above and followed a similar pattern in which we discussed their own particular experiences of deliverance. My interviewees regularly explained their experiences in sensory terms with bodily sensations creating certainty about that which lay beyond. The experiences discussed included some I had witnessed publicly and many more that either lacked publicity—such as having sex with spirits in their bedroom—or that had happened at another ministry.

During the first few deliverance services I attended in Accra, the ubiquity and creative application of sex in possession and deliverance surprised me. The crude specificity, embodied evidence, and voyeuristic pleasure in human-cum-demon sex was explicit and public. Furthermore, I was uncomfortable witnessing how the prophets used their power to peep and prod through voyeuristic and physical methods. That discomfort exponentially increased as I tried to write about that which expressly played on shock, titillation, and force. This book provides thick description of sex in deliverance, which will at times, undoubtedly, make the reader uncomfortable. This is, in many ways, a trigger warning as some of the sexual descriptions and violent deliverances may evoke trauma and pain.

Additionally, what was rarely a conversation with my interlocutors in the field but has obsessed me and worried me ever since is race. As a white ethnographer I have to acknowledge the long history of the racializing sexualities of modernity/coloniality that precedes me not as some distant past but as a contemporary reality into which I find myself entangled.[115] I remain convinced that telling these stories, sharing these scenes, has the potential to explode human sexuality as that which was "systematically designated for white bodies and sexual savagery for non-white ones, Black bodies most of all."[116] My intentions aside, I have written this book with the question "how do I avoid the racializing ethnopornographic gaze?" at the forefront of each decision I have made in constructing this text. While I will critique moments when power was imposed in unjust or problematic ways, the more time I spent in these communities watching, listening, and feeling, the more I became convinced that this was not only about the sexual fantasies of a few but was an amalgam of sexual fantasies, desires, fears, and sensations that helped many to understand their own bodies and how those bodies interacted with others in the world around them and the worlds beyond them.

Further, while modernity/coloniality is overly obsessed with African and black sexuality, contemporary Africanist and Pentecostal scholarship has swung too far the other way in its sexually conservative nature. There is a risk in the silence. Neither obsession nor silence is the appropriate tact. *Seductive Spirits* is wholly committed to not replicating the obsessions of modernity/coloniality which were rooted in taxonomies and hierarchies for the purposes of white supremacy. But Pentecostalism is not asexual, and its erotics are not confined to the personal or the private. Pentecostal erotics are a rich means of worldmaking, of offering vibrant alternative possibilities, and of rethinking the world within which we exist. And so, my plea is that *Seductive Spirits* be read through this lens. It is certainly the approach I took in writing the book, though any failings to adequately do so are my failure to accurately capture otherwise possibilities.

———

Christianity, especially with sexual demons, is about embodied experiences and practices "for getting in touch with an 'elsewhere,' an 'otherness,' or a 'wider self' that lies beyond the horizons of one's immediate lifeworld."[117] In that sense, *Seductive Spirits* represents the contributions of my interlocutors, conceptualizing interdependent, sensual, and sexual relationships between spirits and humans as described to me. Still, there is something more, and *Seductive Spirits* pushes beyond what many of my interlocutors were able or willing to consider, into the ambiguity and open-endedness of these sexual experiences. To push into this indeterminacy is to both read bodies and bodily sensations as "indexes of spirit presence and agency" and to embrace the surplus of meaning in spirit-cum-human erotic encounters.[118] Where I push beyond the worldviews of my interlocutors is when I introduce theoretical conversations to augment, challenge, and explore their experiences. This melding of theory and ethnography is a novel approach to Pentecostalism and one of the ways that I avoid the ethnopornographic gaze. I explore sex with demons because I firmly believe that sex with demons in deliverance-dominant Pentecostalism challenges social norms and moves toward a new framework of being, belonging, and intimacy. Each performance, from public masturbation to trans-mogrification into animals, demonstrates how sex is used to expand the definition of the body beyond its fleshy boundaries and to make spirits immanent.[119]The performance of sex with demons in deliverance rituals stretches and shatters normative definitions of sex. In fact, it pushes even further by crafting decolonial sexual worlds. The innovation and creativity of these sexual worldings demand exploration.

Seductive Spirits begins with a chapter on the various influences that have shaped the contemporary Pentecostal scene in Ghana, with a particular emphasis on those sources that influenced demonic sex. The sources are wide-ranging, from biblical exegesis to *The Exorcist,* Western preachers to West

African tell-all books. In chapter 2, "Indecent Scenes," I develop pneumo-eroticism as a hermeneutic for reading sex with demons. This largely theoretical chapter brings together a story of a spirit of masturbation named Maggie with Marcella Althaus-Reid's theorizing of the orgy. In so doing, I aim to develop a capacious hermeneutic for reading sex with demons that takes sex seriously.

Chapters 3 through 6 follow a similar pattern. Each chapter combines a loose sexual category with a unique sense practiced by Ghanaian Pentecostals. These chapters are heavy on ethnographic data, filled with experiences with demons that present a cosmos of limitless sexual possibilities. Every scene in this text is an example of the boundless and spirited sexualities performed in deliverance. In chapter 3, "Singular Scenes," I explore the spirit of masturbation through the sense of touch. In chapter 4, "Scenes of Struggle," I explore queer sexualities through a choreosonic sense. This chapter is unique in that it centers around a failed deliverance which strengthens my case that deliverance, in these cases, is about the performance of sexualities and not primarily the defeating of demons. In chapter 5, I explore spiritual marriages between demons and humans through the sense of metakinesis. These sexual experiences often occur in hazy dreamlike states. For Ghanaian pneumatic Christians, these dreams are real embodied experiences, distinct from Western ideas of dreams as imaginary and inconsequential. In chapter 6, I explore a particular genre of spiritual marriages in which the demons manifest as animals. Here I rely on the portmanteau demonologeyes to describe the non-occularcentric sense of sight on which Ghanaian Pentecostals rely.

In the conclusion I depart from the thick description of the previous chapters and explore how demons, in the words of Corten and Marshall-Fratani, arouse a "messy exuberance of meaning."[120] In that exuberance I find that demonic sexual worldings challenge much. Among those things that are challenged are modern/colonial understandings of good and evil, especially with regard to sex. As such, it is absolutely vital that academics explore Pentecostal demonologies not as another form of redemption but as decolonial possibilities. I do so by engaging a variety of theorists and theologians including but not limited to Frantz Fanon, Katherine McKittrick, and Marcella Althaus-Reid.

This book has been a surprise to me at every turn, from the content to the conclusion. I imagine some of it may come as a surprise to you. My purpose is relatively simple, to demonstrate that the subject exists and matters. I have not tried to exhaust the subject, much remains to be explored. *Seductive Spirits*, then, is much more an invitation than a definitive declaration, an invitation for you to think, feel, and imagine the world through sex with demons.

ONE

HISTORICAL AND CONTEMPORARY SCENES

The sources that make up the content of *Seductive Spirits* are multiple. I've already mentioned the many interviews, mining my interlocutors' stories for details of their encounters with the demonic. I've alluded to the participant observation, though much more detail on the research sites can be found in the coming pages. But there is a wealth of history, literature, film, and story that constructed the conditions for the worldmaking I found in deliverance-dominant Pentecostalism. So while this chapter is a recounting of my sources, it is also an explanation of how Pentecostalism arrived at its current place, and it is a de-exoticizing of the content of *Seductive Spirits* by demonstrating just how prevalent such ideas are.

RESEARCH SITES

As previously mentioned, *Seductive Spirits* is made up primarily of ethnographic data I collected from four deliverance ministries in greater Accra, Ghana. I attended each of these sites on a weekly basis in such a way that Mondays were spent with Kwofie, Wednesdays with Emmanuel, Thursdays with Ofori, and Saturdays with Nikoi. The other days were still often spent at deliverance services as Tuesdays were often spent at one of Emmanuel's other sites in Tema, Friday nights were often spent at all-night prayer services in Accra and Tema, and Sundays were spent visiting Pentecostal churches other than the four that make up the data herein. While the point of this text is not strictly a comparison of the four sites, indeed I spend most of my time articulating what they had in common, it is necessary to paint a picture of what each deliverance ministry was like to help set the context for the scenes within. Despite holding much in common, it will become clear that each site offers a unique approach to the demonic.

I first met Kwofie by chance, though he would claim it was divine. Aware of his name as it figures in the works of two prominent Ghanaian scholars of Pentecostalism, Opoku Onyinah and Kwabena Asamoah-Gyadu, I set off walking about Madina, the bustling suburb of Accra where Kwofie had previously ministered. As I walked the streets asking about him, most people were convinced that he was still imprisoned for defrauding a congregant of a large sum of money. I had information that he had been released, so I ventured on undeterred. I walked for hours. I finally happened upon someone who took me to his church, which was in a state of disrepair. It was late on a Saturday afternoon. I was dusty and dirty from the hours of walking the neighborhoods desperate to find Kwofie. I walked into the seemingly empty church to find a lone figure sitting in a plastic chair that bent and curled under his weight. I introduced myself and explained that I was looking for Kwofie. "I am he," he said, "I have been waiting for you." His prophetic utterance sent this researcher askew, worried that perhaps I was ill-prepared for the consequences—supernatural and otherwise—of my fixation with Pentecostalism. But from that moment, our relationship flourished and resulted in hours upon hours discussing deliverance and demonology. We would regularly review various episodes and performances I had witnessed, and accordingly, his interpretations and ideas imbue much of what follows.

Kwofie's church was one of Ghana's first deliverance ministries. He is an imposing figure standing over 6'6" with broad shoulders and a booming voice and is synonymous with the early years of Pentecostal deliverance in Ghana. His knowledge of demonology is expansive, and before prison, he was regularly visited by those who then went off to start their own deliverance ministries. My friend Philip, a junior deliverance minister at another sizeable Pentecostal church, called Kwofie a "pioneer in demonology and deliverance." As Kwofie tells it, he inaugurated deliverance in Ghana, and he will occasionally claim he was the first to do deliverance in Africa. This is an exaggeration; he did not start deliverance in Ghana, but he was undoubtedly one of the earliest practitioners of the popular ritual. Most prophets and prophetesses I met had attended Kwofie's ministry in the past and learned from his demonology and deliverance. Even though his congregation has dwindled considerably, at least at the time of this writing, as supplicants hop from one deliverance site to another in search of the proper antidote, they are undoubtedly encountering Kwofie's impact on Ghanaian deliverance.

Emmanuel, the prophet whose deliverance performances are most prevalent throughout this book, is no less controversial than Kwofie. His charismatic excesses also briefly landed him in prison. Emmanuel is a young, stylish prophet who has irked the more established stars of the Pentecostal constellation in Ghana. He is infamous for both his deliverance methods and his various scandals, including impregnating and then cursing the wife of one of his junior pastors. His outsized personality with the press is incommensurate with the kind, soft-spoken, almost shy manner he speaks to me as a friend and a "spiritual son." His church, which is a large congregation, is set in a compound in Ashaley Botwe, a suburb of Accra. He lives on the compound along with his television station, employees, and a variety of pastors and prophets. The compound is littered with life-size kitsch figurines of Jesus and Mary alongside life-size portraits of Emmanuel and his wife, who is a well-known gospel singer in Ghana. The church was in the midst of expansion the first time I was there. It seats a few thousand persons on red plastic lawn furniture and is nearly always full well in advance of the service. People will occasionally camp out inside the building waiting for his miraculous deliverance services.

Emmanuel is, undoubtedly, one of the most notorious contemporary Pentecostal prophets in Ghana. Along with dismissals from other Pentecostal prophets, the church is the frequent target of memes and other critiques through social media, is regularly adjudicated in the media, and is used in many ways as the example par excellence of Pentecostal excesses. Accordingly, the church is often scorned by traditional Pentecostal pastors and prophets for a variety of extremes, most notably for its troubling use of violence within deliverance rituals.[1] In particular, Emmanuel is often accused of being an *azaa* (fake) prophet whose spiritual prowess came by way of the "occult."[2] Such critiques doubt the source of Emmanuel's spiritual wares but not their power.

Emmanuel leads three congregations that each number in the many thousands. Deliverance happens in Ashaley Botwe every Wednesday and is attended by more than three thousand people and, according to the participants, many more spirits. Most of those three thousand persons are not church members but are people in desperate need of deliverance, often coming from other churches and occasionally from different religious traditions. Emmanuel also has a large number of exclusively male acolytes, pastors of varied ages, who act as aides in deliverance but to whom he gives a fair amount of agency and responsibility during deliverance services. At times, he watches his pastors while they perform the deliverance rituals. He, though, is considered to be the most potent prophet by his followers and to possess a close and direct relationship of communication with Jesus, his "spiritual father," who gifts him his spiritual powers. Most notably, Badoe is the senior pastor at the Ashaley Botwe location and will play a prominent role in this book. Badoe has been earnest in his support of the prophet standing next to him in triumphs and trials (once literally while police handcuffed the prophet).

Much more restrained than either Kwofie or Emmanuel—noted, for example, by the fact that he has never been arrested—Nikoi provides another perspective. Nikoi is the junior pastor of one of Ghana's most established Pentecostal figures. His position is of some repute but belies his real passion for deliverance. Every Saturday for approximately six hours, Nikoi enacts deliverance for those who seek it in a dilapidated tent in back of an opulent church building in Adenta, a district further down the Accra-Aburi highway than Madina.

The service here is part of a concentrated deliverance experience whereby participants must attend five services to guarantee deliverance. The service is exclusively for deliverance. Unlike many places that use deliverance as the climax following corporate prayers, singing, testimony, and a sermon, Nikoi's service begins promptly at 8 a.m. and immediately launches into intensive deliverance. The milieu and atmosphere change abruptly from the drudgery of early morning to something matching the intensity of a Black Stars match.[3] Nikoi and his pastors have the deliverees stand huddled in a group at the front of the tent where they are to be in constant prayer. While the deliverees pray, each pastor grabs—often forcefully—one of the deliverees and attempts to deliver him or her. Deliverance is performed in many ways, but in Nikoi's tent it always includes the spilling of copious amounts of oil and the deliveree vomiting into garbage-bagged-lined cardboard boxes. Vomiting is considered a primary way in which demons make their exit. The sounds of people vomiting, prayers exhorted, and screams all punctuate the air and can be heard as you approach the church from the road. These were marathon puke-and-rebuke sessions.

In deliverance centers like Nikoi's, delivered persons continue coming to sessions for five weeks in order to establish protection from demons who might return. There is a great fear that if delivered persons are not well established in their deliverance, then the demons will return, perhaps more viciously than before. Often people mention that Jesus said demons previously cast out return to ruinous effect, citing Luke:

> When the unclean spirit has gone out of a person, it wanders through waterless regions looking for a resting place, but not finding any, it says, "I will return to my house from which I came." When it comes, it finds it swept and put in order. Then it goes and brings seven other spirits more evil than itself, and they enter and live there, and the last state of that person is worse than the first. (Luke 11:24–26, NRSV)

The delivered body is described as empty, so the five weeks of teaching inculcates tricks for self-deliverance, receipt of the Holy Spirit's gifts, and learning what to avoid (bathing naked outside, sexual sins, etc.) to make one's body impenetrable. Despite the promise of five weeks to freedom, most attendees at Nikoi's tent stayed long beyond the allotted term. Demons abide in such a way that deliverance is never complete and so deliverees often stay beyond their five weeks or return for another five week set at the onset of a new demon.

The final prophet comes from a prayer camp, a much less friendly affair than the others. Prayer camps are perhaps the most intense way of dealing with demons, as they involve a residential period. Once a week or more, I would take a two-hour *tro tro* ride (the local mode of transportation) up the mountain, past the Aburi Gardens, to a prominent prayer camp. I would sidle past the goats and roosters that convened at the prayer camp and amble toward the center of the compound where sat the church building—a simple building with plenty of openings that made it feel as though the building was embraced by the rich green foliage of the hills. The outer ring of the camp has housing options that, depending on one's ability to pay, range from quite comfortable to nothing more than a dilapidated roof.

This particular prayer camp is overseen by the prophet Ofori. He is well known and revered; in the past, his prayer camp has been visited by such illustrious characters as the president of Ghana. Thursday mornings are when deliverance occurs at the prayer camp. The service starts with singing, testimony, and a sermon, but the highlight is when Ofori performs mass deliverance. Ofori's deliverance is far less individualistic than the other deliverances discussed above. Ofori tends to work the entire congregation into a frenzy so that the whole building is littered with bodies slain in the spirit. It is far less ordered and controlled than the other deliverances.

Deliverance with Ofori also happens in a one-on-one setting, which I watched on occasion. Three times per week, people can approach the prophet for counseling, which involves waiting for hours for a mere thirty seconds of the prophet's time. As people wait, they pray. When they finally meet the prophet, they discuss their particular issue. He then counsels them on how to receive deliverance. Most often, the counsel is that they should spend either twenty-one or forty days at the prayer camp fasting (though porridge and drinks are allowed). He will then pray with them, with the odd person falling out and experiencing deliverance on the spot. Usually, though, this is merely a diagnostic step that leads to a residential period at the camp.

While it is still busy and bustling, in many ways, the prayer camp has been overtaken by a miasma of internal paranoia. Most of that paranoia is justified, rooted in the reality that this prayer camp—and many others— treats people with mental health issues quite poorly. I was only allowed to do my research there on the condition that I would not seek out those with mental health issues. I did not. However, midway through my time visiting this prayer camp, things changed dramatically when a rather compromising document was published by a prominent nonprofit organization concerned with human rights. The report outlined the horrific conditions of people struggling with mental health issues at the camp, including details about how they are chained up and provided with very little in the way of material support. The report dramatically altered my relationship with the prayer camp and made research there quite difficult. My friend Mary, who has long lived at the camp and runs the convenience store on the compound, helped me navigate the difficult terrain and convinced people to talk to me. Her help and support did not alleviate everyone's distrust, and I was physically threatened by a junior pastor from America and eventually banned from the site. Nonetheless, there are many stories throughout this book from this particular research site.

GHANAIAN DELIVERANCE HISTORY

Each of these deliverance-dominant ministries claim that the foundation of their ministry is the model provided by Jesus. But the development and transformation of deliverance over thousands of years, the ebb and flow of its popularity, is impossible to track. Stephen Hunt writes, "Tracing the origins of deliverance is rather like embarking upon a subterranean voyage where some very dark crevasses may be encountered. The vast majority of leading advocates are themselves unsure of quite how things developed."[4] This claim is true of much of Pentecostal Christianity, which, regardless of context, is always an outgrowth of, in the words of Ogbu Kalu, tangled roots.[5] Still, the rhizomatic development of deliverance, especially sexual deliverance, must be outlined for it is replayed, with slight variation, again and again.

Besides its tangled history, the historical excavation of deliverance is made more difficult by virtue of often being dismissed as unrespectable and unworthy of attention. This is true of even the prophets in this book, each of whom are (or were) enormously popular but would not necessarily be considered mainstream. While most Pentecostals believe in the need for deliverance and indeed see it as one of the gifts or charismata, more established Pentecostal traditions in Ghana find some of the practices of my interlocutors to be off-putting. Off-putting, though, has also long been the sociological reaction to deliverance. In America, deliverance, a prominent element of the earliest instantiations of Pentecostalism, was forced underground in the middle of the twentieth century for approximately thirty years.[6] There was a revival of deliverance and demons in the 1970s and '80s, just as Pentecostalism began to rise in Ghana. Nonetheless, respectability remains a concern, and with the prophets in this book, Pentecostals and non-Pentecostals have voiced displeasure with their deliverance methods, with some excesses causing uproarious discord concerning the viability of deliverance itself.

To be clear, I am not providing a comprehensive history of demons from within Ghanaian Pentecostal practice. This is not a genealogy but an outlining of variegated influences as described or witnessed in the field. Such a genealogy is impossible. Pentecostal history does not work in genealogies; it is recursive. Prophets plagiarize each other and their predecessors in piecemeal and creative ways. The same goes for congregants; each sextifying narrative is the purview of the storyteller but revisits the sextifying of others. Nonetheless, it is worthwhile to collect some of the contributing factors even though a causal history is impossible.

This incomplete history is rooted in fieldwork. I often witnessed Ghanaian Pentecostals carrying two books to church, their Bible and something concerning demonology. Demonological and deliverance literature is always readily available at churches and street stands.[7] Most prominent prophets have added their own works to the genre, though there is significant overlap (read: plagiarism) between many texts. Nonetheless, there is a seemingly insatiable appetite for the genre, which extends into films. I constructed this particular list of influences in multiple ways. First, I read and watched every deliverance resource that Onyinah or Asamoah-Gyadu—early documenters of Ghanaian deliverance—cited as popular in Ghana. These sources were primarily Western and West African. I also read or watched all the resources that were named in the course of interviews or that I saw people carrying in church. Being exposed to these sources was not easy for this author, who has avoided frightful movies and books since a scarring preadolescent experience! I then curated the texts and films explored herein because they bear significant similarities to the deliverance and sexual demonology I found so prominent in Ghana.

By avoiding genealogy and honing in on the sources cited or witnessed in the field, this history is dramatically different from a history of demonization. Demonization, or diabolization in the words of Meyer, was an act of modernity/colonialism that rescripted African notions of religion, sexuality, race, culture, and being as evil.[8] Missionization assumed Africans were, in every way, unconsciously serving the devil before the arrival of colonialism's vanguard—missionaries.[9] In the words of Jomo Kenyatta, traditional African worldviews were regarded as "savage and barbaric, worthy only of heathens who live in perpetual sin under the influence of the Devil."[10] Demonization is not disconnected from the sources for sex with demons, but pursuing both developments would quickly become too unwieldy and expansive.

It is, though, worth establishing that missionization in Ghana played a significant role in the obsession with demons generally. Christian missionaries taught two conflicting theories about indigenous religions. Nineteenth-century Christian missionaries argued that indigenous spirits were mere superstition. Yet they simultaneously argued that these spirits were real manifestations of the devil and were the devil's demonic minions. The latter claim flourished, as Opoku Onyinah writes, "By the introduction of a personalized devil and the association of the gods with demons, the missionaries had unconsciously strengthened the belief in these gods and witchcraft, yet they had failed to provide for the holistic needs of the people (such as protection, healing, and deliverance). For the Africans, these images were real, life-threatening forces."[11] A manichean dualism was established between indigenous spirits and Christianity. Accordingly, exorcistic activities emerged in anti-witchcraft shrines, then African Initiated Churches, and eventually most prominently in Pentecostal churches.

In the dualism between demonic indigenous spirits and the Christian Holy Spirit, deliverance ministries manage to take indigenous worldviews and history seriously and simultaneously provide the succor that Onyinah claims missionaries could not. Deliverance offers the desired holism, and accordingly, the manichean demonization of indigenous spirits reached an apogee in deliverance ministries. Meyer concurs, writing, "During deliverance session, people (re)enact their possession by non-Christian powers, thereby integrating these entities into Christian worship, albeit in a subordinate sense."[12] Onyinah recaptures this unique demonological cosmos in the neologism *witchdemonology*. Witchdemonology maintains the Western term *demonology*, while the term *witch* stands in for the traditional Akan worldview.[13] That the witch is much more than a witch is illustrated by the fact that among his interlocutors Onyinah found no clear definition for terms like *witch* or *witchcraft*. They were instead used synonymously with demons and evil spirits of all sorts, but primarily in the demonization of Akan traditional deities.[14] With the association between the demonic and their African origins, indigenous spirits now needed to be fought to death, exorcised from a people and continent seen as more possessed than anywhere else.

The kind of Pentecostal development that led to the scenes herein can largely be traced to a boom in the 1980s, especially through parachurch organizations and global Pentecostalism.[15] What follows is a description of some of the resources that have been used in constructing the sexual-spiritual cosmos I encountered. I will outline three categories that influence much of African Pentecostalism: the Bible, West African sources, and Western sources. These categories are major shapers of every element of Ghanaian Pentecostalism. I will demonstrate just how prevalent sex with demons are in these wells from which deliverance springs. Ghanaian Pentecostals, long familiar with deliverance and spiritual warfare, used these sources to shape a comprehensive sexual demonology and catapult deliverance to the very apex of Pentecostal rituals.

Biblical Influences[16]

The Bible plays a role in sexual deliverance, but a relatively small one. When it comes to the Bible and deliverance, pneumatic Christians spend most of their time in the Old Testament. This Old Testament focus is entirely consistent with my argument that Pentecostals are not particularly interested in ridding the world of demons, but in engaging and encountering the demonic. The New Testament is a story of exorcisms, with Jesus casting out a variety of demons from a diverse group of people. The Old Testament is not a text of exorcisms, but it does contain a host of demons. It is those demons, and not Jesus the exorcist, about whom my interlocutors are obsessed.

Among Ghanaian Pentecostal Christians, Genesis 6 remains the primary textual source, and often the only textual source cited, for their theology of sexual spirits. In Genesis 6 the sexually insatiable "sons of God"—traditionally associated with some kind of lascivious angels—consorted with human women and produced giants. Early Jewish and Christian interpretations of this story concentrated on the sexual intercourse between fallen angels and humans, constructing, as Jennifer Knust has argued, a fear of miscegenation with supernatural beings.[17] My interlocutors were absolutely convinced of the realness of Genesis 6 and its continued reality all around them. To this end, a prominent demonologist in Ghana told me that "the marriage of sons of god to the daughters of men in Genesis 6 is a pollution agenda. The products are pollution par excellence." The "is" in "is a pollution agenda" importantly points to the present, not the past.

First Enoch adds specific details to the story, features that are prominent in Pentecostal retellings. While most Pentecostals would not be familiar with this noncanonical book, the details show up in sermons, personal narratives, and dire warnings. In First Enoch, a group of lustful angels led by Semjaza and Azazel were ejected from heaven and traveled to earth to have sex with human women. Solomon, a Ghanaian prophet who specializes in spiritual marriages, summarized the tale of lustful angels as the origin of spiritual marriage: "These women were harassed sexually by these fallen angels and by that spiritual marriage was introduced into the human race." Pentecostals believe this original sexual encounter between cast-out angels and human women led to the birthing of giants, which eventually led to the emergence of evil spirits and demons. Demons carried on the sexual tradition of the lustful angels and possess a desire and ability to seduce humans.

Like the manner in which Genesis 6 looms over Pentecostal practice, the figure of Asmodeus also plays an outsized role in demonic sex due to his role as ruler over the principality of sexual spirits. He was often considered by my interlocutors as one of the worst demons. The *Malleus Maleficarum* calls him the demon of lust, the devil of fornication.[18] Again, the stories of Asmodeus that are repeated throughout deliverance-dominant ministries come from a noncanonical text, Tobit. Like First Enoch, Pentecostals do not consider Tobit to be canonical. Despite it not being canonical and not being specifically cited by anyone I interviewed, the story of Asmodeus in Tobit acts as a template for deliverance from sexually insatiable spirits.

Tobit begins with a character named Tobias who desired to marry Sarah. This desire was a risky proposition as Sarah's seven previous potential husbands had been murdered on their scheduled night of matrimony. The murdering jealous lover was a demon named Asmodeus. Asmodeus loved Sarah and thus, as a jealous lover, thwarted these men's carnal desires. Although the story does not state whether Asmodeus slept with Sarah, as he does a great many Pentecostals, he was, in the original text at the very least, a demon obsessed with her sex life. Tobias, according to the story, required supernatural assistance to defeat Asmodeus. Supernatural aid comes to Tobias in the form of the angel Raphael who helps Tobias avoid becoming the eighth dead groom by exorcizing and binding Asmodeus.

Asmodeus, though, is not merely a mythical character bound to history by Raphael's spiritual strength but remains a spirit spouse among charismatic Christians in Ghana, a spouse who sleeps with humans and refuses to allow human marriages to occur. Stories of Asmodeus get replayed with new inflections in the lives of the faithful. Asmodeus, in particular, is a helpful guide to how Pentecostals imagine and approach the supernatural as a terrifying, ambiguous possibility that can and does impinge on the quotidian elements of being human.[19] Like Sarah, humans in spiritual marriages have less success in amorous relationships because their spirit spouses are jealous lovers. With heartbreaking details of repeated failures, many people described to me how their spirit spouse—their Asmodeus in some form or guise—was destructive to their loving relationships. In some cases, the spirit spouse would merely make it impossible for the person to enjoy human company and sex. In other cases, the jealous spirit spouse threatened their human lovers with pain or death if they continued to sleep with the spirit spouse's beloved. In extreme cases, human lovers disappeared entirely at the behest of the spirit spouse. Jeanne Rey tells the story of a Congolese woman who would wake up to her husband lying on the floor. While neither husband nor wife could figure out why he was no longer in bed, they eventually concluded it was because the wife was in a severe spiritual marriage and the jealous spirit spouse was ejecting the earthly husband from the bed to have intercourse with the wife. The woman reported that the spirit that slept with her was headless and regularly had sex with her to the point where she could identify his "sperm on her body while taking a shower."[20] The specter of Asmodeus continues to work in these stories—destroying, threatening, and dispatching human lovers.

Adam and Eve also play into the Pentecostal exegesis of sexual demons. The Prophet Ofori spent almost an entire morning outlining a complete biblical genealogy for spiritual marriage that started not with Genesis 6 but instead with Adam and Eve and continued into the present. In particular the story of the fall in Genesis was the provenance of spiritual marriage. Ofori told me, "When the devil came into the Garden of Eden that relationship there when you go deeper, you know in my own conscience, it is about spiritual marriage." In a not entirely novel reading, Ofori implied that Eve and the serpent had sex, something he confidently referred to as "the generation of spiritual marriage." Things worsened in Genesis 6, and the genealogy continued until it infiltrated Jesus's family. It is unclear how exactly many of the stops along the genealogical timeline constitute spiritual marriage. For example, he included the story of Judah sleeping with Tamar in Genesis 38 as spiritual marriage, but the text itself includes no evidence of spirits. Still, he was adamant: "When you trace spiritual marriages, they come through the generations. Jesus came to break spiritual marriages in his family."

Sometimes, after having delivered the congregants at his prayer camp from evil spiritual spouses, Prophet Ofori instructed the congregation that they needed to "Enter a spiritual marriage with Jesus." The crowd cheered at this possibility. Ofori told them, "Jesus is going to be your spiritual marriage. You will enter a soul tie with Jesus." This is interesting language in the context of spiritual marriage. In the context of Christianity, Jesus frequently makes an appearance as the metaphorical bridegroom for whom Christians should wait. Phillip said, "We are married to Jesus Christ only." Likewise, Nikoi, in the middle of delivering a woman from a spiritual marriage, yelled, "Jesus, come and marry her" before launching into a sermonette about Matthew 25. Ofori explained to me, "God loves us, so He married us. Spiritual marriage is not all evil. The original spiritual marriage is what we have as Christians to enjoy."

In conversations with Ghanaian Pentecostals, this relationship was often referred to as a positive spiritual marriage, the ideal supernatural human exchange. However, this spiritual marriage was rarely discussed and never performed in the manner demonic spiritual marriages were. I frequently asked how one differentiates between good and bad spiritual marriages, and the most common response was that betrothal to Jesus does not involve sexual intercourse; it is an asexual relationship. Or, as Ofori stated, "The Bible says in Isaiah 54:6 'Your creator is your husband,' that is why we are Christ's bride. As a Christian, we are married to the Holy Spirit. The Holy Spirit does not have sex with us; it marries us to help us." The limited talk of positive spiritual marriages and the repeated emphasis on the Holy Spirit's asexual nature reminded me of Okot P'Bitek's *Song of Lawino* which parodies the third member of the trinity as "the Clean Ghost."[21] The Clean Ghost and this asexual marriage is quite the opposite of spiritual marriage to evil spirits, which is always and explicitly sexual.

This sexual demarcation between good and evil spiritual marriages has not always been the case for Pentecostals. Sean McCloud has curated a number of occasions in which people explicitly articulated a sexual connection to Jesus, the Messianic bridegroom. One woman shared about being aroused by Jesus and taken to the bridal chamber of love. The beauty of the experience convinced the woman that it was God uniquely loving her. Another group of intercessors all had the same dream, "in which Jesus appears and begins to touch them physically and sexually."[22] Of course, each of these examples had their naysayers who believed that such sexual interactions must necessarily be from demon lovers and accordingly subjected the women to deliverance.[23] Nonetheless, it is noteworthy that some find the experience too beautiful to be imagined as demonic.[24] While I found nobody in Ghana who articulated marriage to Jesus in sexual terms, almost everyone I interviewed was adamant about the pleasure—extreme pleasure—that resulted from the sexual encounters with demons.

West African Influences

While it is important to note the persistence of sexual spirits throughout Christian texts, it is equally important to note that such spirits are littered throughout most religions. The Islamic *jinn* and Greek *satyrs* are prominent examples, but various West African religious traditions also contain include spirits sleeping with humans.[25] The penchant for spirited sexual partners as an explanatory framework within West Africa is rooted in the indigenous worldview. One such prominent West African deity is Mami Wata who Pentecostals have dramatically sexualized. Mami Wata, by far the most common sexual spirit in Ghana, is a mermaid-like spirit who dwells at the bottom of the ocean. On earth, there are shrines in her honor, mostly located in the Volta region. Alternatively, for Pentecostals she is a universal demon—a kind of succubus—believed to be a fallen angel. Pentecostals fear her sensuality and sexuality for she is, as Birgit Meyer referred to her, "Satan's most seductive demon."[26] Chimaraoke Izugbara writes of Mami Wata's abode that it is a "fantasy space located at the bottom of the sea, where money and commodities are generated in exchange for sex and sometimes blood."[27] The erotic Mami Wata uses her wealth and wiles to "bait her adepts into orgiastic sexual encounters."[28] In this account, after sex with Mami Wata, or the equally seductive spirits under her control, the human lover can no longer have sex with other humans. They are then sexually covenanted to Mami Wata, and the consequences of breaking the covenant are severe, ranging from a quick descent into madness to death.[29]

Mami Wata is usually represented as a woman. Prophets I spoke to described her fair skin, large eyes, and exquisite, long hair. Joseph, Kwofie's junior pastor, told me, "Mami Wata is a person with details of a fish, the tail of a fish, but from the stomach up to head it is a woman, a very nice, fair in complexion." When she manifests, her appearance is always described as excessively beautiful, almost too beautiful to behold. Her beauty plays a significant role in her ability to seduce men and women. Joseph continued, "Normally you see her naked, to attract people she is like a magnet, you can't even turn your eyes away. Slim, not big. Everything is accurate, but you cannot figure out the beauty of her. You'll begin to think about immoral things, sexual things. That might not even be in your mind, but seeing her, because of that charming ability in her, you will follow her." Such descriptions, almost verbatim, were common among the churches I frequented.

Despite the feminine magnetism that Joseph described, my interlocutors ardently believe that Mami Wata is not just a woman or even a woman at all, but a demon. Her gender is a mystery as she can woo human spouses indiscriminately, gender having no influence over who she claims as a spouse. Sometimes interviewees referred to her as female, sometimes as male, and sometimes simply as demonic. In the history of incubi and succubi there were innumerable musings about their ability to transition between male and female. However, due to the manner in which demons gender-bend in the narratives of my interlocutors, I think there is no need to tie Mami Wata, or any other demon, to binaries. Mami Wata, and all Pentecostal demons, are gender fluid. For example, she is not perceived as having ordinary genitalia but a form of genital fluidity. Images of Mami Wata tend to gender-bend by wrapping a snake in an erect phallic position around Mami Wata's waist while also emphasizing her breasts. In this image, neither male nor female sex is clearly inflected. Mami Wata in this depiction is first and foremost a demon or a spirit who then bends gender to her whims and goals. Mami Wata appears and reappears again and again in Pentecostal fantasies.

One of the most common West African sources of information on sex with demons are the ever-prevalent tell-all books which go into extensive details about sex with demons. In order to better understand these sexual tell-alls, it is important to explore the model each one follows, the 1988 publication of Nigerian evangelist Emmanuel Eni's *Delivered from the Power of Darkness*.[30] Eni's testimonial text has, for over thirty years, dramatically shaped the cosmos within which deliverance occurs. Eni's tell-all, published by Scripture Union, was and is read by many prophetic practitioners and believers alike.[31] Atiemo claims, "Its influence on the Ghanaian Christian psyche was great. For example, people refused to buy a brand of sardine called 'Queen of the Coast' because of allusions in that book to a spirit-being called by that name."[32]

In the book, Eni recounts his deep involvement with the spiritual underworld—especially under the sea—and how he escaped through deliverance. His storytelling is vivid and dramatic. The book explains how Alice, Eni's lover, introduced him to the underworld after he uncovered a collection of human remains insider her refrigerator. In the story, Alice revealed to Eni her illicit powers, and he, trapped by his love for her, surrendered himself to whatever and wherever his receiving such powers would lead him.[33] Once he succumbed to Alice, Eni's new and prodigious spiritual powers quickly defined his life, allowing him to meet Mami Wata.[34] Mami Wata visited Eni regularly disguised as a beautiful woman. Eni emphasizes that their relationship was nonsexual. She supposedly instructed Eni never to touch a woman, and he was faithful to this command. This kind of sexual control by Mami Wata is common, but Eni's not having intercourse with Mami Wata is unique. Often in Pentecostalism the sexual covenant with Mami Wata—that is the promise to not touch another—is concretized through sex between human and spirit. She is usually highly eroticized and sexually charged.

In Eni's story, Mami Wata invited him to visit her underwater abode.[35] The spirit world under the sea was vast, filled with science labs, design labs, a theater, and endless wealth. He stayed in this world for some time and then acquired the power of trans-mogrification into animal forms and escaped as a crocodile.[36] As Eni describes the journey into the spirit world, he emphasizes that these were physical experiences, a common plea among those who experience demons and deliverance. There is a certain realness—"these things are real"—attributed to the physical and material as opposed to the imagination. For Eni, this is not just a story but an accurate description of how his body traveled through space and time, encountering humans and spirits alike. The same certainty holds for the experiences described by my interlocutors throughout this book.

Eni's narrative, though, is nearly sexless, which makes it unique among firsthand stories of demonic interaction. Usually books such as Eni's are highly eroticized. But even in this rare example of spirit-human sexual abstinence, sex plays an important role. Eni describes one of his demonic roles as seducing pastors or acting as a sort of spiritual pimp to tempt clergy. Eni, in the employ of Mami Wata, explains that he would send beautiful women to specific churches where they would pretend to convert. After feigning conversion, the women would use the guise of spiritual immaturity and the need for discipleship to remain close to the pastor. Eventually, in this scheme, the assigned woman would begin sexual liaisons with the pastor, thus squelching the pastor's anointing. Sex was spiritually weaponized. According to Eni, once fornication with the pastor had commenced, the woman would depart, leaving the pastor's penis engorged and possessed.

Eni also describes sexual dreams (wet or otherwise) as the most common demonic tool for oppressing Christians. Such dreams are a defining feature of spiritual marriage—a kind of spectrophilia that largely takes place in a dream state. It is crucial to emphasize that in the Pentecostal worldview, these are not merely dreams that float away with the rising sun but are considered real sexual acts performed by demons. Those in spiritual marriages believe that they are not simply dreaming about enjoying coitus with demons but are experiencing the act of or material performance of a demon having intercourse with a human. Ignoring the reality of such dreams or dismissing them as normal is done at one's own peril.[37]

Eventually, Eni finds salvation and then deliverance. The entire second half of Eni's text is about the power of Jesus Christ to overcome all the evil that is laid out in the first half. After the evil has been exorcised from Eni's life, he becomes an active member of the Assemblies of God.[38] But in many ways, this is anticlimactic. For deliverance ministries, the exciting parts all occur in the first half of the text as he charts the realm of Satan. As Meyer writes, "The popularity of confession stories stems from the fact that they brighten the dark and make visible what happens therein."[39] The most striking and vital aspect of all texts in the deliverance genre is the fascination with the devil and the devil's agents.[40] Deliverance ministries claim their power by stating that they are the only religious groups capable of charting this realm and effectively responding to such evil.

A text similar to Eni's and also quite popular is Kalu Abosi's *Born Twice: From Demonism to Christianity*.[41] Like Eni, Abosi claims to have achieved a nearly unparalleled rank among the demonic and worked closely with Mamy Water and Satan moving between Nigeria and Benin to persecute Christians.[42] In question-and-answer format Abosi writes,

> Why is it that a Christian gets involved in having sexual intercourse in the dream? As. Remember that temptation is an advancement to spiritual life. Without examinations, no promotions for students. It is a spiritual attack by the devil. If he wants to get a believer, he will firstly lure him with sex in the dream. Depending on the believer's reaction (without serious prayer), the devil will wear and appear physically with the shape of a woman in order to tempt him to have it real. This will evolve the desolution [*sic*] of the ring which marks the presence of the Holy Spirit.[43]

Abosi makes it clear that sex with demons, especially through spiritual marriage, is fundamental to the Pentecostal understanding of the world.

One of my primary contacts, Kwofie, also wrote a book about his own tales of the underworld. A generous reader would note that the book contains marked similarities to Emmanuel Eni's work. A less charitable reader might accuse Kwofie of plagiarism. The basic outline is that Kwofie visited the rich spiritual underworld in the sea, met with Mami Wata and an assortment of other demons, and after years of intense deliverance was eventually delivered. His book is noteworthy not for its novelty, but for the marked way it describes the sensual elements of deliverance. This emphasis on the sensual is significant because Kwofie undeniably played a significant role in defining demonology in Ghana, most specifically in the greater Accra region.

Kwofie was born into a family of witch doctors and wizards. As he tells it, he was dedicated to demons before being born: "I remember my Mama told me that she felt the demons enter her womb and heard the devil say, 'he is our son.'" His childhood was filled with demons manifesting as shadowy figures, which felt more real to him than the natural world. Demons, as he tells it, are unique in size and form, but are remarkably consistent in function. They can be microscopic or gargantuan. They can take the bodies of humans or materialize in the bodies of animals. Sometimes they appear as combinations of animals and people, half humanoid and half animalistic, taking on the appearance of mythical creatures. Despite this variety, the function of each demon is to pursue and enter human bodies; to accomplish their evil deeds, demons need access to and control of human bodies.

Kwofie's book tells of visiting the city under the sea and seeing merfolk. He speaks of many cities under the sea, but the particular one he inhabited was off of the coast of Ghana.[44] Like most testimonial works, the second half of his book is about his conversion. But as he tells it, his conversion story is one of salvation and deliverance: "After salvation, it took about six months before I had a human heart because my heart was so demonized. So, I could not feel anything." The whole text turns on these five words: "I could not feel anything." For a while, at least, demons had completely befuddled his sensuous capacities. In these words, Kwofie articulates how the entire cosmos is in a battle over and for the human senses. Through deliverance Kwofie began to feel. This most notably manifests in the way Kwofie tells his story: the first half of his book—the possessed part—is almost entirely absent of bodily descriptions. The only description of bodies is the penetration of his body by demons. Kwofie's story does not describe how penetration felt, merely that it occurred. As soon as Kwofie begins talking about salvation and deliverance the text becomes rife with embodied descriptions.

Perhaps the most embodied description occurs when he is forced toward salvation. He bathed—a bodily cleansing that was not available to him as a witch doctor—and afterward heard a disembodied voice that instructed him to go to the Assemblies of God church. Before he could make any movement toward the church, he explains that he felt a big invisible hand grab his belt and push him across the street to the church. He tried to resist, but the hand kept pushing him forward. He became increasingly nervous as his body neared the church, and his "hands were trembling and then my arms began to shake. What was happening was I could not keep myself still." The kinesthetics of his bodily movement signaled to him that something different was happening to him. All around him he heard demons shrieking and moaning.

Kwofie experienced salvation and deliverance as an awakening of his senses. While embodied, these senses interact with the spiritual realm in a way that challenges conceptions of the body and its senses. Kwofie eventually made it into the church but not without more experiences in which the spiritual impinged on his awakening senses: "It was like an unusual spiritual force that hit me in the face when I slipped through the door." As the pastor invoked Jesus, Kwofie began to sweat. His body trembled. His mouth was dry. His throat was tight. His hands became clammy. His body became stiff. He felt a serpentine spirit moving up and down his spine. And Kwofie's body responded on its own, taking Kwofie to the front of the church where he converted. He was consumed by feeling in the body, which is the key to understanding his dramatic transformation. Of course, this was only the beginning of his deliverance, and Kwofie's text spends ample space reiterating the various demons he was delivered from over a two-year period.

The thing about Kwofie, and I deeply cherish the time we spent together, is that he is enigmatic. Stories told one day changed dramatically the next. Ideas expounded upon with dissertation-level detail were contradicted the following week. This inconsistency does not necessarily make him unique among Pentecostals; the centrality of spontaneity and creativity in Pentecostal rituals often leads to inconsistencies. But there are two critical details I gleaned from the significant amount of time I spent with Kwofie. The first is explained above in the sensuousness of his narrative, the centrality his senses play in understanding the complexities of the spirit world. Theologically, he was assured, demons play with the human sensorium. He stated so specifically, and repeatedly, "Demon entities use many different forms of control of humans, including having control over all the five senses." The second important detail Kwofie emphasized in his theologizing and in his deliverance practice is that deliverance is almost always sexual.

The most powerful of testimonies that probe the threshold between transcendence and materiality are sexual. Sextifying allows for a kind of performance of that threshold, remaking the visible and invisible as real. Nobody has sextified with quite the specificity or influence as Victoria Eto. While Eni was undoubtedly a more famous author, a case can be made that the demonology and ethos of deliverance in Ghana actually more closely resemble the cosmos as described by Eto, who was intimately and sexually involved with Mami Wata. Eto, importantly, illustrates the sexualization of deliverance rituals where "almost everything is subjected to a sexual interpretation."[45]

I contend that Eto, despite her somewhat muted status among the constellation of deliverance figures, constructed an entire cosmos of sexual demons
that continues to influence and shape deliverance-dominant Pentecostalism
in West Africa.

Victoria Eto was a Nigerian evangelist who lived and studied in Ghana
for a time.[46] Eto's videos and books are quite popular and surpass Eni's in
graphic detail, but also, I would argue, in their beauty, prose, and creativity. First published in 1981, Eto's *How I Served Satan Until Jesus Delivered Me*
follows the standard structure of the testimonial genre, beginning with a detailed account of her involvement with the demonic, which is followed by an
account of how she received deliverance. Eto states that the purpose of telling
such a tale is to "glorify His Name the Lord" who "opened my eyes to see everything that happened during my deliverance. I saw and understand all the
demons that left my body."[47] In chapter 6 I will further develop this extraordinary sense of sight that Eto describes, something I refer to as demonologeyes.
But what is worth emphasizing in her description of purpose is that the telling
of the tale, despite its lofty divine ambitions, is really about reveling in the
demonic. In protesting that the testimony is for God's glory she acknowledges
that her story could be read differently, that indeed the demons seem to be
center stage. In fact, her protestations seem to preemptively assume that the
titillating details will be read as glorifying the demonic. The succor of deliverance is secondary to the pleasure of revisiting Eto's very sexual demons that
she saw with supernatural clear-sightedness.

Eto's spirited sex scenes begin, as many do, with an intimate relationship
with Mami Wata. Eto explains that she was not the first in her family to have
this spirited intimacy; her father's spirit wife was also Mami Wata.[48] According to the book, the relationship between Eto and Mami Wata was fiercely
erotic. They exchanged bodies and spirits, indicating a kind of continuity
between the demonic and human worlds. This dramatic relationship of rec-
iprocity suited both parties, such that, "When I started astral-traveling she
possessed me fully so I could use her spirit as if it were mine and she could use
my body as if it were hers."[49]

Eto explains that she was sexually involved with other spirit forces as well.
When she was seven years old, she entered into a sexual relationship with the
demon Asmodee.[50] While a young Eto slept, Asmodee would have sex with

her. In a sentence that perfectly captures the paradox described by many of my interlocutors, Eto says, "It was like a dream, but it was real demonic contact."[51] Eto emphasizes how she experienced a mix of nocturnal secretions and tactile perversions at the hands (and other body parts) of Asmodee. Whatever this was, Eto makes it clear that it was embodied—both in her body and Asmodee's. The marital relationship was a contract of exchange; Eto received academic success and distinction and, in exchange, became a "sex weapon, used by the powers to drag men into demonic bondage."[52] Eto's sexual appetite became insatiable, requiring plenty of diverse partners, both material and demonic. In the book she writes that Asmodee rewarded her sexual insatiability by gifting her command of one thousand demons.[53] Eventually, Eto had sex with Lucifer, who bequeathed her even more demons.

Tactile intimacy was only enhanced when Eto became a lesbian, yet another sexual demon in the Pentecostal pantheon. As she said, "My eyes, ears, nose and skin had acquired such extrasensory powers."[54] In this phrase, Eto captures the reality of so many of my interlocutors, which is that sex obliterates sensual limitations. As such, in this portable Pentecostal sensory dynamic, the traditional senses are inadequate. The senses of sight, hearing, smell, taste, and touch do not describe Eto's experiences with Asmodee, Mami Wata, or the spirit of lesbianism.

It is not only the traditional senses that are inadequate to describe her sexual escapades; our ability to understand and define what constitutes sex is also obliterated. Eto writes, "The combination of spiritual and physical sex broke down my sex horizons."[55] The image of sex horizons is an interesting one, already demonstrating an expansiveness and inexpressibility. In the breaking down of those horizons, Eto points not to binaries or heteronormativity but infinite and boundless sexual possibilities. Sex with Satan, specifically, inaugurated what Eto describes as a period in her sex life whereby no level of creativity or volume of partners could satisfy her voracious sexual thirst.[56] Her sexual desires and possibilities were limitless.

As Eto explains, it was an inexplicable sexual encounter with another woman that led to her conversion. One of Eto's lovers converted to Christianity, and sometime after her conversion, Eto's partner stopped mid-coitus and explained why she could not continue and then left. Eto could not understand anything powerful enough to arrest sex and was left curious how and why someone would end such a relationship. Amidst exasperation, dissatis-faction, and desperation, Eto found Jesus. In a sentence dripping with innu-endo, she writes, "I was still probing when Jesus touched me."[57] Jesus's touch inaugurated a lengthy conversion for Eto from someone who self-identified as a "highly promiscuous . . . nympho . . . lesbian, as well as some-one who masturbated" to a Christian evangelist. Slowly she was freed from her various sexual demons.[58]

As with the texts described above, Eto's book is divided roughly into two: the first half is the life of sin, and the second half is the escape to freedom. However, even the section of the text that describes deliverance mostly reit-erates erotic—though not necessarily pleasurable—experiences. Ostensibly, the thesis of Eto's book is deliverance: deliverance is possible for everyone because it was possible for me, since I was possessed by more demons and more sex than anyone else. And Eto certainly wants the reader to believe she was among the most possessed: "Unlike most agemates of darkness I did not have a charm, but my flesh was so impregnated that it was a charm by itself. In fact, I was a satanic synagogue on legs. But I give glory to Jesus who has cleaned me and has made me a temple of the living god."[59] The critical component to this argument is not the cleansing but reiterating of her em-bodied cavorting with the demonic, her flesh impregnated with evil, and her existence as an embodied satanic synagogue. In reiterating and reliving the demonic, Eto reminds us that these demonic experiences, felt deeply in the body, are those that make sense of the world.

Eto continues to make a case for her embodied and sensual fascination or obsession with the demonic by describing her deliverance, erotic detail after erotic detail. The first demon to leave her was the spirit of prostitution. While pleading the blood of Jesus, Eto felt heat and pain in her vagina. When she was delivered from that pain, something else became wedged in her vulva. Deliverance eventually arrived through urinating a dense fluid. The spirit of prostitution had entered her body through the vagina and exited through the same orifice.[60] As she cast out the spirit of prostitution into the "bottomless pit in the name of Jesus," another spirit injected something into her thighs. In similar tales, she fought off the spirits of lesbianism and sex with men.[61] Her story is a steady stream of deliverance from one sexual demon, only to reveal another one.

In Eto's story, the spirit of masturbation posed a severe challenge, lingering in her body for years after her conversion. She nearly left the faith because she could not stop masturbating. She would abstain for months, sometimes literally inserting the Bible as a foil. This insertion of the Bible is not about *logos* but about the materiality of the Bible pressing against her genitals to help defeat the demon of masturbation, a connective tissue between the spirited and embodied. In describing the freedom she found, she cites Romans 6:6, which states, "For we know that our old self was crucified with him so that the body ruled by sin might be done away with, that we should no longer be slaves to sin." Her new self was finally masturbation-free; she successfully crucified the Victoria Eto ruled by the stubborn spirits of masturbation.

But Eto had not vanquished all of her sexual demons. Finally, she had to confront Mami Wata, her sensual spirit counterpart and spouse. One day while looking in the mirror, Eto explains that she saw a woman who looked exactly like her, except evil and untamed. Eto knew this was Mami Wata fixing for a fight over her conversion. During the violent deliverance, Eto convulsed, foamed at the mouth, and was "seized by an intense sexual desire." Deliverance is less about freedom and more about concupiscence. In common deliverance parlance, Eto pleaded with God to send down a fire that would consume Mami Wata and her sexual demons. As she prayed, she saw a scorched worm fall from her pelvis, and then more worms fell until a heap had gathered at her feet. As they were cast out, she "underwent a sexual paroxysm."[62] Freedom, though, was illusory, and the following morning Eto writes that she woke up in heat with a male demon stuck in her vulva. The orifices are always the threshold, the site where the transcendent (demon) encounters the material (her vulva). As she pleaded for deliverance, the demon turned into a distended phallus hanging from her vulva. "In Jesus' name" she severed the distended phallus and was finally free. And yet the precise and exhaustive sexual details throughout Eto's story of deliverance demonstrate that this is not a story about incredible freedom. This is a story of sensuous and sexual worldings, for every element of her narrative provides a chance to reiterate demonic erotics.

In her 1983 text *Exposition on Water Spirits*, Eto provides less sextifying and more theory, establishing an erotic demonological cosmos pivoting primarily around Mami Wata. This book is not a recapitulation of her autobiography, but a description of how to combat the demonic and their efforts to possess bodies and spread "sexual pollution."[63] In Eto's estimation, Mami Wata is the most pressing problem in West Africa, pressing her demonic body against human flesh in a variety of sexual acts.[64]

Eto's narrative and theoretical arc attempt to squash any accusations of pornographic voyeurism. However, it is hard to read the texts and not notice the pleasure and gratification in so many of the erotic details. Deliverance in this context is as much a reiteration of the erotic than anything else. She discusses demonic dogs that haunt a great many persons, including some of the prophets I spent time with. In describing deliverance from demonic dogs, she emphasizes their sexual organs and potential to utilize the dog's tail and tongue for sexual satisfaction.[65] In fact, the physical manifestations that result during deliverance are an embodied reiteration of sexual possession: "Some may roll their bodies as if under strong sexual urge, some will have sexual paroxysms, others will behave as if they are having sex, so will have a discharge and others will have a dry orgasm."[66] Deliverance is not a facsimile of demonic sex, it is a public performance of such sex.

The details of Eto's world tidily line up with the experiences, characters, and expressions of my interlocutors. She lists demons who sexually frequent human dreams. She discusses demons who weaponize human sexualities. She describes the jealous marine spirits Asmodee and Mami Wata who sensually and sexually wed demons to humans.[67] And she articulates how some demons impart animal sexuality into human bodies, which leads to an uncontrollable, almost violent need for sex.[68] These sexualities—sometimes by different names and forms but performing the same function—define the highly sexualized world of deliverance I experienced in Ghana.

Beyond textual sources, the Ghanaian popular film industry—Ghallywood—has spent many reels exploring demons of all stripes. The most popular of these films was probably the 1991 film *Diabolo* directed by William K. Akuffo. The film pivots around the idea of satanic wealth and the efforts of Diabolo—an attractive man—to gain this wicked wealth. But the means of acquiring such wealth are highly sexualized. Birgit Meyer describes the opening scene:

Diabolo approaches a prostitute, offers her some 30,000 cedis and she willingly agrees. They drive to his elegant villa outside town. There he hands her a drink, which almost immediately makes her faint. He carries her up to the bedroom and binds her to the bed. After drinking a strange bubbling concoction he starts trembling and shaking until he is transformed into a python. In that form he enters the prostitute's vagina. In the next scene he has become a human being again. We see him sitting on the bed by the woman, who is vomiting banknote after banknote. Impatiently Diabolo slaps her cheek whenever things don't go fast enough. He fills a whole suitcase with neatly stacked 1,000 cedi notes. When the stream of money comes to an end he sends her away. Groaning she stumbles through the streets until she collapses, dead, in her mother's compound, vomiting a few last coins and red slime. In the shape of the snake Diabolo visits her Christian burial, which is conducted by a catechist. He is discovered and the preacher shouts at the snake to go away. He chases it away as if to cast out an evil spirit.[69]

The film includes multiple scenes like this where Diabolo, in his evil moneymaking schemes, has sex with women. He eventually meets his match, and as he burns to death his human head emerges, illustrating the human-animal combination that Diabolo has become.[70] The deliverance cosmos in Ghana is fascinated with such animal-human possibilities, and I mention *Diabolo* here because repeatedly throughout *Seductive Spirits* we will witness performances of sex with snakes.

Western Influences

To be clear, the sources from West Africa, especially Victoria Eto, most closely represent the world of my interlocutors. However, one must acknowledge that as deliverance became a widespread phenomenon in West Africa during the 1990s, there were significant Western influences.[71] Paul Gifford concluded, "Undoubtedly, the U.S. charismatic demonology has traditional African beliefs; but the demonology of Africa's contemporary charismatic church may well be getting its special character through the power of American literature."[72] While I would quibble over where responsibility for the growth of deliverance lies, Gifford is undoubtedly correct that Western literature, theology, and film have contributed to deliverance thinking and practice in Ghana.[73] There has been a varied and sustained Western influence on deliverance in Ghana, mainly from pre–Third Wave or Third Wave Pentecostalism—or post-denominational neocharismatic ministries—who emphasize spiritual warfare against the demonic as a divine mandate.[74] Sean McCloud has provided an extensive look at the Third Wave in the context of America, where "the Third Wave's primary focus is spiritual warfare, the purpose of which is to banish demons from human bodies, material objects, local places and whole regions of the globe."[75] This focus describes much of Ghanaian Pentecostalism.

North American influence over Ghanaian deliverance began with visits from several figures from the Latter Rain Movement. Members of the Latter Rain held meetings in Accra, Kumasi, and Cape Coast with reports of deliverance, healing, and miracles.[76] In response to the Latter Rain meetings, healing and exorcism began to flourish in Ghana. However, the Latter Rain Movement was uninterested in forming organizations or churches, so deliverance remained largely a parachurch movement in its earliest manifestations including but not limited to Scripture Union and the Full Gospel Businessmen's Fellowship International.[77] And yet, in many of these earliest deliverance movements sex with demons was a common reality.[78] As the parachurch movement grew and hosted additional impactful Pentecostal figures such as Morris Cerullo in 1977 and Benson Idahosa in 1978, new deliverance-dominant churches and prayer camps began to emerge.[79] Slowly but surely deliverance became the dominant mode of Pentecostalism, especially popular in cities such as Accra and Kumasi.[80]

Nobody, though, has influenced deliverance with quite the geographical breadth or for quite as long as Derek Prince. Prince was a Cambridge-educated Pentecostal minister who established a high-profile deliverance ministry of his own.[81] James Collins calls Prince "the most significant Charismatic practitioner of deliverance ministry."[82] Prince's significance extends into Ghana, where his 1987 teaching tour and ubiquitous books continue to shape deliverance.[83] The Ghana Pentecostal Council hosted the Prince meetings in Accra and Kumasi. Onyinah writes that "undoubtedly, Prince's contribution to deliverance ministry in Ghana was very great."[84] Prince's visit to Ghana came at a critical juncture in deliverance history for the country. At that time, the overwhelming preponderance of demons and the significant interpretive latitude made many wary of a practice prone to subjective whims. But after Prince's visit, resistance to deliverance disappeared.[85] Even those who claim to have originated deliverance in Ghana, such as Matthew Addae-Mensah, will admit that the practice remained on the fringes of Pentecostal culture until Prince's visit.[86]

Abamfa Atiemo unequivocally states that "Derek Prince's teaching tour of the country aroused the interest of many pastors and evangelists in the deliverance ministry; and the knowledge he imparted built their confidence. Even now many pastors recommend his book and audio-cassettes to clients."[87] Atiemo's evaluation was consistent with what I found at each deliverance site. Nearly every deliverance proponent I met with cited Derek Prince as a significant influence. Kwofie—who influenced the others I researched—called Derek Prince his spiritual father and repeatedly emphasized that Prince had prophesied over him. Kwofie was extremely specific that Derek Prince was the only demonologist that he had read, though he could not remember the name(s) of the Prince texts he had read. Though possible, it would seem that Kwofie's claim about only having read Derek Prince is doubtful considering the closeness with which his testimony mirrors Emmanuel Eni's and his theories on sexual deliverance duplicate Victoria Eto's. Nonetheless, the influence of Derek Prince's demonology and deliverance instruction looms over most deliverance ministries in Ghana.

Some of Prince's most lasting beliefs that influenced deliverance ministries include his demonic ontology, where demons are disembodied spirits who are desperate for human bodies to most fully express their evilness. For Prince and his acolytes, spirits are always and everywhere traversing the world looking for bodies that they can penetrate. Each demon is then related to a particular sin or affliction that can only be expressed through the inhabitation of bodies. The body is always at risk primarily through acts that are commonly described as sinful. As James Collins summarizes Prince's impact, "Prince leaves one with the impression that we are all surrounded by an unseen spiritual ether, which is teeming with evil spirits longing to get inside the bodies of human beings."[88] This is the deliverance worldview where everything is enchanted and everyone—especially through bodily orifices—are always at serious risk of possession. To this end, Prince was an early advocate of physical and material manifestations of departing demons. For example, he encouraged the art of vomiting demons out of the body.[89] In Ghana, as Onyinah points out, it is very common to see performances where demons exit via the various orifices in the human body.[90] I witnessed or was told of demons departing through vomit, urination, defecation, and bleeding. Prince very much contributed to the construction of the Pentecostal body with its penetrable orifices as sites of possession and dispossession.

Another vital Western source is a slim deliverance manual entitled *Pigs in the Parlor,* written by a charismatic American Baptist couple Frank and Ida Mae Hammond. *Pigs in the Parlor* was widely popular in Ghana. Gifford cites a Ghanaian interlocutor, exclaiming, "Some of those Nigerian books are not well based, but frightening. Some are weird and exaggerated. We don't take them as true, especially Nigerian books. We just concentrate on Frank Hammond's *Pigs in the Parlor* book."[91] I saw copies of *Pigs in the Parlor* for sale on the street in Accra and, on more than one occasion, saw someone carrying a copy to church. First published in 1973 and now boasting more than a million copies in print, *Pigs in the Parlor* was designed as a practical guide to deliverance. It oscillates between claims that range from the ludicrously open-ended to the impossibly specific.[92] Sex, though, appears often and is one of the seven most common symptoms of demonic possession. Sexual perversions immediately make one a prime candidate for deliverance, including "fantasy sex experiences, masturbation, lust, perversions, homosexuality, fornication, adultery, incest, provocativeness and harlotry."[93]

Of North American books that were popular in Ghana, in addition to *Pigs in the Parlor,* perhaps the most notable were Rebecca Brown's texts.[94] Gifford notes that in 1995 Brown's works were the fastest selling at the Evangelical Challenge Bookshop in Accra.[95] Particularly popular was Brown's tell-all *He Came to Set the Captive Free,* an account of the deliverance of Elaine. Elaine was allegedly a top witch in the United States, and her story is notable for its claims of an elevated status as the Queen of Satan and its intense sexual entanglements. While Queen of Satan, Elaine writes that she was worshipped by many and possessed immense power both materially and spiritually, and she also had sexual roles to fill. According to the book, she was put on a stone altar, stripped, and then Satan, along with many humans and demons, had sex with her. The watching crowd cheered ferociously, the sex whetting their voracious appetites for the orgy that would ensue.[96] Sex with Satan was not a one-time proposition for Elaine, who explains that she was repeatedly subjected to rit-ualized and violent sex. After she wed Satan in an elaborate ceremony in the hills of California, Elaine writes that she was forced to have "brutal" sexual intercourse with Satan, whose previous princely appearance was dislodged by a horrid, monstrous creature. She claims that the sex was violent, and she was left with a plethora of sexual wounds.[97] Other sexual brutalities were frequent, but what primarily bothered Elaine in this account was sexual intercourse be-tween humans and demons. She describes these sexual demons as "demons that could be seen and heard and felt in a physical manifestation." In this worl-dview, sexual demons are sensed, they are felt, and for Brown, they are terrify-ingly arousing. Some of the demon-human sexual encounters in her book were between consenting demons and humans, but demons also regularly had sex with nonconsenting humans as a form of punishment, sometimes while making human spouses watch while their partners were sexually violated and raped.[98]

In Brown's 1987 text, *Prepare for War*, Brown revisits the fantastic conse-quences of fornication, calling demons a "'venereal disease' much more dev-astating than herpes or AIDS!"[99] Here she is not talking about the demons of spiritual marriage—whereby the demons and humans are conterminously ex-periencing sexual satisfaction—but is referring to demons spread via "sexual sin" between humans. Demons are said to be transmitted very much like a disease from one person to another via sexual intercourse.[100] And so Brown suggests that participation in sexual sins or perversions including but not lim-ited to masturbation, sex with someone of the same sex, or sex with animals leads to a demonic infestation.[101] While in America Brown should be read as a terrifyingly effective proponent of satanic ritual abuse and one who contrib-uted to the satanic panics, she is read in Ghana as correctly understanding the centrality of sexual demons to the construct of evil. Onyinah laments that "unfortunately many Christians uncritically accepted the testimonies presented in these books and cassettes."[102]

Films also conclusively demonstrated the centrality of sex to evil. In the 1970s, *The Exorcist* spoke poignantly to Ghanaian ideas about a world filled with evil spirits that can make the human body possessed, distressed, and grotesque. Most importantly, the film aligned with a commitment that Chris-tians must, at all costs, fight evil principalities.[103] *The Exorcist*, based on Wil-liam Peter Blatty's book by the same name, was loosely rooted in the 1949 exorcism of a fourteen-year-old boy in Maryland. Michael Cuneo writes of the popularity of the film in America: "As if by alchemy, the dramatic and seductively grotesque arrival of demons on the screen and the bestselling page resulted in demons rampaging through the bedrooms and workplaces of Middle America."[104] Both Asmoah-Gyadu and Onyinah point out *The Exorcist's* popularity in Ghana and its contribution to the societal acceptance of deliverance.[105] There are several aspects of the film that are well established in Ghanaian deliverance. That is not to spell out a causal relationship but to merely emphasize the similarities that people witnessed when they lined up at theaters to watch Linda Blair play twelve-year-old Regan. Most notably, *The Exorcist* sexualizes possession in perhaps the most memorable scene of the film when Regan masturbates violently with a crucifix while yelling, "Let Jesus fuck you!" In another scene, she accosts another character with the phrase, "Your mother sucks cock in hell!"[106] This kind of sexualized language is often part of deliverance and is seen as a sure sign of possession.

While the history of the demonic in Ghana is layered, with a great many sources, there are two related critiques of this history that are worth noting, especially in advance of this book's conclusion. One was raised by Pentecostal mega-pastor Mensa Otabil who noted that the centrality of the demonic, and corresponding deliverance, in Ghanaian Pentecostal Christianity was largely used to alienate Africans from their culture.[107] Otabil is not wrong when figures such as Rebecca Brown preach that "almost every single thing done in African culture is to do with demon worship."[108] Similarly, O'Donnell has demonstrated that the West, in particular American Evangelicals, have long relied on places and people such as Ghana as the other, "demons or the abodes of demonic presence."[109] The fact that Kwofie's story is now a book sold exclusively by a Florida-based pastor demonstrates just how reliant on these stories Western Pentecostalism is. Both complaints address the perniciousness of modernity/coloniality in the realm of the demonic. And yet, I remain convinced that the sexual worlds my interlocutors have constructed with demons are not only defined by modernity/coloniality but can be read as resisting such impositions. There is no doubt that the history of sexual deliverance in Ghana is a strange assemblage, influenced, shaped, and molded by a great many forces and more potent than any of the sources on their own.

TWO

INDECENT SCENES

Giorgio Agamben writes, "In Christianity, hermeneutics has replaced prophetism; one can practice prophecy only in the form of interpretation."[1] Agamben did not write of contemporary Pentecostalism, but it could have been, especially in deliverance-dominant Pentecostalism. Pentecostal pastors are notorious for claiming all sorts of titles, whether or not they have the qualifications or office that might traditionally bestow such honor. In this book, Emmanuel alone has oscillated between self-identifying as a doctor, a prophet, a bishop, and an angel. But every leader in this book has at one point or another called themselves a prophet, and they certainly all consider themselves prophetic. Their prophecy, though, is interpretation. It is the narratival interpretation of moving bodies, short testimonies, and mere nods of assent into grand cosmic battles and, simultaneously, earthly possibilities. In each deliverance the prophet gloms onto some piece of information, however received, and turns it into a story from which they hope to emerge the victor. Theoretically, I find something meaningful in the conflation of prophecy and hermeneutics, the idea that prophecy is hermeneutics. New hermeneutics are needed. If we assume that prophecy is something radical that inherently contravenes the orders of modernity/coloniality, then a kind of prophetic hermeneutic might just offer something helpful.

As mentioned in the introduction, this book aims to take sex seriously and not hastily rush past the sex to name it is as something else. That is not to deny that sex is polyvalent in interpretive possibilities but to emphasize that in order to truly capture such meaning it is necessary to start with the sex. This is particularly important in sex with demons because it does not lend itself to assumptions about what constitutes sex. In order to take the sex of Ghanaian Pentecostals seriously, one must then also take the demonic seriously as a significant player in all things sexual. Ghanaian Pentecostals do not simply demonize sex, but are convinced that demons are involved in having sex with humans. With prophecy as hermeneutics, I wrestled to find a radical hermeneutic capable of understanding sex with demons in all its complexity. To take demons and sex with demons seriously requires new interpretive approaches. I found myself in need of interpretive tools that did not merely parrot the claims of the faithful nor dismiss their ideas about sex and demons. I could not find such a hermeneutic and therefore set out to construct one that would aid in consideration of the many scenes in this book. Accordingly, I will apply a hermeneutical portmanteau, *pneumoeroticism*, in my efforts to understand this phenomenon.

Pneumoeroticism combines the capacious categories of spirit (*pneuma*) and eroticism (*eros*) to interpret sexual relationships between bodies and spirits. The point here is not to fit Pentecostalism into one predetermined category or another, or even to create a new and smooth system, but to provide diffuse keys that illuminate the uniqueness and possibility of sex with demons. Pneumoeroticism, then, is comfortable with disparate, potentially incompatible ideas about sex, the body, and demons. And while pneumoeroticism is not entirely contained by Pentecostalism, indeed, a great many sexual possibilities combine *pneuma* and *eros* in some manner, in this book, it is how I analyze the sexualities I saw performed that were shared with me and that play a significant role in deliverance-dominant Pentecostalism.

Sexual encounters with demons have not yet been adequately theorized due to their inability to align with the religious, sexual, and bodily order of things. The very nature of these human-cum-spirit and spirit-cum-human sexual encounters is deemed unthinkable, demonic, indecent. While this inability to be contained by specific constructs has left the phenomenon undertheorized, it is also what provides significant power within Pentecostalism for it is what creates the possibility of otherwise.[2] The point of Pentecostalism's inability to align with specific orders, read: modern/colonial, is not to find a way within those orders but to organize, perform, and produce alternatives.

Sex with demons upsets the modern/colonial lexicon of sin and perversion by embracing that which is used to dismiss African sexualities, African bodies, and African religiosity.

Sex with demons upsets the religious order, especially missionary Christianity, by refusing the manichean split. While many, including many Pentecostal insiders, rush to interpret everything as strictly good or evil (or sinful), in practice they tarry with evil and all that is hidden, ambiguous, and polyvalent within it. Sex with demons even transgresses traditional, approved sites of religious interpretation. This is not biblical exegesis, nor is it prophetic preaching, though the various prophets are prominent in the deliverance experiences. Instead, interpretation happens in bedrooms, in public, in bodies, in fantasies, and in dreams. This dislocation of hermeneutics from its normal locus dislocates assumptions about the world and interactions in the world and offers fantastic possibilities.

Sex with demons displaces an assumed heterosexuality, refuses an ethos of reproduction, and introduces new questions about the human role in sex. The location of sexual practice is expanded in this revelation, especially away from religiously endorsed sites. Sex is controlled by the spirits, escaping religion's heterosexual core. Sex with demons enables different perspectives on sex not as new identities but as possibilities, not as reproduction but reimagining, not as discipline but excess.

Finally, Pentecostalism claims that meaning happens in ritual, in the uncontrolled and excessive body. This challenges the theological order of restricting the body, especially sexually, stripping the body of its materiality and sensuousness.[3] In so emphasizing the sensuous body, Pentecostalism constructs new dynamic bodily configurations. It is not about rationality but enacting and performing that which lies beyond the reach of rationality. Pentecostalism sees the carnal body in all its fleshy materiality as interpretation.[4] The carnal senses excited through co-participation between humans and demons are already interpretation and a way of seeing the world. These corporeal sensations, which already "transcend the traditional dualism between understanding and embodied sensibility," are interpretations.[5] In following these physical sensations, the body provides meaning, and the body is meaning, that is to say, the body is signifier and signified at once.[6] In a line that my Pentecostal interlocutors would agree with, Marcella Althaus-Reid writes that "the theological scandal is that bodies speak, and God speaks through them."[7] Of course, deliverance-dominant Pentecostals would emphasize the even more scandalous corollary: the scandal is that bodies scream in a variety of ways—from movement to docility, with great volume or in silence—and that demons speak through them. Pentecostals believe that this bodily crying out is significant, and it signifies an entire unseen realm—from demonic to divine—that is continuously assailing the vulnerability and openness of the human body.

PNEUMA + EROS

Pneuma, the ancient Greek word for spirit, is a useful marker of these human-spirit relationships because of its ambiguity. *Pneuma* can be used to describe spirits good, bad, and otherwise.[8] I lean heavily on this descriptor because while Pentecostalism pays homage to the Holy Spirit, in deliverance-dominant versions it is the demons who play outsized and intimate roles. I point this out not as a critique or to pejoratively label demons as bad. Demons are otherwise. This very much aligns with the spirit of Marcella Althaus-Reid's queer theology which characterizes demonologies as "the art of being rebellious loving spirits."[9] Sex with demons is indeed an artful performance of rebellion by interminably revisiting spirits who have been cast out or disallowed.

Eroticism offers rich demonic interpretive options as well. Armando Maggi, in a story of spirited love if not sex, has pointed out that "the Symposium Diotima defines *Eros* as a 'great demon,' which connects men to the gods."[10] *Eros* is a threshold phenomenon that defines unashamed, material, sensuous sex. Eros also arouses immaterial implications, weaving its way through the beyond and back to the body. Those immaterial implications of *eros* include, according to Georges Bataille, the calling into question the nature of one's very being.[11] Sex with demons is an act of questioning one's being.

Eros in relation to sexuality is excessive or extravagant. *Eros* is more than. It is not merely interior or exterior but more than, saturating both the interior and exterior with meaning. *Eros* is not what theorists like Bataille refer to as animal sexuality because it is more than mere sexual mechanics, but it is certainly at times animalistic. It is more than the body, though certainly embodied. It is more than spiritual, though spirituality is deeply implicated. *Eros* offers much because it does not necessarily sexuate; that is, it does not inscribe male or female, nor is it necessarily genital. That is not to say that reproduction and genitals do not appear in the scenes that follow, but only in an *eros* that refuses to be defined or identified by those features. In the sexual realm of spirits and humans nothing is assumed, and the capaciousness of *eros* serves us well in this pursuit.

Others have similarly theorized the sensuousness of eroticism hermeneutically. For example, Keguro Macharia uses the term *frottage* to help unwind the way bodies, sensations, and sexualities rub up against one another.[12] Frottage does not only capture the violent rubbings of modernity/coloniality, but also the centrality of sex, gender, desire, and eroticism to black freedom struggles. While frottage is not the perfect metaphor or method for Pentecostals, its creative ambiguity is worth emulating. In frottage, Macharia does not make totalizing claims or teleological promises. Instead, frottage demonstrates the creative ability of sexualities to imagine and construct new worlds, however incomplete. In *eros*, despite its very Western etymological origins, I hope to emphasize the capaciousness of sexualities that necessarily challenge modernity/coloniality's "yoke of sexual terrorism, violence, and colonization."[13]

The point of pneumoeroticism is that traditional orders fail when they encounter bodies they cannot discipline and spirits they cannot tame. In utilizing *pneuma* and *eros* the point is not to capture any singular truth but to multiply interpretive possibilities. In many ways pneumoeroticism pluralizes Bataille, "The meaning(s) of eroticism(s) escapes anyone who cannot see its religious meaning(s)! Reciprocally, the meaning(s) of religion in its totality escapes anyone who disregards the link it was with eroticism(s)."[14] Pneumoeroticism, then, is a practice of interpreting Pentecostal spirituality differently by taking sex and demons seriously.

This chapter outlines a hermeneutic of pneumoeroticism and traces its interpretative possibilities through an indecent analysis of a particular scene, Priscilla's deliverance from a demon of masturbation. This is not intended to be a definitive proposal but the commencement of a conversation about the possibilities that emerge when we take sex with demons seriously. The goal is not to limit how the reader experiences the scenes within but to create a method that illuminates important markers in order to envision new possibilities and worldings. Because sex with demons refuses the modern/colonial orders of religion, bodies, and sexuality, pneumoeroticism must begin by emphasizing indecency. Decency—or the modern/colonial order of religion, bodies, and sexuality—is stifling and oppressive and would immediately silence the experiences of sex with demons.[15]

Spirited sexual experiences are inherently indecent, in both Pentecostal practice and story. Indecency in deliverance is multifarious. Some of how these experiences are indecent are relatively superficial. For example, in deliverance Pentecostals simultaneously, unwittingly, and impressively embrace Althaus-Reid's indecent challenge to utilize sexual and explicit language. Words like "cunt," "cum," "eat out," and "cock" are thrown around deliverance services with reckless abandon, echoing through the church via booming sound systems. More profoundly, in the deliverance process, social norms and boundaries are consistently transgressed. These boundaries include: masturbating with a demon in public, which disturbs societal discretion around sex; trans-mogrification of human bodies into animals, which explodes continuity of being; and bodily and demonic secretions on a Bible, which transgresses that which is considered sacred. Sex with demons pushes—sometimes literally—against normative orders. Most poignantly, sexual demons, as they manifest within the deliverance apparatus, perform a different way of life, being, and meaning. In this way, the sensing bodies throughout this book tell stories of indecency, challenging and sometimes obliterating normative boundaries.

The theoretical way I want to orient this study toward the indecent is through the orgy. I believe that the hermeneutical lessons of orgy, especially as outlined by Marcella Althaus-Reid, illuminate the sexual components of deliverance.[16] Orgies broadly defined include sexual and sensual experiences collectively aimed at excess and confusion, a mingling of bodies, and a blurring of lines around what is natural. Orgies are intense experiences of bodily pleasure.[17] Deliverance, similarly, combines bodies crying out, some manifesting their aberrant sexualities, various intimate physical combinations, and intense voyeurism. In both, more bodies lead to more senses, lead to more realities constructed, shaped, and performed. I do not apply the theory of orgy flippantly. Orgy is neither inherently good nor bad; it is merely a theory, for as Karl Toepfer states, "People contemplate orgies far more than they ever actually participate in them."[18] But the orgy is a rich theory that opens up indecent sexual possibilities and challenges heteronormativity's limited couplings with unending permutations and combinations. The goal here in embracing orgy as a model for pneumoeroticism is to illuminate transgressive desires and bodies tarrying in rebellious ways beyond the opaque and limited discourses of modernity/coloniality.

I use orgy not to concretize contemporary sexual categories but because it allows for innumerable permutations and combinations that open up possibilities. In the orgy, "all things are permitted, even perversions and sins against custom."[19] By using orgies as a hermeneutic model the goal is to demonstrate that excess and extravagance can resist cisheteropatriarchy. If pneumoeroticism instead used hetero couplings as a model, the poignancy of sex with demons would be blunted. If instead we use orgies as the model we begin with the assumption of dynamic and ever-unfolding sexual possibilities.

This turn to orgies, though, should not be particularly surprising, for orgies are religious—traced to festivals and rituals.[20] The Greek term *orgias* originally referred to worship in mystery cults and religious ecstasy in the worship of Dionysus.[21] Dionysiac orgies sometimes included *maenads* who climbed Mount Parnassus and, in a state of drunken stupor, engaged in various sexual activities with the divinity.[22] Orgies are a spiritual tradition where spirits and humans intimately meet at a threshold or a "crossroads."[23] None of this historical evidence makes orgy an inherently natural theoretical fit for Pentecostalism, but it certainly points toward a theory of rich possibility in ecstatic religion.

Orgy did not enter the English lexicon until around 1589, and by then had shed some of the religious ritualistic thrust and meant something approximating ecstatic group sex. Nonetheless, deliverance and possession certainly conform to this orgiastic variable. Deliverance is an intense zone of co-participation, never practiced alone but instead publicly mediated by interactions with others.[24] As the scenes emerge in *Seductive Spirits*, as the sex is laid out, it will become clear that orgiastic indecency, broadly approached, sensuously frames spirituality and bodily materiality for Pentecostals.

Here, as I embrace orgy to theorize pneumoeroticism, I again bump up against the long history of Western stereotypes about Africa. Modernity/coloniality imagined African religious rituals as raw, unvarnished orgiastic feasts and dances.[25] Modernity/coloniality haunts. But this is kind of the point. I imagine the Pentecostal demonic cosmos as reshaping haunting so that sex is no longer defined by the limited terms of modernity/coloniality. In order to do so we must subvert modern/colonial assumptions. Such subversion happens in *Seductive Spirits*, most especially in the conclusion, by recounting some modern/colonial impositions not to embellish hoary stereotypes but to demonstrate otherwise possibilities. To think with Pentecostalism is to think otherwise sensually in the celebration of black bodies.

In embracing indecency, I wish to riff on Marcella Althaus-Reid's approach to sexual hermeneutics in her book *The Queer God*. In her book, Althaus-Reid provides five hermeneutic keys that work as "a sexual hermeneutics which provides us with body-maps, with a cartography of wild dreams, of transgressive movements in search of radical breakthroughs in our ways of thinking."[26] Althaus-Reid's hopes for her sexual hermeneutics echo what I hope pneumoeroticism describes: a redefining and expansion of the body that challenges and reshapes approaches to being human. Pneumoeroticism does so not by abandoning the explicitly erotic but by interpreting those indecent bodily sites of sexual exchange with demons. I do not strictly stick to Althaus-Reid's keys, instead mingling a variety of authors and fusing their approaches into a hermeneutic that helps us both note and interpret some of the more meaningful interstices of sex with demons. This textual promiscuity has left me with five characteristics of the orgy that are helpful in understanding sex with spirits and its public corollary of deliverance: theatrical programmed scenes; bodies transgressing limits; carnal pleasure in worship; violence of desire; and combinative reduction. I will apply these pneumoerotic keys to the story of Priscilla's deliverance from Maggie, a spirit of masturbation, to illuminate the interpretive possibilities within sex with demons.

FIVE PNEUMOEROTIC HERMENEUTICAL KEYS IN PRISCILLA'S DELIVERANCE

On a blazing hot Tuesday with the sun perched high over a set of tents assembled in an industrial city close to Accra, Prophet Emmanuel educated the congregation on the perils of masturbation. He began by plainly articulating, as if it was a scientific fact, that masturbation causes brain disorders and "madness." But more frighteningly, masturbation was cited as "one of the main tools" available to marine spirits and demons, especially Mami Wata, in destroying mortals. The dire, apocalyptic warnings were immediately followed with the promise of a remedy. He was the remedy. Prophet Emmanuel could break everyone's masturbatory problem. "Just as Jesus gave me many spirits, Satan has given many spirits to the marine gods. I can use mine to overcome theirs," he promised. The spirited boasts were Emmanuel's description and prescription of deliverance for all those who masturbate.

Emmanuel started by calling everyone forward who masturbates. He had his pastors organize the supplicants in groups according to the spirits that plagued each supplicant: the demons of lesbianism, gayism, or masturbation.[27] In a vibrant, ironic statement, he said, "If you are a lesbian, masturbator or gay, come; for the Lord has spoken." The pastors, sensing Emmanuel's impatience, moved much more efficiently than usual and quickly divided the gathered congregants by their respective spirits. It was rather easy to do, as nobody claimed the spirit of gayism, and only one woman described being in a relationship with the spirit of lesbianism. The other fifty or so, approximately 80 percent of which were female, were all plagued by the demon of masturbation. Emmanuel turned to the gathered masturbators and said, "May the Lord touch you all." His hope for those who touch themselves was that the divine touch, which would be mediated through the touch of the pastors, would heal and replace self-touch. Emmanuel then unleashed the pastors onto the masturbators, instructing them to "try to deliver them from that spirit." It was the typical frenzy of pastors pushing bodies around, bodies shaking on the floor, and a boisterously praying congregation. Emmanuel tried to restore some order by commanding everyone who had been touched with deliverance to return to their seats. The chaos dissipated as they moved back toward their seats.

Orgies Are Programmed, Performed Theatrical Scenes

Deliverance rituals, like orgies, are "programmed carefully, to the last detail."[28] This emphasis on programming immediately seems to contradict deliverance ministries, which emphasize spontaneity as the primary characteristic of both the demonic and the Holy Spirit. It does not. Grant Wacker corroborates these pronouncements, stating, "Pentecostal worship oscillate(s) between antistructural and structural impulses. Planned spontaneity, we might call it."[29] Much within pneumatic rituals that appears spontaneous is not; repeated observation of deliverance rituals attunes one to the rhythms that repeat themselves over and over again. As Michael W. Cuneo writes of exorcism, "Strange assemblage that it was, the ritual played out seamlessly, like a finished stage performance whose kinks had been ironed out through endless rehearsal."[30] And indeed, there is a lot of rehearsing because everyone involved has most assuredly attended many performances, witnessed many deliverances, and trained their bodies accordingly. The reason why the scenes are effective is that they build on previous performances that have all been staged very publicly in deliverance.

In broad strokes, the opening portion of Priscilla's deliverance is the standard theatrical manner in which deliverance scenes are programmed and performed: Demons are identified and demons are combatted. Often, demons are defeated, but not always and never completely.

But deliverance always erases the difference between public and private. Meyer has pointed to the publicity of deliverance. "Significantly," she writes, "demonic possession is not confined to the individuals experiencing it, but rather it is a matter of public interest. The exorcism of demons takes place in front of the congregation and churches offer their members the possibility to listen to testimonies from people who were involved with evil spirits in the past."[31] All that is usually considered private—sexual intimacy, in this case masturbation—is immediately thrust into the public sphere. Privacy is obliterated. The most intimate details of one's life are on display, denuded. Sometimes bodies even end up unclothed.

Althaus-Reid utilizes *covenant*, a profoundly theological term, to describe how orgies are organized in deeply binding agreements constructed around what is going to occur. It is difficult to ascertain what covenant looks like in the context of deliverance due to the fluid and transient nature of deliverance. People seek out deliverance anywhere and everywhere. Unlike church membership or loyalties, people are likely to seek deliverance in multiple places from multiple prophets, if not through multiple religions. Accordingly, people appear and disappear with regularity. Often when interviewing people who had experienced deliverance, it had been their first time visiting that particular site and they had no previous engagement with the prophet.

With the only contact happening between deliverer and deliveree in the throes of performance, what constitutes covenant in the deliverance milieu? Presence constitutes covenant for both deliverers and deliverees alike. Being present is a covenant with all those involved promising an openness to the potential moving of spirits—good or bad—and a covenant to the leadership of the church, allowing them to marshal, interact with, or evacuate these spirits by any bodily means possible. Presence is a pact that one is content to have their spirits revealed, manifested, or tested. It is not an insignificant covenant as it is an agreement to have the personal details of one's life revealed or physically confronted. I use the term *covenant* and not *consent* because covenant describes an overarching framework in which porous and penetrating beings encounter one another. Consent occurs between two bounded entities. Consent needs to be regularly reevaluated. Covenant instead embraces a refusal to be a bounded individual entity; it is an embrace of porosity.

Sex with demons is at its core a covenant. According to Pentecostal beliefs, while spirits are ever-desiring of the ability to enter the human body, they can only do so under certain conditions. Demons follow careful rules, laws, and prescriptions about how and when they may enter the human body. Each prophet in this book emphasized that demons are stridently legalistic about entering human bodies. Kwofie was particularly adamant in reiterating that demons exclusively enter human bodies at the invitation of the human, stating it so often that I can still hear his voice repeating "demons are legalistic." This kind of legalistic language is common in Third Wave Pentecostalism, which says that demons cannot enter one's body unless gifted the legal right to enter, though humans are often unaware of exactly how they provided that right.[32] The inability, often, to successfully identify how one provided the right of entry to one's own body demonstrates that this is a broad covenant structure rather than consensual. Spiritual marriage, for example, is a covenant between spirit paramour and human lover. Being possessed by the spirit of masturbation is a covenant between the spirit and the masturbating human. It is these covenants that are the focus in deliverance-dominant Pentecostalism.

All of these covenants are founded on an acceptance of the human body's fundamental porosity. Pentecostals play with ideas of consent and power in a way that challenges ideas of a bounded self. The body is instead open and multiple, dependent, and inviting. As such, all interpretations of sex with demons must banish the assumption that sex is an individual act between two bounded entities disconnected from other acts. Instead, sex with demons is an experience of porosity as the fundamental embodied reality that necessarily impinges on other acts, other people, other things. Covenanting should not, then, be viewed as limiting or closed off to generative desires. Instead, covenanting is itself a form of pleasure, a multiplication of pleasure that creates a forum where nothing is off limits.

Repetition is vital to deliverance. But it is always repetition with variations, however slight. The variations are especially revealing. Within this programmed framework, variety is created by small surprises or little contraventions, creating various permutations. These artful variations construct "mini-mirrors for different people to keep seeing and re-creating themselves in their relationships."[33] In the masturbatory deliverance, there was a slight variation. As the front of the church cleared, everybody who had been touched left except for one, a single body left lying on the floor. The prostate woman, Priscilla, was wearing a white and blue dress, and effortlessly rubbed herself as she raised her hips up and down. Amidst the frenzy of the deliverance it was unclear how she had ended up in this position, but the offending spirit was plain for all to see through her bodily movements. Priscilla was masturbating with a spirit that would eventually reveal herself as Maggie.

"Badoe," Emmanuel called out to his second in command, "try to raise her up." Badoe moved toward her while two ushers dressed in identical blue shirts with white floral print picked Priscilla up by her arms. While the sartorially twinned ushers picked Priscilla up, another woman wrapped her lower body in a wrap. The ushers held Priscilla unsteadily on her feet, one hand under her armpit and one holding her wrist so that they could move her with ease and easily combat her feeble attempts to return her hands to her genitalia.

Emmanuel turned his attention to the spirit: "Who are you?" The query was unquestioningly addressed to the spirit because Emmanuel knew Priscilla well; she is a prophetess and an acquaintance. It is common in Ghana for prophets and prophetesses to attend the services of well-known or well-established prophets in the hope that they pass on their unction. Emmanuel knew this woman, so the question of identity was hurled toward the spirit.

Crying, Priscilla responded with "I won't let her marry." She added something that the prophet did not hear clearly. He asked her to repeat it, and she obliged: "It has been a long time since she started it." The cover of discreetness was minimal; everyone knew exactly what "it" was: defilement of the vagina by the hand or object. She added an even more specific timeline to the statement when she said, "I made her start at Primary 6." The prophet feigned shock at this early starting point by repeating "P6" again and again. Each time he repeated "P6" he became louder and shook his head more dramatically.

Priscilla's head tilted back, and she moaned before adding, "I won't let her to marry, she wants no man."

Prophet Emmanuel responded by asking, "Who are you? What is your name?"[34] This question added an extra layer of specificity to his previous statements about needing to know the spirit before being able to destroy it. Not only was he required to know that it was the spirit of masturbation, but he also wanted to know the personal information of this particular spirit of masturbation.

"Me, ha ha, my name is Maggie," she responded, swallowing the *ma-* and emphasizing the *-ggie*. Priscilla was suggesting that she masturbated with a female spirit named Maggie. In this framework, gender is an incredibly complicated category when moving back and forth between humans and spirits, as spirits gender-bend and do not always abide by human categories or binaries.

In Orgies, Bodies Transgress Limits

In order to understand sex with demons, one must pay attention to the ways that bodies transgress limits. In particular, the unfolding story of Priscilla and Maggie demonstrates at least three ways in which bodies are transgressed: through the porosity of orifices, through melding of materiality and the supernatural, and through the transgression of assumed heterosexuality.

In the teachings of the prophets, the demons enter the body's orifices where the boundedness of the body is confronted with its porosity. Demons enter the body through nine orifices on the human body (eyes, nose, mouth, skin pores, penis/vagina, anus, ears).[35] Unsurprisingly, erogenous orifices are the most frequent orifices of exchange. Given Maggie's nature as a spirit of masturbation, Pentecostals believe she would have accessed Priscilla's body through the vagina. Pentecostalism, though, imagines all orifices as holding erogenous potential. For example, the ears are at risk of demonic penetration when listening to sex-talk, the eyes through pornography, etc. While the Pentecostal imagination depicts all orifices as materially penetrable through sex, such penetration is not proper and is not to be pursued. The only sanctioned penetration is strictly a penis penetrating a vagina within the bounds of heterosexual marriage. The best example of this obsession with and fear of orifices is found in an Oral Roberts sermon that reemerged and went viral years after he delivered it. In the sermon he pontificates:

> There is one place in the women's body and one place in the man's body that creates multiplication. There are not two, there are not three, there are not four places, there are not ten places, there is one place: in the women's vagina and the man's male organ. There is only one place in the woman's body where the male organ was designed to penetrate: the vagina. Only one organ named to bring forth life: it's the male organ. It is not in lesbianism, where the tongue of a female goes into the vagina of another female. It's not in the male, where the male organ goes into the part of the body where the waste matter comes out of the body, this poison, and he penetrates that part of the body in homosexuality. It is not to be put in the mouth of the man or the woman. It is the male organ penetrating the vagina of the woman: the male and the female. Look at the orifices of the body, the openings in the body. Certainly you can't put the male organ or the woman's tongue in the eye, touch the ear, certainly not in the orifices of the nose, or the navel, but there are a couple or three other places: there is the mouth; there is the anus, where the poisons of the body are excreted.[36]

This titillating of the orifices, the voyeurism toward non-heteronormative sexualities and the reveling in the pornography of the body's penetrability, are mainstream in Pentecostalism. Most meaning-making for pneumatic Christians occurs in experiences of the demonic interacting with human orifices and protuberances.

In my research I was told that the orifices are not merely entry points, but through deliverance act as the points of exit as well. Demons enter and exit through the same orifice. If a demon came through a person's mouth, then it will exit much the same way in vomit, screaming, coughing, etc. As Abamfa Atiemo points out, "A person being prayed for may also vomit or urinate in the process."[37] If a demon entered through a person's anus, it exits through the excretion of feces. If a demon entered through the eyes, extreme crying would occur as an exit. In the case of Priscilla, it is unclear when she was delivered whether or not there was a material marker of deliverance.

Orifices, then, are sites of revelation where the transcendent becomes immanent. Wariboko writes that "revelation is in the body, an art of bodies, at the body's limits. Revelation is the body extended, and this embodiment is what escapes it sometimes. Or may we say revelation is the process of the body's escape from itself?"[38] In these sensual experiences, Pentecostals crack open their subjectivity, interpolate the demonic, and importantly transgress the body. It is all quite Bakhtinian, as Nimi Wariboko has illustrated in his exploration of the pneumatic obsession with coprophilia and the anus.[39] The grotesque body is never complete but always becoming through the bodily orifices and apertures. In pneumatic Christianity, the grotesque body unveils the demonic.

Additionally, the Pentecostal body is a polyvalent one, always mediating the material and nonmaterial, the physical and the spiritual; it is "a complex and multifaceted entity that functions in the Pentecostal cosmological system as a mediating site for material and non-material domains."[40] This mediation is always treated as transgressive of the two orders, transcendence and immanence. This transgressive embodiment is simultaneously material and immaterial, a duality captured in Lisa Blackman's prose. She writes about bodily possibilities that extend far beyond fleshy boundaries. Instead, she recasts the body "as process rather than fixed entity, whilst retaining a focus on the more lived or phenomenal dimensions of experience."[41] Bodies as processes are open and lack stability as they entangle with the human and the demonic, material and immaterial.[42] As Florencia Tola writes, "The conception of a body in permanent connection with other bodies (humans and non-humans) which are also conceived as multiplicities and possessing other's extensions, is coherent with an ontology that puts more emphasis on transformations and multiplicity than on stability and on individual entities, more on processes and relations than on substances and on given or natural things or beings."[43]

The body is continuously transforming, oscillating between possessed and dispossessed, and in possession multiplied in connection with a variety of spirits.

For pneumatic Christians, bodies are constituted by both human and nonhuman elements. Spirits dissolve boundaries between "self and other, inside and outside, and human and non-human."[44] Corporeality is not limited by boundary placement that constrains the body but is instead opened up to alternative possibilities. Otherworldly bodies—like spirits—indicate that instead of being bounded, the body is defined by co-participation.[45] Possession in this way is what Blackman calls a "threshold phenomena," which describes any phenomena that operate "across and between the self and other, material and immaterial, inside and outside."[46] Sex also acts as a threshold phenomenon such that the scenes of demonic sexualities and sex with demons are a kind of doubled threshold, intense and intimate co-participation between body and spirits.[47]

But possession gives each spirit a moment of materiality, however brief. Each embodied action of a person possessed exposes the spirit. For example, when Priscilla masturbated, her self-touching was not merely her own exposure, but the exposing of the spirit of masturbation. The spirit's exposing itself, in the deliverance performance of Priscilla's self-touching, is deeply embodied. Spirit materialization complicates what is human and what is spirit, and how expansive the body is. For Pentecostals, the differentiation between spirit and human, which is never finally a differentiation as the two entangle in various ways, helps illustrate how the body is transgressed. For example, the human—Priscilla—is used to make the spirit—Masturbating Maggie—temporarily material. The impossibility of differentiation is concretized when Prophets Badoe and Emmanuel repeatedly hurl the question "who are you?" at Maggie. After obfuscating, Maggie reveals herself through Priscilla's body and voice. Discovering the name of the spirit is a process of knowledge augmentation; at that moment, we can name both Priscilla and Maggie, but the differentiation between human and spirit is impossible. They are two and they are one. In these spirit materializations, we see "spirit biographies intertwine with the autobiographical trajectories of religious practitioners, who sense and narrate the agency of spirits in their lives."[48] "Who are you?" is an ontological question. In answering, Maggie reveals herself to be a spirit, though the spirit had already become embodied when the masturbation commenced. Priscilla is shown to be possessed. The ontological boundaries of Priscilla are expanded, altered even. Naming is how demons are rendered intimately and immanently for the congregation. Still, Maggie had long been rendered in Priscilla's body during their coterminous masturbation, with both demon and human receiving pleasure in the act.[49]

Maggie, though, is always relentlessly contingent, contingently embodied, imbricated in Priscilla's masturbating. She manifests in masturbation and in naming herself. The bodily boundaries during deliverance are still unclear until the final—which is rarely actually the ultimate—articulation of the docile body, which is the demonless body. How does one define the body as Priscilla strokes herself, each stroke reaching far beyond her body into the spiritual cosmos? Or is each stroke Maggie reaching toward Priscilla? Clearly, Priscilla's body is not fixed, and its boundaries are regularly, if only temporarily, transgressed.

Finally, sex with demons transgresses the Christian assumption of a hetero-reproducing body. Theology demands heterosexual bodies. As Tom Beaudoin writes, "Theology's official heteronormativity is tightly interwoven with colonialism and the silencing of non-Euro, non-modern, noncapitalist 'others.' Systematic theology is a way that church intellectuals keep sexuality from the ambiguous, polymorphic expressions—that 'others' press and sublimate—that would otherwise open new vistas on divinity."[50] The a-theology of Pentecostal bodies in sexual relationships with the demonic is definitively ambiguous and polymorphic and forces us to think about the body in ways otherwise than heterosexual. This should be obvious from the start since the paramours being discussed are demonic and not of the human order. But even when translated into the language of human sexuality, the sexualities performed are not of the cisheteropatriarchal order. While there are phallic scenes—for example, a demonic penis holding a knife—there are also scenes where male spirits have female genitalia; wind creates orgasms; men are passive victims; and women have sexual agency over powerful demons. As the various sexual experiences with demons were shared with me, I kept coming back to Robert Reid-Pharr's definition of queer: "If there's one thing that marks us as queer, a category that is somehow different, if not altogether distinct, from the heterosexual, then it is undoubtedly our relationships to the body, particularly the expansive ways in which we utilize and combine vaginas, penises, breasts, buttocks, hands, arms, feet, stomachs, mouths and tongues in our expressions of not only intimacy, love, and lust, but also, and importantly shame, contempt, despair, and hate."[51] I am wary of any claim that Pentecostalism is feminist or queer in the modern Western sense of the terms, but attention to the ways it combines bodies certainly transgresses heteronormative understandings of the body. In the realm of the sexual, it provides a transgressive model that transcends the phallic.

Often when I have presented the materials of this book, I have received complaints about my misapprehending Pentecostal sex, that it is always and only singularly obsessed with reproduction. In one way, this complaint is correct: Pentecostals are obsessed with the production of progeny. Miracle babies are a whole industry—spiritual and economic—unto themselves.[52] But, in the ubiquitous sexual encounters with demons, when demons approach gaping bodily orifices, this is unproductive. Sure, there are claims about carrying the babies of demons, but this is a relatively rare and underdeveloped idea in pneumatic Christianity. Sex with spirits is very much unattached from reproduction, as the sexual relationship between human and spirit is delinked from the possibility of creating working, subservient humans. This kind of demonic sex is not about the reproductive but the transgressive.

A-satiability is much broader than reproduction. The demon-sex-deliverance apparatus does not stop; there is no determined resolution; the point is not to exorcise the demons but to intimately encounter them, again and again. Michel Maffesoli writes, "The rites whose religious—or more precisely, orgiastic—basis is understood consist of fantasy incarnate. The word incarnate here carries its full semantic force: it indeed refers to aggressive, caressing, colliding, loving bodies. And before they were sanitized in the familiar political and religious rituals, these rites were truly and intimately a violent or tender confrontation involving fantasy, exertion, loss—in a word—the unproductive."[53] Much of Maffesoli's description has already been explored in this chapter, but it is vital that reading sex with demons start with the assumption that such sex is unproductive.

Orgies Are the Carnal Pleasure of Worship

In order to interpret sex with demons, one must continually center bodies seeking pleasure and demons allegedly doing the same. The pleasure-seeking and pleasure-feeling elements of sex with demons are easily lost if one assumes demons are bad. However, watching and listening to many experiences of sex with demons makes it clear that pleasure is primary. In order to understand the pleasure of which my interlocutors speak, it is important to think about what that embodied pleasure is and where it comes from. Karl Toepfer writes, "Orgiastic experience entails an erotic, carnal pleasure in worshipping some-one."[54] There is no doubt that pneumatic Christians experience carnal plea-sure in worshipping someone—it is, indeed, one of their defining features. To best understand this, it's helpful to look at the origin of sexuality according to the strictures of pneumatic Christianity. Accordingly, there are two distinct readings of the origin of sexuality, one that reads the divine origin as heav-enly and one that reads its inauguration as demonic. In order to interpret sex with demons, one must emphasize the latter.

The first reading is that sex is a gift from God. That is to say that sex in its most pure form—in this case reproductive sex in the bounds of marriage—was created for humans by God. The emphasis here is on the word *for*—it was created for humans as opposed to with humans. Humans have since sullied this gift and, thus, the introduction of various sexual demons. Sex originated outside the material cosmos.

While there is no doubt that this kind of lapsarian reading is the the-ology preached, in practice, one could argue that the scenes throughout this book imagine sexuality in all its variety as emanating from a kind of mutuality between demons and humans. In this interpretation, sexuality is seen as originating from both the demonic and the human in cove-nants. It is the demonic beings that find pleasure in sex with humans, who seek out sex with humans, who encourage sex with humans, and who through mutuality find sexual gratification with humans. And humans find demons capable of the best sex, or at least inducing the most pleasure. Almost everyone I spoke with discussed how sex with spirits was more pleasurable than human sex and that human sex paled in comparison. Most poignantly, there was the woman who described to me how she could differentiate between her spirit spouse and a dream about her human hus-band because one was far more pleasurable, resulting in copious amounts of orgasmic secretion. The pleasure was measured by its source, the more pleasurable encounters being with demons. Human-cum-human sex then is a mere facsimile of human-cum-demon sex. The emphasis here is on the mutuality, the sex with.

This demonic construct is not a simple dismissal of sex as bad. Instead, the import that these sexualities have in the construction of this cosmos leaves no interpretation available except that they are foundational to an entire worldview. In this way, while transgressive, these sexualities are not deviant. There is an odd acceptance or peace with transgression in deliver-ance ministries, an awareness that they are always only animated by trans-gression and that transgression teaches as much or more about the cosmos than the alternative. In this interpretation, sex originates with the demonic. Sex is not only a human impulse or act but also a demonic one. By sexually integrating the demonic and the human in the body, Pentecostals demon-strate a kind of carnal worship of both the demonic and themselves. Again, the weight of Christian history requires that I reiterate that such statements throughout this text are not value-laden or pejorative. The worship occurs in a relationship of honor and mutuality whereby the continuation of sex is as-sumed as a sort of rite. So even if one does not accept the argument that the origin of sex in and of itself is an act of worshipping the demonic, the exclu-sive "soul-tie" certainly seems to be an adequate example of carnal worship. In the descriptions of sex with demons, without the assumed manichean split, interlocutors expressed their desire "to feel a divine energy within the body."[55] It need not be repeated that the scenes in this book display a deep desire for intimacy with the metaphysical or divine. It is, though, worth repeating that for deliverance-dominant pneumatic Christians, this desire does not manifest for the Holy Spirit or trinitarian God as the deliverance model purports, but for the demonic. It is the pleasure, desire, and sexual energy of encounters with the demonic where the most profound intimacy is simultaneously sought and resisted, abhorred and desired. Bataille describes the power of such carnal worship in *Erotism*:

In universal religions like Christianity or Buddhism terror and nausea are a prelude to bursts of burning spiritual activity. Founded as it is on a reaffirmation of the primary taboos, this spiritual life yet implies a celebration, that is, the transgression, not the observation, of the law. In Christianity and Buddhism ecstasy begins where horror is sloughed off. A sense of union with the irresistible powers that bear all things before them is frequently more acute in those religions when the pangs of terror and nausea are felt most deeply.[56]

In sloughing off the horrors of the demonic, in instead embracing transgression of the law (or multiple laws) by having sex with that which was taboo, Pentecostals find transgressive erotic union with that which is disallowed, the demonic.

Returning to Priscilla's deliverance, the prophet addressed Maggie: "How has the sister wronged you that you ushered her into such an act?"

Maggie did not answer and instead provided more detail, "I won't allow such a noble lady to attract wealthy men. She masturbates each night before sleeping and also at dawn." She tried to move her hand toward her genitals, but the ushers skillfully redirected her hands away from her body and clasped her wrists so she could not touch herself.

The prophet repeated the last sentence showing shock at her masturbatory profligacy, "Each night and at dawn."

Maggie was angry at this and lashed out at the prophet: "How does it concern you? Are you her relative?" She accentuated her questions by apoplectically hurling the invective "Swine!" toward the prophet.

The prophet deflected the name-calling by dismissing her, "Do you understand the word swine?" and then to the raucous cheers of the congregation stated, "She's not my relative, but everyone here is spiritually my relative." The cheers got louder, and Emmanuel added, "Jesus has given all of them to me to save in his name." The prophet turned back to Maggie and asked, "Maggie, how has the sister wronged you?"

Priscilla presumably speaking as Maggie transitioned from Twi to English and firmly stated, "Don't worry me."

The prophet, responding in English, said, "I will worry you."

"I prepare myself," he added while fidgeting with the gold buttons on his suit, "I prepare myself to fight you."

Maggie laughed maniacally and promised to fight back, "Prepare yourself for a battle today. Do you want to take her from me just like that? I'm not done with her; she'll masturbate until she dies."

Before the embodied battle of deliverance commenced, the conversation took a brief but essential deviation. As mentioned above, Priscilla is a prophetess. She is not a famous prophetess but is known within the context of her community. Since much of Prophet Emmanuel's preaching about masturbation made it clear that masturbation is an extreme sin that completely and utterly cuts one off from the divine, he struggled to come to grips with how Priscilla could be possessed with the spirit of masturbation. How could a woman of God masturbate? If this masturbating prophetess could still perform miracles, deliverance, and prophecies, then Emmanuel's whole enterprise would be troubled. It would leave open the possibility that Emmanuel himself might be a masturbator. Emmanuel asked, "She now has a church where she helps people, and you still do this to her?"

Priscilla speaking as Maggie explained: "We have attempted to quench the fire of her anointing, but we don't succeed."

Emmanuel understood: "You've attempted quenching her anointing, and yet you don't succeed, meaning this woman is free when she goes to church, but when she comes home, she is married to you." In her church, Priscilla does not touch herself; she touches others. She can keep from touching herself in that sacred space. However, that boundary had just been transgressed when Maggie manifested in Emmanuel's church; Priscilla had masturbated in a church. The relationship appeared to have ruptured.

An agitated Maggie became worked up: "What do you want? Keep deceiving yourself, yeah, yeah."

The prophet also became agitated: "You abusive demon . . . how dare you insult the great prophet?" referring to himself in the third person. "You will leave her to marry and continue her godly work," implying compulsory matrimonial heterosexuality.

Maggie shrieked: "You lie; I'll never leave. She will continue to masturbate forever." The stakes were higher now. Previously she had promised she would masturbate until she died. Now she was promising that Priscilla will masturbate forever.

Orgies Rely on a Violence of Desire Counterbalanced with Time Delay

Orgies are defined by a violent hurry-up-and-wait pattern, or in the words of Althaus-Reid, "an ethics of passion and urgency is systematically contradicted and played against an ethics of delay."[57] Deliverance mirrors this pattern. There is a multiplicity of ways in which delay and desire are effected in deliverance spaces. Everyone attends deliverance desiring freedom from something, and yet despite the deep, metaphysical desires, they are left to the whims of spirits and prophets who determine who is delivered.

The urgency and violence of desire in Priscilla's story is extravagant. First, there is Priscilla's desire to masturbate, a desire so strong that she would put her entire career as a prophet at risk, potentially even her own soul at risk, according to the Pentecostal worldview. We see the urgency in the case of Priscilla with the violent and threatening claims of desire (i.e., "she'll masturbate until she dies"). Returning to Bataille's religious eroticism, he says, "Let me stress that in this work flights of Christian religious experience and bursts of erotic impulses are seen to be part and parcel of the same movement."[58] In pneumatic Christianity, this is not something that needs to be stressed but is evident as religious experience and erotic bursts are part and parcel of the same thing. The desire is deep and sexual. Bataille defines religious intentions as those reaching beyond the immediate world.[59] Pneumatic Christians yearn for this by pursuing, desiring, and fantasizing about sexual encounters beyond the immediate world. This is the desire.

But there are also Maggie's desires as the spirit of masturbation. Maggie's statements suggest that the spirit's being, Maggie's being, is dependent on Priscilla's masturbating. The implication is that if Priscilla ceases to masturbate, Maggie ceases to exist, since she comes into being as herself through masturbation. This exchange between the prophet and Priscilla speaking as Maggie indicates that Maggie hopes that that symbiotic relationship will continue until Priscilla's death, which will also be Maggie's death, and the cessation of Priscilla's masturbation.

But all of this happens in a kind of delay, a tarrying. The scene began with Priscilla masturbating, or at least something that approximated masturbation. The performance, the wrestling with evil, is just a means of delay from either the orgy of more masturbation or the orgy of deliverance. Further, the deliverance drama plays with the desire for deliverance and a delay in performance; docility—the bodily goal—rarely comes immediately but only after a long-protracted scene. Tarrying is delay. Whether one is tarrying with or waiting upon the divine presence, it is to delay moving on to another place, situation, milieu, or experience. To tarry is to delay finishing, in fact it is completely unconcerned with finishing. This is true of both deliverance and the erotics of demons. The performances are often slow, with pauses and repetition. There is no rush to move beyond delay despite the intensity of desires. In tarrying with demons Pentecostals delay.

Desires named and delays complete, the prophet then instructed Badoe to "cast out her spirit." Badoe walked briskly toward her. He put one hand on Priscilla's forehead and one on her waist, still held by the sartorially identical ushers. While Badoe commenced deliverance, the prophet, confident in Badoe's prophetic abilities, moved on to invite those with spiritual marriages to come forward. The episode was mostly complete as far as the prophet was concerned. Meanwhile, Badoe pushed Priscilla's head back so that her neck strained and her upper body bent backward. As Badoe pushed her backward, her body resisted and snapped forward, pushing Badoe away from her. Badoe returned and hit her forcefully with an open palm in the waist. Badoe again hit her, this time in the vaginal area. He grabbed her forehead and pushed her backward, her body bending dramatically away from her arms, which were still held up by the ushers. They tumbled four steps backward, and the ushers lowered Priscilla slowly and gently to the floor, with Badoe never taking his hand off of her forehead and face. The ushers let her arms fall limp beside her body. Meanwhile, Badoe yelled "out," but it lacked the earlier demanding tone, no longer a question but now a declaration: the spirit was gone! Her body went docile; Maggie was dead. The prophet yelled out a celebratory "heh," and the band played a song to which the congregation swayed, most with their hands raised. Priscilla lay docile for the duration of the song, nobody paying any attention to her, and then quietly returned to her seat.

Combinative Reduction

Combinative reduction is the dissolution of the orgy as meaning has been saturated. Nothing more exciting lay ahead. Combinative reduction only happens after everything has been explored, after meaning has been optimized. In this way, pneumoeroticism, like an orgy, requires an ideology of "more than enough." Orgy functions on the ideology of "more than enough pleasure."[60] This is a dramatic change from most sex, which pivots around an insatiability or "never enough." Orgy is different. And in the scenes that follow, there is "more than enough"—whether that be information, bodily encounters, violence, or meaning. Deliverance saturates.

The conclusion of that particular scene has been reached but it is not the end, for it "usually gives way to another scene, subject to the laws considered before, that is, counteracting excessive limits with minor variations and delaying the sense of urgency."[61] And then everybody moves on to the next body—the next person and the next demon—and does it all over again. There is no ultimate desire for an end to this cosmic battle, for the point is not ultimately defeating the demonic but instead constantly encountering, sexually, the demons that inhabit this world and the next.

The reduction in the apparatus being explored herein is docility. The bodily goal of deliverance is to turn a convulsing body into a docile body. In Marcella Althaus Reid's queer theology, a materialist theology rooted in embodiment, the bodily goal of the demonic is rebellion in contradistinction to docility.[62] But deliverance is marked by a restrained body, the quieting of the excessive body. The rhetoric of the prophet and the spirit are far less demonstrative of success than are bodily reactions. Foucault cites docility as a marker of the "subjected, used, transformed and improved" body.[63] In many ways, this is how prophets utilize docility. Docility, the accurate marker of deliverance, marks the body that is controlled and transformed. The body remains on the ground, not rigid as though dead, but a mere inert object.

The lack of interest or care showed toward the docile body indicates a lack of interest in the Holy Spirit by deliverance Pentecostals. Additionally, the Holy Spirit is not imagined with nearly the creativity or iconography of the evil spirits. The Holy Spirit is, in many ways, an absence. Meyer points this out, stating, "The Holy Spirit is a generalized antipode to the differentiated domain of Satan."[64] That is to say that the Holy Spirit is less a thing itself than it is the negation of the demonic. In Pentecostalism, demons come with specific ideas, attitudes, desires, and personalities. Demons are creative. The Holy Spirit lacks all such things. Meyer again captures this beautifully, saying, "Possession by the Holy Spirit alone is comparatively dull and meaningless. It lacks the possibility of articulating forbidden ideas, wishes, and desires or to express facets of oneself evoking one's actual life conditions."[65]

Docility is a return to the body. At the conclusion of deliverance, if successful, the body lies docile. It is a coming back to the body from the various spirited possibilities that have been visited. But the body is not the same as it was at the beginning—it has been stretched, expanded, troubled, and challenged in spirited ways. To say that pneumoeroticism starts with the body and returns to the body is not to say that it returns to the same, unchanged body. It returns to the body with a new understanding of the breadth and capacity of that body. If body A in some sexual combination experiences spirits, then when that body returns absent the spirits (through deliverance, another spirit, etc.), it returns not as the same body but as body A'. That is to say, it is still a derivative of body A but expanded, stretched, and changed in some way. Likewise, if body A' has sex with a spirit and then the spirit is released, it becomes body A", which is a familiar and unfamiliar body, a significantly expanded body.

The onset of docility makes a body uninteresting and meaningless, until the next time it encounters a demon, when the body, no longer docile, becomes meaningful again. When docility occurs, the conclusion of that scene has been reached but it is not the end, for another scene quickly takes its place.[66]

We will also see, perhaps most poignantly in the scene on spirits of homosexuality, what happens when docility is not achieved. The scene still simply dissolves because meaning has been saturated. The meaning is independent of docility, docility merely standing as the most obvious and frequent dissolution of scenes. But in each dissolution, the possibility of a new scene emerges.

There are a couple of ways in which the possibility of new scenes develop. First, there is the idea that spirits who have been cast out must find another body for continued existence and may enter another person present. The new scene may directly relate to the previous scene. But usually, the new scene emerges with a different spirit being fought by the prophets in some other body. As we will see, the saturated scenes end with the person returning to their cheap plastic chairs, treated as the same person who entered the church but never actually the same.

Mostly, combinative reduction further demonstrates that this whole demon-sex-deliverance apparatus is not about what pneumatic Christians claim it is. It is not, fundamentally, about freedom or productivity. Pneumatic Christians do not desire completion but the continued extension, sexually, into the depths of the cosmos. Deliverance will never be complete because humans and demons will keep having sex.

These pneumoerotic markers, taken from theories of orgy but stretched far beyond, help illuminate the interstices of sex with demons. We are left with all sorts of details to pay particular attention to as the scenes herein unfold. Sex with demons is often a public performance of mutuality in desire and delay. The human body is not bounded but porous, plastic, and multiple. Heteronormativity has no place in these sexual worldings. The sex importantly interacts with, worships even, immaterial possibilities. And sex with demons never ends, simply saturating one scene with meaning before moving onto another. Hypothetically sexual demons could be defeated if all individuals could be persuaded to deny demons entry into their bodies. But nobody truly desires this. The plastic porous body experiencing polymorphic pleasure is too much to deny.

THREE

SINGULAR SCENES

Amidst the mayhem and frenzy of forty bodies spasming, jumping, falling, and punching in a desperate search for deliverance, Martin's masturbating went almost unnoticed. Unlike Priscilla's masturbating, where she was the only body left and was watched by everybody, Martin was one body among many. His act was slightly obscured by the stage's extravagant, shimmering stairway and its accompanying gleaming railing shined religiously by a few women in the congregation. In fact, Martin's very physical reaction to deliverance went ignored multiple times as it sputtered, died out, and then would slowly arouse until it dramatically burst into a paroxysm of passion. It followed this pattern numerous times until a panicked junior pastor noticed Martin's inflamed loins and ran to extinguish the problematic physical proclamation. After multiple crude, unconsummated erections of the spirit, the congregation was finally made aware of Martin's act when the prophet yelled a shocked "whoa" at the site of his junior pastor battling Martin's manifestation.

The prophet, himself unaware until that moment, aimed the congregation's gaze at Martin's genitals with a nod of his head and a rhetorical question uttered quickly and excitedly, "Do you see how he does it?" The prophet followed up with another query, this time expecting an answer, "What did I say it is called?" The crowd responded confidently and assuredly in one loud voice, "Masturbation!" The prophet agreed by repeating it, "Masturbation." And indeed, as he had multiple times throughout the deliverance session, there was Martin vigorously masturbating, two hands planted firmly on his bulging erect penis. Thousands of spectators now scanned Martin's body, following his caressing fingers twitch and burrow around his penis.

While the human eyes were slow to recognize what was occurring, the whole scene invoked multiple unseen viewers and participants. Someone or something was always watching, maybe participating. The public setting and spirit-infused atmosphere indicated that Martin's self-touching exceeded the solitariness of the vice. And as the pastor frantically and frenetically tried to curtail the masturbatory manifestation, he used his touch to try to reach the engorged spirit. Touch—of self, of other, of spirit: by self, by other, by spirit—became the frenzy of the invisible, making visible all that was ineffable from pleasure to shame. This chapter continues the exploration of masturbation through the sense of touch.

TRACING THE HISTORY OF RELIGIOUS THOUGHT ON MASTURBATION

Prophet Emmanuel asked the congregation about masturbation as if he had named the sex act himself. Still, masturbation has a long history that, at times, has relied on religion and religious ideas. Yet, the history of masturbation is not always an easy one to follow. And while masturbation has not always been a religious preoccupation, nor imagined as a spirit, the history of the act has constructed a complex and powerful cultural phenomenon that Martin and the prophet battled on this sweaty Wednesday afternoon.

Throughout much of history, masturbation was treated with indifference. And among Ghanaian Pentecostals I was told that, until recently, masturbation was a mere triviality, "probably the type of sex least talked about." How then did the masturbator, or "onanist," become condemned and pathologized as sexually deviant, as someone in need of bodily control and discipline? Even more extreme, how did masturbation become a spirit that possesses human bodies? Among Ghanaian Pentecostals, how did masturbation move from a discrete act to a scourge filling churches with chronic masturbators convinced they required deliverance? While impossible to definitively trace, there are several transformational moments.

While rare, there are ancient examples that combine masturbation and the spirit world. In ancient Egypt, there were cosmological beliefs that a masturbating god, Atum, created the universe by ejaculating. The Nile was said to flow with the rhythm of his masturbation. Pharaohs ritualized this gift by annually masturbating into the Nile. In ancient Greece, spirits and masturbation were connected in a myth shared by Diogenes of Sinope. The satyr Pan—half-goat, half-human—was sexually frustrated. All of the nymphs, especially a particular nymph named Echo, were resistant to his sexual advances. Pan's father, the god Hermes, took pity on Pan's sexual dissatisfaction and taught him how to pleasure himself. Pan was so taken with this sexual release that he also showed it to the lonely shepherds of the field.[1] Satyrs were seen as the link in this cosmic circle of masturbation: the gods taught the satyrs who then passed the gospel of masturbation on to humanity.[2] There are ancient vase paintings that clearly illustrate three satyrs voraciously masturbating their exaggerated, large, erect penises.[3] The names of these satyrs further the connection between spirit and masturbation: *Terpekeleos* (shaft pleasure), *Dophios* (to knead oneself), and *Psolas* (erect).[4]

In ancient Jewish literature, there is remarkably little content concerning masturbation. Most famous is the well-worn story taken from Genesis 38:8–10, whereby Onan is struck dead by God because he "spilled his seed upon the ground." But the spilling of the seed was coitus interruptus, and there "is no hint that he masturbated."[5] Rabbis offered a plethora of interpretations of what exactly Onan did to offend God, but masturbation was not the focus of their interpretive work.

Similarly, in early Christian traditions, explicit treatment of masturbation was rare. Onan was utilized as a problematic figure but not to inveigh against masturbation. For example, Martin Luther despised Onan because "it was a most disgraceful crime to produce semen and excite the woman and to frustrate her at that very moment."[6] For most Christians from the twelfth century until the eighteenth century, masturbation was problematic because it was "ontologically yoked to sodomy."[7] Pentecostalism similarly associates "gayism, lesbianism, and masturbation" in a triad of sexual spirits. However, for the most part, before the eighteenth century, masturbation was rarely discussed and certainly was not expressed as demons haunting the world.

On rare occasions, though, there have been glimpses of Christians tying spirits and masturbation together. The writings of the late-thirteenth century Dominican Thomas de Canimpre included four stories of spirited masturbators. Thomas Laqueur describes Canimpre's style as having a "confessional kiss-and-tell, can-you-top-this energy," a phrase that aptly captures Pentecostal sextifying during deliverance.[8] In one story, a woman regularly masturbated in her bed. As she masturbated, the "devil made loud cries of 'fi, fi, fi' and made signs of indiscrete insertion."[9] This idea of devilish pleasure and involvement in the act of masturbation is prevalent among Pentecostals. In another story, a man of the cloth, the Bishop of Lausanne, reached down to masturbate and instead found himself holding a snake.[10] Again, while there is no causal relationship, a prophet told me, "Masturbation, it is always a snake spirit." There are parallels between the stories told by Canimpre and the contemporary pneumatic imagination.

Masturbation took a decidedly religious turn, and one far away from the spirits mentioned above, in the eighteenth century. Masturbation, Laqueur announces in his book *Solitary Sex: A Cultural History of Masturbation*, became a problem "in or around 1712."[11] It was around this year that masturbation was concocted in the best-selling anti-masturbation jeremiad *Onania*. Similar works denouncing the solitary vice followed. Masturbation became a hideous sin. Laqueur and others have argued that it became this way because masturbation was central in the construction of the modern subject. Björn Krondorfer similarly states, "Auto-erotic sex became conceivable as a distinct entity among sexual sins only when the autonomous self emerged."[12] On the contrary, for pneumatic Christians, masturbation reveals the limits of such autonomous thinking, imbricating demons not in some aloof sense, but sensually involved in everything from arousal to climax. A significant leap through history is required to find out how spirits and masturbation became wed in Pentecostal self-making. Masturbation and spirits in the Pentecostal imagination merged in the 1970s and 1980s.

The requirement of deliverance from the demon of masturbation in Ghana appears to be rooted in the teachings of famed deliverance minister Derek Prince. Prince writes about masturbation in his influential deliverance text, *They Shall Expel Demons*. Despite the 1998 release date of Prince's deliverance book, the spirit of masturbation is one that haunted his own ministry due to his slowness in taking masturbation seriously as a spirit. With deep regret, Prince tells the story of a young Christian masturbator named Roger. Roger's deliverance is cited as the struggle that revealed to Prince that masturbation was a spirit and not merely a sin.[13] Prince was fond of Roger's religious zealousness and was particularly determined to help deliver Roger of unidentified demons that plagued him. During one late-night prayer session, after hours of prayer, Roger exclaimed, "It's leaving me, it's leaving me! Don't stop praying; I can feel it. It's in my fingers; it's going!"[14] The "it" that Roger was feeling was the spirit of masturbation. Nonetheless, victory over the demon of masturbation was elusive, and Roger never received his release he so desperately sought. Prince indicts himself over this, stating, "I failed to help because I did not deal with their problems as demonic."[15]

After failing Roger and his vexatious masturbating fingers, Prince vowed not make the same mistake again, and masturbation became firmly entrenched in his demonological pantheon. Roger's cries stayed with Prince and became the model for how that particular demon interacted with the human body. He heard in many others the same refrain, "I can feel it in my fingers. They're tingling. They're getting stiff!"[16] Prince determined that the demon of masturbation penetrated the human body through finger pores and left similarly.[17] Armed with this new information, Prince delivered hundreds by performing deliverances where he demanded of masturbators, "Shake it out of your fingers until you can feel they're free."[18]

Prince delivered one of anthropologist Thomas Csordas's informants from the spirit of masturbation. The event is referred to as early as 1988 in Csordas's award-winning article "Embodiment as a Paradigm for Anthropology," illustrating that indeed this spirit was a part of Prince's spiritual worldview well before he published *They Shall Expel Demons*.[19] Csordas's informant described Prince's masturbation deliverance thusly: "[He said] 'You've known this was a sin, but you did it. You did it deliberately. If you acquired a spirit, it becomes compulsive and you FEEL that compulsion.'"[20] The emphasis on feeling is original and yet wholly consistent with the argument of this book: in a deeply embodied sense, these sexual spirits are felt. Feeling here describes the differentiation between sin and spirit. When you feel the need to masturbate it is a spirit moving in your fingers and in your body.

When Prince invited all those possessed with the spirit of masturbation to be delivered, the informant stood up with twenty or so others, and Prince launched into his deliverance diatribe toward the spirit: "You foul spirit of masturbation. I'm taking control of you in the name of Jesus and by the power of His precious blood. I cast you out in His holy name."[21] In the case of Csordas's informant, the spirit of masturbation departed. He knew the demon was leaving when a series of unique bodily experiences occurred, including "spontaneous elevation of the arms, with hands bent way back, farther than a person could normally bend them of his own accord" and a "sort of an electric feeling, like a mild electric shock."[22]

Csordas argues that any academic interpretation of such an event must take the body seriously in order to come to a complete understanding of the experience. Csordas relies on the body—the motion of the hands and the bodily sensations of shock—to argue that spirits are not seen as interior/exterior but rather in a relationship of bondage and release.[23] Relying simply or solely on the prophetic rhetoric of Derek Prince cannot reveal such a relationship that is ultimately only revealed in and through bodily feelings and expressions. But even as Csordas argues for the centrality of the material body, he spends a limited amount of time actually talking about it, leaving many questions unasked and unanswered. For example, masturbation involves not only hands, which Csordas uses in his interpretation, but also genitals. I have witnessed services like the one Csordas cites, and there is often an emphasis on the hands, including a well-meaning youth pastor who closed such a prayer session with the song "Give Us Clean Hands." However, when the prophet Emmanuel delivers congregants from the spirit of masturbation he focuses on—and indeed, touches—the genitals of those plagued by such a spirit. The primary issue in Csordas using this example is that he relies on a textual testimony that inherently obscures the parts of the body that the supplicant wishes to obscure. In deliverance, the whole body must be considered, and only then can the experience be given serious consideration.

Like his idol Derek Prince, Kwofie is unequivocal that masturbation is a spirit. He repeated himself multiple times, saying, "You may think you are not doing anything with anybody, it is just you acting alone, but it is a spirit." Kwofie theorized that this particular spirit plagues so many people because of its seeming solitariness. He argued that Ghanaians are pious and religious people and are not prone to the usual sexual chicanery of spirits. Ghanaians, he believed, would at least try to resist the sexual wiles of demons. But masturbation, he feared, seems harmless, "So if you aren't a serious Christian, you might not even think it is wrong. A-ha! It is solitary; it does not hurt another person." But, again, he repeated himself, "Masturbation is a very serious and a very powerful spirit."

Everyone I spoke with stridently believed that masturbation is a spirit. This unwavering belief was evidenced by the vociferous reaction to one popular Pentecostal figure, Pastor Chris Oyakhilome of Christ Embassy, when he preached that masturbation is not a sin but a habit.[24] During the "Pastor Chris Live Show," a man from Ghana called in to ask how he could overcome his masturbation habit. Oyakhilome responded by trying to convince the caller that "God is not worried at all about persons who masturbate because it has got nothing to do with Him [God]." Oyakhilome's pneumatic misstep was stridently communicated to me by my informants through disapproving apocalyptic statements. Such leniency and permissiveness were seen as a sign of the last days and a sexual gateway to a plethora of additional sexual spirits.

I am not the first scholar to comment on masturbation operating as a spirit in Ghanaian Pentecostalism. In his 2004 *Ghana's New Christianity,* Paul Gifford cites a Derek Prince–like sermon preached at a well-known Accra-based ministry led by Prophet Elisha Salifu Amoako.[25] The preacher stated unequivocally, "There's a spirit behind masturbation."[26] Birgit Meyer similarly outlines a case of spirits and masturbation whereby the spirit instructed a woman to masturbate, and she did so.[27] These are not isolated examples; every prophet I spoke with shared a similar masturbatory worldview, with slight variations and riffs. Nikoi, who could become quite frustrated with my questions when he thought the answers were self-evident, sighed, "It is a spirit in charge of masturbation." He then went on a diatribe about how the spirit of masturbation made men avoid their wives sexually. He also added, as if he were following the material to its logical conclusion, that masturbation "can also lead you to trying to rape people and all that and you can end up in prison." For Nikoi, if a man masturbates, the spirit takes over his life, leading him not to desire his wife and to desire everyone else with horrific and violent consequences. Emmanuel told me that "masturbation is a spirit, actually." There seemed to be little doubt among the prophets that masturbation was a stubborn, sinful, sadistic spirit.

MARTIN'S DEMON

On the stifling Wednesday morning of Martin John's deliverance, Emmanuel started deliverance by appealing not to a particular person but to all congregants struggling with the spirits of "gayism, lesbianism, and masturbation." This was the first time I witnessed Emmanuel making a mass appeal. His usual mode of operation was to identify sexual spirits within particular individuals; Emmanuel would pace around the entirety of the church, and when his spiritual father, Jesus Christ, revealed a case of possession he would immediately launch into a deliverance sequence that corresponded with the type and strength of the revealed demon. He would often verbalize directions—"left," "right," "three rows back," "at the front," "outside,"—as if he was repeating commands from his spiritual father. For example, during a previous deliverance service, he whispered from the back of the congregation "left." He turned to his left and immediately pointed at a young woman he identified as being plagued by masturbation. He instructed a pastor, one of his many acolytes who follow him around during deliverance, to deliver the young woman and "pray and protect her against chronic masturbation. Pray and cast out that bad spirit from her." The pastor immediately seized upon the woman, grabbing her petite forehead in his hands and shoving her backward as he demanded that the spirit of masturbation leave. The woman's body offered little resistance, and in no time, she was lying docile on the ground. However, mass appeals emerged as a pattern for dealing with the demon of masturbation presumably because the ubiquity of such a chronic and widespread spirit made such an approach economical.

On the day of Martin's deliverance, Emmanuel initiated a widespread assault on masturbation. The offensive was suffused with a sense of urgency, as Emmanuel considers the spirit of masturbation to be genuinely vile. If Prophet Emmanuel had a scale of depravity for sexual sins, gayism, lesbianism, and masturbation would fall among the supremely reprehensible. On the contrary, Emmanuel preached that fornication is a sin easily forgiven by God. Perhaps this was because of his own history, which famously involved impregnating the wife of one of his subordinate pastors and then placing a curse on the resulting child, or the ever constant rumors about his notoriously prodigious infidelity. But the spirits of gayism, lesbianism, and masturbation are not so simply dispensed with. In Emmanuel's teachings, the masturbating body is slavishly subject to evil spirits, and as such, simple forgiveness is not possible. Only the difficult execution of deliverance can free the possessed party; there is no mitigation of masturbation, no penitence for pleasuring oneself. Emmanuel believes that masturbation is a sin against the body, one's own body, by inviting spirits of the night to invade that body. As such, masturbating subjects the body to evil and shuts oneself off from God who abhors masturbators.

Many in Emmanuel's congregation, like Marianne, a young woman in her late twenties, were extraordinarily anxious about masturbation and the chasm that pleasuring oneself constructs between God and masturbator. I met Marianne at a week-long deliverance service for spiritual marriage during which Prophet Badoe, Prophet Emmanuel's second-in-command, delivered her from a spiritual marriage passed down through her family's matrilineal lineage. But possession through spiritual marriage did not haunt Marianne nearly as indomitably as the spirit of masturbation. She simply could not defeat the masturbation demon. Early one evening, we were talking at her house, *Keeping Up with the Kardashians* was playing quietly on the television in the corner, and she described some of the effects that masturbation had inflicted on her. She said, "After doing it, I can't even pray, I'll be off. For like three days, like, I've committed some big sin. It is a big sin."

Before I left, Marianne shared with me a prayer that someone had given her to use in her battle against the spirit of masturbation. The prayer clearly explained that true worship, worship worthy of the divine, was not possible if one stimulates oneself with their hand or objects. It read:

God, I ask that I be delivered from the spirit of masturbation. I will not have sex outside of marriage. With the help of Jesus, I will die to my selfish fleshy desires. I repent of my sins of masturbation. Sexual immorality is a sin against my own body. I will never get to a place where I don't need God. I will no longer stimulate myself with objects or my hand. I will not let the spirit of masturbation rob me of true worship. I declare that I will be intimate with God until my mate arrives. I will be sensitive to the touch of God. Only God alone can give me the desires of my heart in Jesus's name.

The prayer contains an ambivalent approach to human agency in masturbation. On the one hand, the masturbator is repenting of their sins. On the other hand, the spirit of masturbation imposes its will evident through the description of it robbing the masturbator. So, is masturbation an act of human agency, a demonic imposition, or some combination of both? This complicated dance between human agency and spiritual force recurred throughout the course of my research in Ghana. Concerns about whether or not the human has unimpeded masturbatory agency is mostly irrelevant in the pneumatic worldview. Nothing is solitary, not subjectivity or agency. Often, as in this case of spirited masturbation, individuality is not defined via self-determination or self-definition. In Pentecostalism, though, this is not lamentable but embraced. One's existence is always in assemblage, in one way or another, with the spirit world. Subjectivity is necessarily relational, and agency is always negotiated within these various relationships. Aisha M. Beliso-De Jesus uses the term *co-presences* to describe the complex interaction of beings, seen and unseen, as they interact with people, things, and bodies.[28] It is crucial to acknowledge that co-presences explain a receptive subjectivity in contradistinction to passivity. As Zakiyyah Iman Jackson has written, "Receptivity here should not be confused with passivity. Receptivity is the processual experience of embodied humanity—the active, but not always conscious, process of receiving and participating in an encounter—not the totalizing identity implied by the term 'passive.'"[29] As such, masturbation is a participatory act that engages and is engaged in by spirits. For Pentecostals, this is not simply a religio-sexual myth but an approach to the world that challenges the possessive individualism and self-determination of modernity/coloniality.[30]

Further, Marianne's prayer imagines the spiritual connection between her and God as parallel to her experience of masturbation. The pleasurable autoerotic experiences, or "selfish fleshy desires," ruined "true worship." In the place of masturbation, she promised to be "intimate with God," "sensitive to the touch of God," and to have her desires satisfied by God. The divine touch, which is an intimate touch, is deemed acceptable, while the touching of oneself is policed and outlawed. The correlation seems to indicate that intimacy with God satisfies on a similar register as masturbation.

The prayer, though, provides very little in the way of details about the touch of God. How is this touch experienced? And what, other than the source, is different between Godly intimate touch and demonic options? Marleen de Witte argues, "Such descriptions should not be understood only metaphorically. They inform techniques of the body and, as such become literally embodied and produce bodily sensations as they tune the believer's senses to the working of this invisible yet tangible power."[31] De Witte's observation combines well with Kathryn Geurts's argument for *seselalme*. *Seselalme* is an Ewe term for the sense of feel-feel-at-flesh-inside, as a pan-African mode of signifying.[32] In each of these scenes, it is *seselalme* (viscerogenic feeling in the body) that defines how each masturbator experiences senses as intersubjective and interrelational.

Perhaps most revealing is that in Marianne's prayer, masturbation is imagined as a sex act outside the bounds of marriage, a telling characterization of masturbation for pneumatic Christians. By invoking the limits of marriage—a heterosexual relationship of orgasmic mutuality in sex—the prayer is pointing to masturbation as something more than autoeroticism. Masturbation is not simply autarky because it is not a solitary vice. Masturbation is an act of sexual consummation with the spirit of masturbation. Masturbation is a relationship of orgasmic mutuality between human and demon.

Sitting outside a dingy coffee shop close to Accra's circle interchange, a young interlocutor named Yaw shared a group text that was circulating between his Pentecostal friends. Always well-dressed, Yaw's brightly colored tunic moved as he laughed while he scrolled through the phone, sharing the highlights of this Pentecostal warning. Yaw simply did not take the spirit of masturbation as seriously as Marianne and others do. The prayer started with the normal heterosexist standard that pneumatic churches glorify: "Sex is between two people, a man, and a woman." This standard invocation is noteworthy not only because of its heterosexist logic, but for how the first clause emphasizes proper sex as a human exchange. Sex is not assumed to be an exclusively human endeavor. Such a claim goes unstated in most contexts, but Pentecostalism imagines sexuality in ways that explode standard assumptions.

The prayer continued, "If you are somewhere alone masturbating it means you are having sex with a spirit and when at long last you have a satisfaction, that was because you are having sex with a spirit that you don't know or you haven't seen. The spirit is where you are getting satisfaction from . . . you are doing it with a spirit." Nikoi, as he was wont to do, reacted with incredulity and frustration when I posed the question: if masturbation is a spirit, does the spirit experience pleasure during masturbation? By asking the question, he believed, I revealed that I had not grasped the demonic at all. "Yes," he said firmly, "spirits get sexual pleasure when you masturbate." Nikoi added, "A spirit will come upon you and will do whatever it wants." Emmanuel and his assistant Badoe, very different prophetic figures than Nikoi, confirmed the same.

In this view, the relationship between spirit and matter is upset by touch: the human touch that pleasures a spirit stretches the body far beyond its material bounds, and the spirit experiences masturbation as immanent. Such threshold-crossing touch exposes the inadequacy of the terminology, broadly conceived, surrounding sex. For example, there are no terms that adequately define spirit-cum-human sex, and indeed, most of the terms surrounding sexuality are limited to the interaction of bodies and exclude the possibility of spirits. Scenes such as these are sexually transgressive, for example, in the way they relocate sites of sexual pleasure, creating scenes where sexual pleasure is felt in human bodies but also by spirits who feel and instigate the most intense sexual pleasures.

MARTIN'S DELIVERANCE

Returning to Martin's day of erotic reckoning, the prophet made a brief speech as he invited the depraved to the front of his church. He repeatedly admonished them not to be "shy" and promised to "break that spirit for you." Masturbation is a problem to be solved, a spirit to be destroyed. Emmanuel's capacious speech on solitary pleasures with its ambiguous twists and turns actually began as an invitation for those identifying with non-heteronormative sexualities. But when he added masturbation to the list, the speech pivoted to exclusively address the spirit of masturbation and provide particular illustrations of the severity of the problem. He stated,

> It has become a spirit in you. Don't be shy. Maybe you started from school or home. Come if you are a lesbian, gay, or involved in masturbation. Do you know where it will land you? It has destroyed many marriages. Some

are caught in the bathroom by their husbands doing it.[33] She'll say that's why I do not achieve orgasm when we have sex. Then she'll tell the source. Some men also do masturbate even after sleeping with women. If you have such a spirit, don't be shy and come; let's break it for you.

In his invitation, Emmanuel imagined female masturbation as a means to not only pleasure but bodily learning, an act that allows women to identify the erogenous zones of their bodies. This knowledge—or at least the impartation that she has such knowledge to the husband—is related to a lack of orgasm in sex and ruins marriages, though exactly how is unclear. The problem of women masturbating is the spirit-induced orgasm that deprives men of that experience. The masturbating spirit visits her before her assumed wifely duties of orgasming to her husband. The problem is an orgasm with someone—a spirit/oneself—other than a man. For men, the order is reversed. The problem is masturbating after having sex with a woman, which appears to communicate either an excessive amount of libido or the failure of one's wife to adequately pleasure to completion. By ordering masturbation in this way—prior to sex for women, after sex for men—Emmanuel is absolving men from any blame for women's lack of pleasure in conjugal acts.

Regardless of the interstices of Emmanuel's invitation, his core message was clear: masturbators are possessed by a spirit that only he was capable of defeating. As Emmanuel spoke, men and women responded to this invitation. They made the arduous trip from their seats toward the front of the church, navigating the tight quarters of worshippers crammed into the space, young children sleeping on the floor, and the various paraphernalia of pneumatic deliverance that littered the floor including stickers, fans, and bottles of oil and water. By the time he completed his message on masturbation, a group of forty had gathered, all eager and consenting to have their "spirits of gayism, lesbianism, and masturbation" broken. The gender dynamics of the group closely resembled the ratio of the broader congregation: one-third male and two-thirds female.

With the group assembled—only a few stragglers slowly augmented the fringes of the group—the prophet asked his pastors to ascertain and then enumerate which spirit each person was struggling with. At first, the pastors carefully asked each participant what spirit bedeviled them. A junior pastor dressed atypically in a subdued grey suit with no flashy accouterments volunteered the first person. Putting his hand on the small of her back and pushing her a step forward toward the prophet, he stated she was a lesbian. After the pastor had announced this, the woman grimaced, nodded her head, and covered her mouth with her hand in a look that mixed consternation and stupefaction. The pastor lightly guided her out of the way toward the right of the stage.

The pastor in the grey suit then moved on to a young man in a sharp white tunic with turquoise trim and extravagant buttons. In a phlegmatic manner, the pastor stated, "Masturbation, ten years." As he said this, his right hand held the microphone while his left hand made a slow and small jerking motion, a motion most often associated with the act of masturbating. To each pronouncement, the prophet vocalized his sympathy with a simple, if disinterested "uh-huh."

Lurking over the right shoulder of the young man in the tunic was the man whose experience is central to this chapter. Wearing a bright green collared shirt with a brown print, slacks, and black leather sandals, Martin John stood contentedly, perhaps abashed, in the back row, making no effort, unlike most others, to push forward toward deliverance. His clothes drooped around his large frame. His hands remained still at his side, and his vision sunk toward the tiled floor, unlike others who confidently stared the pastors in the eye as their sexual baseness was publicly announced. Nonetheless, the grey-suited pastor reached out his hand and put it on Martin's shoulder and dispassionately said, "The same thing: masturbation." Martin John, now marked as possessed of masturbation, shifted to the right with the others whose spiritual ills had previously been identified. Nothing in the encounter foreshadowed the unique experience Martin John was about to have.

The microphone was passed to another pastor whose first congregant was "gay," and then with an exaggerated and melodramatic jerking motion— larger and longer than the first pastor—he identified a few male masturbators. The next pastor made jerking motions for his male and female masturbating congregants despite the action making very little sense as an enactment of female masturbation. Only one pastor dressed in a fire-engine red suit with a large watch that jingled every time he acted out masturbation enacted anything bearing a resemblance to female masturbation, stroking the air with his fingers as opposed to the ubiquitous jerking action.

Later, Emmanuel described the plight of women who masturbate. He said, "We have several married women who are being tormented by those things. Some are married, some who have boyfriends are being tormented by those things. If your man finds out, he'll divorce you; come, let's break it for you." Whereas much of the religious imagination was phallic, for example, the jerking motions, the consequences were borne by women. And the effects, in this case, were enacted by men against women. If you masturbate, your male partner will leave you. Male masturbation is envisioned as a sin against one's own body. But female masturbation is to sin against one's own body and the male partner.

Worried that his congregants were unsure about what titles were associated with each act, the prophet interjected a clarifying piece of definitional sexual education: "If you play with yourself and ejaculate, it is masturbation. But some call it homosexual. Homosexual is a meeting of two male partners." He ended the explanation with an exclamatory "Gay!" as if yelling the word was descriptive.

Emmanuel reiterated that "this is not a matter of shyness, there are spirits behind those things." Ironically, within this sentence he did not name that about which he instructed people to be unabashed. His concealing masturbation behind the phrase "those things," combined with his fear that people might be too shy to come forward, indicated a strong current of societal discretion concerning the public discussion of masturbation. The unambiguous claim within the sentence was that spirits are to blame. By transposing the conversation to the realm of the spiritual, Emmanuel hoped to transcend the societal hesitance around such topics. The prophet completed his interjection by yelling at his pastors to go faster in their naming of each person's demons. And so, with less care and consultation than before, the pastors just start calling out lesbian, gayism, or masturbation while pointing at various people. The default spirit was masturbation, wildly outnumbering the other two spirits. Only one man was marked as gay and a handful of women as lesbians, but the rest were masturbators in need of deliverance.

Emmanuel then turned toward the non-masturbating congregants—or at least those who had not come forward during his plea for masturbators—and offered them a stern warning: "If you joke sitting there, the spirit can impart into you. So, start praying and drag your children closer to you. Or else you may see your small child masturbating because of impartation." The idea of impartation is not unique: spirits go somewhere when they exit bodies, usually penetrating another body. But Emmanuel's fear of the masturbating child as something particularly grotesque was gripping. The crowd quieted at this warning against their offspring, parents holding children held them tighter, children sleeping in the aisles were awoken to be hugged by their parents.

This was the first time I had ever heard Emmanuel reference children outside of the ubiquitous references to childbirth. Despite lots of discussion of miracle babies, children are, for the most part, absent literally and theoretically from the deliverance scene. In fact, of the research sites central to this book, only Emmanuel's regularly had children in the congregation. They were explicitly banned from Nikoi's deliverance service, and they did not stay around the prayer camp. It is worth considering why, then, in the context of masturbation the child is invoked. For Foucault, the controls incited against children's "solitary habits" by doctors and educators "combatted children's onanism like an epidemic that needed to be eradicated."[34] But eradication was never actually the goal. Foucault writes:

> The child's vice was not so much an enemy as a support; it may have been designated as the evil to be eliminated, but the extraordinary effort that went into the task was bound to fail leads one to suspect that what was demanded of it was to persevere, to proliferate to the limits of the visible and the invisible, rather than to disappear for good. Always relying on this support, power advanced, multiplied its relays and its effects, while its target expanded, subdivided, and branched out, penetrating further into reality at the same pace. In appearance, we are dealing with a barrier system; but in fact, all around the child, indefinite *lines of penetration* were disposed.[35]

For Foucault, the introduction of the masturbating child is a power-multiplying mechanism. Such an interpretation is effective in this case; the prophet's warning can be read as an attempt to "proliferate the limits of the visible and the invisible." The limitless invisible spirits made visible through masturbation proliferated the power—visible and invisible—of the prophet. And in so doing, lines of penetration are written on the bodies of children.

Emmanuel exhorted those assembled to: "Raise your hands and let's pray for you." Like the others, Martin John raised his hands. He bent his arms ninety degrees at the elbow, his forearms fell slightly forward, and he stretched his fingers apart. The pastors and ushers pushed in, encircling, and kettling the participants into a small, inescapable space. Before unleashing the pastors, Emmanuel asserted one last request and a warning to the congregation. The request was a standard and straightforward deliverance instruction: everyone should "stretch out your hands and pray to deliver them from that spirit." He augmented the request with the caution that failure to pray puts one at risk of contracting the exorcized spirits who will gladly enter the unpraying body. This suggests that masturbation is contagious. Emmanuel teaches congregants that touching oneself can move among people in the form of the spirit. He says that this can happen when the touch of deliverance sends the spirit shooting out of the masturbating body and it lands on an unsuspecting, unpraying viewer. Unsurprisingly, once deliverance began it was accompanied by the loud, fervent prayers of the faithful trying to ward off the spiritual ejaculations of deliverance.

Warnings issued, Emmanuel released the pastors to deliver those assembled. The pastors responded by laying hands on peoples' heads and praying in loud exhortations: "leave," "go," or "die." Deliverance is often the combination of exclamatory prayers and touch. Touch responds to touch, with the touch of masturbation warded off by the touch of deliverance. Prophet Badoe explained what happened this way: "The spirit is in that person, dwells in the person so by touching him or laying your hands on him you are touching that person to release God's power. You are releasing God's power into that person, into the body of the person." Often it is the touch of a pastor that causes the demonic manifestation, which Badoe explained was merely the spirit becoming annoyed and fighting back, refusing to evacuate the body. In this deliverance service, the touch of deliverance rained down upon these forty individuals. Sometimes it was merely a momentary slapping of the forehead by pastors and prophets, and sometimes it involved holding onto the person for much longer. Each one of the forty bodies was touched at least once by a deliverance minister. Touch is complex. Touch is ambiguous. Touch generates feelings of care, pleasure, relationality, violation, and violence. Touch is all these things for Pentecostals, and in deliverance touch (of other) is used to combat touch (of oneself).

Quickly the front of the church was littered with bodies. The pastor who marked Martin John as a masturbator came face to face with Martin, who stood unmoving. He reached out and again touched Martin's shoulder with one hand. He put his other hand on Martin's forehead, the base of his hand firmly planted near Martin's tightly closed eyes. Another pastor standing off to the side stretched out his arm and placed his hand on the top of Martin's head, his fingers overlapping with the first pastor. The pastors pushed Martin backward. Martin almost immediately fell to the ground, and the two pastors gently laid him down.

Once on the ground, and out of the piercing gaze and touch of the pastors who had moved on to deliver other people, Martin rolled over onto his right arm and, with his right hand, began vigorously rubbing his penis. His self-pleasuring went ignored for almost a minute amidst the cacophony of prayers and groans and the frenzy of bodies moving to and fro. Eventually, the grey-suited pastor and two ushers, distressed, ran toward Martin. Without hesitation, the pastor straddled Martin and pushed him onto his back. Standing over him with one foot on either side of Martin's hips, the pastor continually tapped Martin's forehead, hoping that the staccato rhythm of his touch might release the spirit from within. Martin, impervious to the pastor's head tapping, remained immersed in his own masturbatory rhythm as his hand moved rapidly over his pants but firmly on his penis. Martin shifted again to his side and slid his hand into his pants, where he continued the strenuous and robust rubbing action. The pastor hit Martin's hand, now embedded deep in his pants, with an open-palm multiple times, and while he did Martin's rubbing slowed and then ceased. Gently and unhurriedly, Martin pulled his hand out of his pants. His freed right hand met the ground and continued to move about slowly as if it was searching for something to do, something to touch, unsure of what to do once separated from his penis. Eventually, his hand stopped moving, and Martin's body went docile.

Rather, most of his body went docile. His penis betrayed him; his erection pushed the malleable material of Martin's slacks into a bulge on his left thigh. His penis stood as a bodily clue that this deliverance was not over; it presaged a need for more touching. Nonetheless, the pastors moved on to some of the other bodies still standing about and the few strewn on the floor, including a woman quickly stroking herself over her clothes. Martin remained still for a mere twenty seconds, and there was no real transition when he launched from tranquil and unmoving to exerting himself again. He aggressively shoved his right hand back into his pants, his black belt bulged at the movements of his wrist, its silver belt buckle moving up and down to his masturbatory rhythm.

I cannot emphasize enough that for Pentecostals masturbation is simultaneously self-touching and not a solo act. Erica Frueh writes of autoeroticism, "Autoeroticism is important for it affirms the subject's knowledge of herself."[36] Knowledge of oneself in this episode is the unraveling of individuated subjectivity. As Martin reaches for his penis, he reaches beyond his own body. He learns his bodily limits and how little control he has over his actions. To return to Beliso De-Jesus's idea of co-presences, with each stroke, Martin learns that he is not alone.

As the group thinned because those delivered had already returned to their seats, the prophet finally became aware of Martin's struggle. Emmanuel impatiently yelled, "Deliver him," ignorant of all the deliverance work his acolyte had been doing. At this, Martin fell onto his back and his arms stretched out above his head, his spirit induced bulge still visible. Martin cried and his chest heaved furiously as Emmanuel reached out toward him. The prophet yelled "Holy Ghost" but was quickly distracted by another deliverance episode. By the time the prophet's attention returned, Martin was unsteadily standing. He leaned heavily on pastors standing on either side of him. Emmanuel ran at Martin, shouting, "And I deliver this man from that spirit," followed by repetition of the word "out" in escalating volume. Emmanuel pushed heavily against Martin's forehead, stomach, and penis, causing Martin's body to fall flaccid. Touch always matters in deliverance, but the touching of the penis appears to be unique to the spirit of masturbation, a paradoxical response to the allegedly problematic act of touching one's own penis. While touching of genitalia is rare in deliverance—at least as compared to the touching of most other body parts, but especially the head, shoulders, stomach, and feet—it offers an embodied explanation of how deliverance is imagined. The prophet, he with the supernatural touch, engages the penis with his hand. The whole goal of the deliverance is to touch the body until something—in this case, sexual spirits—is released.

While addressing Martin's masturbating spiritual coconspirator, Emmanuel asked, "I arrest you. Who are you?" At this Martin's still and flaccid body spasmed and arched, and his face contorted. The prophet melodramatically grabbed Martin by the collar and yelled in a voice that tried but did not quite reach the intended level of intimidation: "Who are you? Talk to me!"

Martin responded by crying, "I don't speak English!"

For the prophet, this explained everything, so he responded with a confident "ah-ha" and firmly stated: "Meaning you're a non-English speaking witch? Do you see that I've got you? I rebuke you with the blood of Jesus to go out of him." Emmanuel pushed Martin to the floor. He was made to stand up again by a handful of pastors. The prophet pushed him to the floor once more and definitively announced, "It's gone; it won't come anymore . . . The Lord has saved you. You are free forever." Again, as was the pattern throughout this ordeal, Martin's body went docile, became unmoving, but his penis remained erect.

Comforted by Emmanuel's confidence that the spirit of masturbation had successfully been extracted, everyone returned to their respective places in the church. Everyone moved except Martin. He laid still for a moment as the service continued around him, the prophet resumed pontificating with the band playing softly in the background. Slowly Martin reanimated: first, his legs started moving, stretching, then bending so that the soles of his feet touched each other. Then he moved his right hand onto his right hip and began rolling around. The prophet noticed the unsanctioned movement. Martin's movement was problematic because he was supposed to be already delivered and, thus, a docile body. The moving body desperate to masturbate was a direct assault on the prophet's powers.

Emmanuel immediately stretched out his hand toward Martin. Martin responded by shaking his hands with unbelievable rapidity. His fingers scurried, calling to mind Roger's cry to Derek Prince, "It's in my fingers!" As they did, his right arm moved like the arm of a clock moving backward. From a twelve o'clock position above his head, his arm shifted, hand still shaking, all the way around until it met his leg. There his hand loosely held his quad. His left hand did the same thing, though moving clockwise. Then both tremoring hands crawled up from his quads and mounted his penis, rubbing it vigorously.

The prophet yelled, "Whoa," the music stopped, and he instructed the congregation to fix their gaze on Martin's penis, "Do you see how he does it?" While murmurs of disgust remained audible throughout the congregation, Martin struggled on his own against the spirit. He used his left hand to try to pry and pull his right hand away from his groin, but the relief was short-lived and his right hand continued to enact the spirit's wishes. Emmanuel continued to describe what Martin was doing and how it would end, "So he does that, and he ejaculates."

While Martin continued his embodied fight with the spirit of masturbation, Emmanuel made a laconic statement that was both descriptive and prescriptive. Looking down toward Martin the prophet said, "Today I break that spirit. He does that and attains orgasm. It is spiritual. The spirit is crying for forceful separation." The prescription was unsurprising and straightforward: the prophet could destroy the spirit through deliverance, the spirit was fearful of Emmanuel and wanted to be separated from the body, to be less immanent. The description, however, that "He does that and attains orgasm. It is spiritual" is complex and polyvalent. Initially, I thought the statement was referentially ambiguous but probably suggesting Martin's orgasming. But upon reflection and several conversations with Prophets Badoe and Emmanuel it became clear that every element of the statement referred to the spirit. Emmanuel had already articulated that Martin was masturbating and that he would ejaculate as the problematic climax of masturbation. Here Emmanuel was describing how the spirit would attain orgasm, a possibility confirmed by other prophets I interviewed. When this claim is combined with the earlier description of Martin's orgasming, Emmanuel has described masturbation not as a solitary act but one of mutuality, one of coterminous orgasms between the spirit and Martin. This mutuality has significant implications for how one thinks about the relationship between spirit and body. In this cosmos, the body is never just or only pleasuring a human but nonhuman(s) too if we consider that the spirit engages in the very act of masturbation. The body is dynamic and multiple.

Previously we encountered masturbating Marianne, who lamented the chasm masturbation constructed between her and God. Marianne, though, was equally honest about the pleasure that masturbation brought her. Like most others, Marianne experienced a dissonance around such sexual experiences; masturbating with spirits was simultaneously pleasurable and problematic. This kind of dissonance was present among my interlocutors with all the varied spirited sexualities they encountered. Masturbation was personally pleasurable, but bodily pleasure itself erects no ethical, moral, or theological barrier for Pentecostals. The problematic element was that the mutuality meant it was also pleasurable for the spirit.

Another issue, resonant with Victoria Eto's complaints, is that spirits have insatiable sexual desires. Phillip, a deliverance minister under Nikoi, told me, "Masturbation is disastrous. Masturbation is using yourself to get an orgasm. It is sinful because it is influenced by demons; it is not normal. It is always a spirit that arouses the person to masturbate." Marianne confirmed this. As Marianne described it, she usually masturbated at nighttime. However, she found that the spirits would find more and unique ways to entice her to pleasure herself and the spirit. It could be encountering naked pictures on WhatsApp or pornography popping up on her computer, all enticements of the demon at all hours. Marianne took the idea of mutuality further than Emmanuel, suggesting that not only were spirits experiencing orgasm but they were the ones ensuring human pleasure. Marianne said, "At that moment, you are not the one doing it . . . you get it?" I did not understand, so she added, "They tend to manipulate you," while mimicking fingering herself. Her actions helped me understand, but I still sought more clarity: "So who is doing it?" She replied matter of fact: "Them! You get up and then you go and they do it." Marianne's description matches the text message that Yaw shared with me, a firm belief that one is masturbating with a demon.

Emmanuel's discourse about the spirit orgasming with Martin ended with a seemingly contradictory claim that the spirit was also crying out for forceful separation. Why would the orgasming spirit leave the masturbating body that was so intimately related to its own existence and experiences of pleasure? If Martin's masturbating was also pleasurable for the spirit, what was the evidence that he wanted to leave that pleasure-inducing body? After much conversation around this deliverance event at Emmanuel's compound, the evidence appears to be contingent on time and place. If Martin were masturbating at home, the spirit would be content in remaining with Martin's body. Privacy marked the place where mutual satisfaction could occur. But Martin's audacious masturbating in the church during a period dedicated to the deliverance of such spirits constituted a public plea, a public manifestation set off by the touch of deliverance ministers.

This explanation, however, does not account for the forceful element of the spirit's plea. Why could the spirit not leave on its own volition, or at least plead for peaceful passage? In deliverance, forceful separation is the only way that termination can occur. Deliverance, as such, is always a violent encounter. In deliverance services, I observed that spirits do not move on from their human partners easily. They supposedly have no agency to move on from their partners unless they are forcefully removed. From this perspective, for the spirit, remaining with Martin meant continued encounters with Emmanuel, and so the preferential option was actually to be freed from Martin and potentially to then move on to a new partner, perhaps one of the non-praying persons in the congregation as Emmanuel had warned.

Martin began to cry. His heaving chest accentuated just how disheveled his clothing had become with his twisted shirt, undone black belt, and his slacks collected around his bulging erection. He mumbled something that was not caught by the microphone. The prophet asked him to repeat it. The words "I'm ashamed" fell out of his mouth steeped with a sense of sincere regret. The prophet did not hear this confession, this frisson of shame, as Martin's but as the confession of the spirit of masturbation. He warned the spirit, "You are mad! If you don't take care, I'll expose you." Again, Emmanuel's exhortation was richly symbolic. How could the spirit be exposed more than it already had in Martin's masturbating? Presumably Emmanuel meant he would name the spirit, but it remained unclear why that might be threatening. It had already been established that he was going to rid the spirit from Martin's masturbating body. But, deliverance is about performance rather than consistency.

The prophet, patting Martin's erection, turned to the congregation and said, "See how erect his thing is." Again, he directed their gaze to Martin's penis, though by the cries of some in the audience they did not go entirely unscandalized by the request. The request was purposeful, though, as the prophet imposed the erection as the barometer of the spirit's presence. "So, the spirit is leaving," he said while tapping the penis and watching the erection dissipate. He tapped it twice more, his touch representing a spiritual turn-off. The whole episode suggested that the offending spirit was located in the penis. Martin rolled onto his front then rolled onto his back again, and the visible bulge was no longer there. The prophet yelled victoriously and broke into an upbeat song. At the conclusion of the song, the prophet moved on to a new subject, to a new issue, to new people, and new spirits, and Martin's docile body was simply carried away.

I cannot overemphasize the link between touch and deliverance. Years after Martin's deliverance, one of Emmanuel's pastors sent me a video of a masturbation testimony. The man gave a succinct testimony of Emmanuel's power over the spirits of masturbation:

> It all started around 1992 when I was in school. A friend of mine was discussing masturbation. So, when we completed in May 1992, I went to stay with my mother, and one day in the night, I began to masturbate. It has been going on and on and on, and then it came to a point where I tried to stop. I did all that I could, but I could not stop. At a point in time, I started praying to God that whatever will happen and I will stop doing it, even if I should become impotent. It was going on and on, and then finally, I could not stop without doing it in a week. Sometimes every day for months, months! So, in June this year, I came to see the prophet, and he gave me direction to do. When I went home, I started on the second day in the night. I had a dream, and the prophet was standing by me, and he was praying, and then he left. Immediately after you left, I felt worms coming out of my manhood. When I saw it, I jumped, and the worms came out. Ever since, I did not masturbate again. It has been four months, and that is why I came to testify. I do not even feel the urge to masturbate again.

The worms come straight out of Eto's Pentecostal worldings, but it was touch that captured Emmanuel's attention. Emmanuel was impressed with his own prowess and instructed the man to "Come. I want to touch you again." It is always touch that concretizes deliverance. The man came forward, the band played a triumphant tune, and Emmanuel touched him on the head. To touch is to master; this is the lesson of deliverance. To touch oneself in masturbation is to be mastered by evil spirits. But the deliverance touch, the touch of the prophet masters the body in a completely different manner, a controlled manner, a disciplined manner.

STEPHEN

Early one afternoon, as the clouds rolled in over the mountain at Mamfe, Mary—my assistant at the prayer camp—sent me a man named Stephen, whom I had never met before. He came to meet me at the terrace where I was leaning up against the balustrade. While three plastic chairs were lying around, only one was of a sufficient quality to hold a human being, and so I continued to lean against the balustrade throughout the interview. I was exhausted, having taken the early morning *tro tro* ride up the mountain after attending an all-night prayer service. My attention was admittedly more pre-occupied with the goats and roosters traipsing around the base of the terrace than our introductions. Still, I could not help but notice his hands held tightly in his lap, making small movements, a sort of tortured or agonizing hand wringing that continued throughout the interview.

I shook his hand, offering a brief respite from his hand wringing, and started with a seemingly benign question about what church he attended. He immediately launched into an answer dissonant with the question, stating: "As I was growing up and I got to secondary school, I developed an interest in pornographic movies, and when I watched pornographic movies, then I would masturbate . . . [eventually] I started feeling pain in my manhood." The rapidity with which he launched into his masturbatory tales speaks to the anxiety that plagues many surrounding deliverance and sexual spirits. He did not know at that point that my research interest was in sexual spirits but was compelled to speak by the same anxiety that animates much of the discourse. In many cases, the fear of persistent sexual desires and or acts becomes all-encompassing, all one can think about, and all one talks about. In another example, a man who was suffering from spiritual marriage called me every day for weeks sharing with me the details of his sexual dreams. He was hor-rified, anxious, and perturbed that every evening after sharing such intimate information he was revisited by the demons. And yet, he also continually noted the pleasure of such visits.

Not dissimilar from Emmanuel's worldview, Stephen's church, one of Ghana's oldest Pentecostal denominations, taught him that masturbation was not merely a sin, but a sign of possession. Despite these dire warnings, Ste-phen "developed a desire so I couldn't abstain from it." Through his "chronic masturbation" and "pornography addiction," his dreams were plagued by many salacious affairs with beautiful women. The sex would be brief and torrid, almost unbearably intense, and then he would wake up "and realize I've discharged and I am wet." For Stephen, the secretions stood as evidence of an interloping evil spirit and the pleasure she had visited on him.

Stephen concluded that his attachment to the spirit of masturbation hinged on his capitulation to the claims of his science teachers, which had been crucially detrimental to his spiritual development. Science had manip-ulated him into thinking that his groping fingers experimenting with his own body was normal, with damning repercussions. Science is incomplete and "where science cannot operate, where science cannot discover things the su-pernatural takes control . . . we are spiritual beings. Science has limits; the spiritual has no limits." In secondary school his science teachers taught that "when you have these things [masturbation and wet dreams] they will say its normal if you have too much sperm in your system and you don't use it, in the night it will come alive." In church Stephen was taught that spilled seed does make certain things come alive: spirits. Stephen was adamant that his passion for masturbation and enjoyment of pornography was not normal or spon-taneous but related to intimate experiences with evil spirits. Believing that the sperm spilling experiences of masturbation and nocturnal emissions were normal had caused him to misapprehend touch and its supernatural powers.

Onan's specter haunted Stephen, inspiring anxiety and fear about mas-turbation and, most notably, around its seminal climax. Marianne's account of masturbation mirrored Stephen's. When asked what was problematic about the solitary vice, she said: "I don't think you should . . . for you to cum, it should be between you and someone." She was unsure about where the Bible supported such a claim, but she was sure that it did. Most people I talked to were much more like Marianne, convinced that masturbation was wrong but could not point to a theological or biblical precedent as to why. They were convinced that there is some sort of biblical edict against it, but it is not the Bible that provides the most critical evidence. The text is part of what informs their worldviews, but most important is how spirits, especially pernicious spir-its like masturbation, are experienced in, threaten, and ultimately destroy the human body. Stephen, though, named Onan specifically. He believed masturbation was a problem, but it was not the act itself, not the pulling and tugging on his penis, that was so endangering. The truly frightening and fatal element was semen falling freely.

Sperm, for Stephen, was the crux of the issue because spirits desired it and could use it in a myriad of ways: "As for my seed, I don't know what they [demons] use it for." Despite his claim of ignorance, he certainly knew a lot about how and why demons loved his semen. "Semen holds power over life and death," he said. His death. He continued: "But as you do that [ejaculate outside of the vagina], you are contaminating yourself . . . During that time, my manhood, everything could not function; everything became dead over so many years. But as I abstained from those things, as I focused on God, it's only God who healed me now everything began to revive again. So, if you give yourself to those sins you are killing yourself, they somehow take your semen and use it for your death, they start killing you gradually by taking your sperm." Stephen made it clear that he viewed himself and his habits of nocturnal emissions and masturbation as a contemporary Onan. And like Onan, death would be the outcome, a death defined by his flaccid penis. The more he masturbated he noticed he was becoming less and less virile, until eventually, his penis could no longer become erect. He believed that the spirit of masturbation had made him destroy himself and ruined his "manhood."[37] Kwofie confirmed Stephen's narrative as typical: the demonic spirit of masturbation "can just weaken your penis and make it to not ejaculate again." Emmanuel preached a similar mini-sermon one week which tied masturbation—which in a previous example he had linked to madness—to impotence and sexual weakness. In this case, a soft, bloodless "manhood" turned into a robust blood-filled penis through deliverance.

Stephen found freedom in deliverance. But the destruction of the spirit of masturbation did not come easily for him, and it only came through Prophet Ofori's efficacious effort. Stephen had tried many other spiritual options but had never found the succor he sought from the stubborn sexual spirits. He had tried other pastors, prophets, and the Edumfa prayer camp. He even, in what he described as a moment of desperation, visited Juju men who had him sacrifice a fowl and drink a traditional concoction.[38] "I went through all that to no avail," he described, "because nothing was helping me." Ofori was a sort of spiritual last resort. Upon arriving at the prayer camp, Stephen waited in line by the prophet's villa for a brief counseling session with Ofori. When eventually called upon, he shared with Ofori his addiction and its corresponding bodily consequences. Ofori comforted him that he was in the right place and prescribed a common twenty-one-day regimen of fasting and prayer in residence at the prayer camp.

The prescription of fasting and prayers is not unique. Sometimes prayers are prescribed as part of deliverance and sometimes as a means of maintaining the results of deliverance. The prayers prescribed for masturbation all sound markedly similar. One prominent deliverance pastor shared the following prayer with me: "You evil spirits that cause me to be bound to masturbation and pornography—I renounce you and all your works! I command you in the name of Jesus Christ to loose your grip and go from me now!"[39] This language is rich in mutuality, with the demon(s) instructed to "loose your grip." The grip is not merely a metaphor but an actual description of the spirit's touch.

One week at a deliverance service in Mamfe, I watched Stephen receive deliverance. As Prophet Ofori made his frenetic rounds of the congregation, never letting the deliverance stories develop with quite the same amount of detail as Prophet Emmanuel, he stopped in front of Stephen. Stephen was standing and vigorously praying, his eyes closed and his fist pumping to accentuate his supplication. The prophet paused and then stated that the Holy Spirit was at work, delivering Stephen from snakes that had invaded his body. The pain Stephen was experiencing in his "manhood" was a result of the penetrating serpents. Stephen had no explanation for what the snakes represented, but nor was he altogether concerned about his inability to understand. All that mattered was that he knew with certainty that the serpents were in his body as a result of masturbating. Ofori prayed that Stephen would be delivered from the snakes. The prayer was short, and at its conclusion, Ofori held the microphone between his face and Stephen's, so close that it was only the microphone that kept their faces from touching. Ofori then blew into the microphone creating a sonic cyclonic effect. Stephen's body began to shake all over. Ofori blew again, and the shaking became more severe. Ofori blew one more time and pushed on Stephen's forehead, which caused Stephen to take two small hops backward before falling to the ground, his plunging body expertly caught by the ushers. As Stephen would later describe it, "the Holy Ghost brought me down."

The end result was a victory for Stephen, marked by his bodily docility. The following day he found embodied evidence that deliverance had been successful. As he told me, "The next morning I realized I was well. Before blood could not flow through my manhood, but now blood was flowing. I was getting better and better and better." The disconnect between this interpretation and that of Martin's deliverance is part of the creativity of the Pentecostal pantheon of demons. Evil spirits, paradoxically, can both make the penis erect or flaccid according to their needs. According to my interlocutors, the erect penis in masturbation is problematic. The erect penis as a symbol of male virility is a good thing. The flaccid penis as a symbol of self-control is a good thing. The flaccid penis as a symbol of impotence is problematic. But, Stephen was thrilled by his erection. In the twenty-one days at Ofori's prayer camp, Stephen did not masturbate once nor even feel the titillating temptation to do so. For Stephen, this was "freedom." Marianne similarly extolled her ability to not masturbate as a sign of successful deliverance: "[Before] once like someone sends me an image of naked people on my WhatsApp or something, it just arouses me, and I start doing it. You get it. But right now, you can send me porn and everything, and I'll watch nothing." She distinguished her past as one of masturbation and her present as masturbation free.

To touch is to understand deeply but it is also creative. Marleen de Witte calls Pentecostal touch a "theosomatic knowledge . . . a knowledge of God or spirit being(s) gained through and stored in the body."[40] The introduction of masturbation as knowledge into religious ritual is an important signpost of what the conclusion to this book calls decolonial demons. In order to think about masturbation in this context is it necessary to acknowledge where tarrying occurred—in the masturbatory act—instead of the alleged defeat of masturbation. Masturbating in public, in the church, constructs a world of sexual possibility.

Marcella Althaus-Reid was excited by the potential of a demonology of masturbation to disrupt modernity/coloniality. Of course, for Althaus-Reid demonologies are sites of rebellion, pulling and tugging at possibilities that the modern/colonial church outlawed. In this way she viewed masturbation as "a form of postcolonial strategy because it de-territorialises sexuality from procreation, complicating the easy identificatory sexual colonial patterns of what is what (what counts as sex, as communal or as 'solitary' for instance), probematising the processes of colonial constructions as 'discrete biological and social units' and mixing up rights to pleasure."[41] In this way the spirit of masturbation has a past, one outlined in brief in this chapter. Masturbation also has a present in the many scenes played out in Pentecostal climes. But masturbation also has a future as it pulls at some of the core tenets of modernity/coloniality.

FOUR

SCENES OF STRUGGLE

There are specific sounds in deliverance: erotic groans, accompanying music, angry exhortations, and piercing screams. There is also persistent, frenetic, and unremitting motion during deliverance: bodies jolt, punch, dance, spasm, and fall. And there is a deep river connecting the rich, textured soundscapes of deliverance and the bodily paroxysms of dance, violence, and resistance. Sounds move. Sounds move people. And sounds move demons.

The sonic is not a discrete sense. Sonicity has synesthetic qualities, entangling sound, movement, sight, and touch.[1] The sonic has always been central to Pentecostalism, and many have attested to this. David Daniels writes that for early Pentecostals, it was "through the choreography of sound, [that] meaning is internalized."[2] Linda van de Kamp points out that during a Mozambican Pentecostal service, "the use of music during the therapy and services mediates the personal experience of the Holy Spirit. The physical quality of sound, such as the beat, helps one to feel the spirit."[3] Percy argues that immediacy and ecstasy in Pentecostal worship music induce "a sort of 'spiraling staircase to God.'"[4] De Witte poignantly articulates that "sounds are not merely useful as meanings but as vibrations of air that physically contact and include the addressee, human as well as spirit."[5] The choreography of sound, the physical quality of sound, and the vibrations are important elements of Pentecostalism.

The central claim in interpreting the scenes in this chapter is that the sonic is a primary mover of the mobile body. In each scene the sonic and kin-esthetic tell a remarkable story. This chapter is an experiment in synesthesia, undoing the stability of the senses. This experiment occurs through the inter-pretation of acts of deliverance by watching and listening to the entanglement of bodies in motion, in contact and convulsions, and by listening to the sounds and phrases that constitute the affective atmosphere in which these bodies move. It is in the thick textured sounds of charismatic deliverance that bodies are made.

The scenes here, though, embody the second claim of this chapter, and that is one of refusal. Each scene in "Scenes of Struggle" is the story of unsuc-cessful deliverance from the spirits of "gayism and lesbianism." In exploring how the sonic and kinesthetic reveal refusal, this chapter proffers an argu-ment about sensual resistance. In many ways, the chapter on masturbation is a sensual case study of ritual success. Martin, despite the fits and spasms, eventually becomes docile. The spirit of Maggie supposedly departs Priscilla. Marianne and Stephen stop masturbating. That is not the case in the scenes in this chapter, where resistance is spoken and embodied. This argument around refusal emerges in the same way as the first claim concerning sensual synesthesia, through careful attention to the sounds and movements in deliv-erance performance. Those sounds and movements reveal much about the persistent, hoary, and violent Pentecostal scripts of anti-queer animus. While each violent action and shout from the pastorate delineates which bodies are forcibly disciplined—which is a sensually harrowing experience for queer believers—attention to the variety of responses to these scripts throughout deliverance illuminates a crack in those rigid and vicious scripts.

THE CHOREOSONIC

Before examining the scenes, it is worthwhile emphasizing just how import-ant sound and movement are to pneumatic Christianity and to explore the relationship between those two senses. Pneumatic Christians move—a lot. As Daniel Albrecht puts it, "According to traditional Pentecostal ritual logic, God is expected to move, but so are God's worshippers."[6] Pentecostals are not inert in deliverance or its attendant rituals. They jump and shout. They dance to the music. They step—sometimes high-step—to the repetitious rhythms of drums and clapping. Carrie Noland writes, "Kinesthetic sensations are a particular kind of affect belonging both to the body that precedes our subjectivity (narrowly construed) and the contingent, cumulative subjectivity our body allows us to build over time."[7] The kinesthetic is an oft-overlooked component of embodied knowledge, movement knowledge, and all of its somatic subtleties, but Pentecostalism makes such ignorance an impossibility.

Pneumatic Christianity also includes a wide variety of sounds, but relatively consistent among those sounds is the volume. Pentecostal churches make noise, and their role as culturally despised or irritating noisemakers is not a new phenomenon. David Douglas Daniels argues that sound and noise were a primary marker of early Pentecostal identity. In particular, the Pentecostal riot of sound—its sporadic and unpredictable sound—set Pentecostals apart from their Protestant counterparts. And it was not just the types of sounds being made but the decibel level that made it Pentecostal: "volume, a lot of it, was valued."[8] This noise regularly confronted neighbors and was a source of complaint by many. But, as Daniels elegantly states, "Early Pentecostal sound became a means of constructing an alternative soundscape, social space, and religious culture."[9] Or, in the words of Crawley, something otherwise.[10] This something otherwise is otherwise than modernity/coloniality. Noise has long been racialized as other, improper, and irrational.[11] Noise was viewed as an impediment to enlightenment.[12] In this way one watches, listens, or feels the excess within these Pentecostal performances as pushing for something different than the hushed order of modernity/coloniality.

Pneumatic Christianity in Ghana is "often accused of public noisemaking."[13] The sonic history of Pentecostalism in Ghana is a loud and contentious one, especially since 1998. As both Rijk van Dijk and Marleen de Witte have chronicled, from 1998 to 2002, there were occasionally violent confrontations between Ga traditionalists and charismatic Christians.[14] The conflict stemmed from the annual Ga Homowo festival, which demands a ban on drumming, handclapping, and noisemaking to appease the gods.[15] Pentecostal churches are ill suited to abide by such an order and refuse to comply with the prohibition, creating all sorts of issues. But it also spills out in battles with neighbors over what and when Pentecostal sound constitutes noise. Multiple churches in my research struggled to get building permits due to complaints about their noise.

In the West, it might be difficult to imagine an ecclesial soundscape being so overwhelming and occasionally oppressive, but the soundscape of Accra is unique. At times it can feel as though Accra is engulfed in an exclusively Pentecostal soundscape. With their sound systems cranked to levels that encourage the squeaks and squeals of feedback, the noise from Pentecostal churches spills out onto the streets. Sometimes those sounds mingle with the daytime noise of the city, and sometimes during their frequent all-night services they pierce the silence of the dark night. Cars with large speakers troll the streets, hurling prayers, or blaring local gospel music. Even the loud calls of the *tro tro*—another central figure in the Accra soundscape—or the chatter within the *tro tro* fall silent when an itinerant charismatic evangelist hops in and launches into a prayer, sermon, or song.

But there is an entirely different soundscape at play in deliverance, with contributions from the seen and unseen. Sound evokes and invokes the supernatural, the sacred, and the demonic. The potency of sound is consistent throughout the entire service, which begins with corporate prayers that are loud and intense, followed by praise and worship that is usually upbeat. The preaching is "passionate, loud, screaming and agitated, it underscores spiritual authority and embodies divine inspiration."[16] And then there is the deliverance soundscape: back-and-forth discourse between the prophet and the spirit; onomatopoetic sounds; microphones cutting in and out or providing earsplitting feedback; the band interjecting, occasionally misplaced; the syncopation of corporate prayers in tongues; clapping; and the weeping, shrieking, screaming, and moaning of the possessed. Often the sounds layer over each other as one pastor continues with deliverance while another pastor begins a fight with another demon. The brief and abrupt silence of docility is always followed by the exuberant and boisterous cheers of the congregation. The sound of deliverance "penetrates us, fusing the material and nonmaterial, the tangible and intangible, religious sound is a powerful medium for connecting to and accessing the effective power of spirits."[17]And the whole soundscape repeats itself many times during each deliverance service.

The power of the sonic is not merely, or even mostly, through a linguistic mode, but requires an expansive soundscape. As Robert Desjarlais writes of his work in the Himalayas:

It is the music as much as the surface meaning of the shaman's repertoire that one must engage with the flesh. By incorporating a mantra's magic within his heart, throat and limbs, a melody echoing others through its sinewy folds and assonant rhymes, an apprentice healer begins to incarnate a sensibility that goes beyond the linguistic. The play of the drum quickens into a kinesthesia of curing, a mumbled mantra summons the presence of the sacred, rhythms of healing grow more tactile than cerebral.[18]

It is not about the quality or content of the sound but its tactility that makes the spirits feel material. It is not necessarily what the prophet says, but his tone and timbre. It is not the notes of the bass guitar that matter but the deep vibrations that it sends reverberating throughout. It is not the indecipherable tongues but their staccato syllables that create tactility.[19]

Sound also evokes and invokes the body. Each sound throughout a Pentecostal service has corresponding bodily movements. Even the congregation never sits idly by. During prayers they pace back and forth, punching and chopping at unseen forces. During worship they dance, clap, and sing. During the sermon they interject their assent to the preacher's teaching with loud exhortations and occasionally by jumping to their feet, waving a handkerchief, or putting cash at the prophet's feet or on the prophet's body. During deliverance they pray, whoop, and scream. The whole service is a choreosonic medley. Regardless of what combination of sounds constitutes the texture of a particular deliverance service, what is heard is central to how bodies move. Ashon Crawley's portmanteau, *choreosonic*, provides a vital intervention here.[20] In Crawley's *Blackpentecostal Breath,* the Blackpentecostal choreosonic is the "always attendant and interconnected concept of movement and sound."[21] Importantly, neither movement nor sound is privileged in this construction.[22] Choreography and sonicity must be thought about in tandem because Pentecostals always practice and ritualize them in tandem.

The choreosonic is a primary way through which Pentecostals know the world. Daniels argues that in early Pentecostalism, sounds, the unpredictable, loud, and often nonverbal sounds, were a way of knowing. Some sounds were identified with the heavenly, and other noises were rejected as demonic.[23] He writes, "Sound enlarges the scale of expression and allows for broader emotional ranges, more textured vocabulary, tonal diction, affective commitment and fuller embodiment."[24] The fact that sound choreographs fuller embodiment is a fundamental tenant of pneumatic Christianity—a truth from the initial evidence of tongues to the screams of deliverance. The choreosonic is an exploration of how sonic and kinesthetic sensibilities are central to knowing and to experiential truth. The choreosonic is a way of feeling the world, of being in the world broadly conceived. Sound and movement coordinate the body. Through the choreosonic the body becomes penetrable, loosened, and shook. Of the choreosonic, Crawley writes, "Such dancing flesh, such shouting, extends outward and reaches for flesh, for feeling, otherwise."[25] For pneumatic Christians, the choreosonic is how they feel (for) themselves, (for) others, and (for) the transcendent—and how others and the transcendent feel (for) them. The choreosonic is more than symbolic; it is an experienced and embodied knowing. Bodies reaching outward remove boundaries, cross thresholds, and refuse to be limited by anything.

The choreosonic is not merely some ethereal hope but includes a deeply political component. There is something destabilizing about this melding of sound and movement that undoes not only Enlightenment senses, but the attendant racist theologies and philosophies.[26] Crawley writes,

> But even the question—was this choreographic or sonic—veils the truth of the choreosonic. Even if these were merely movements, those movements of flesh would have their attendant sonic registers. And if only merely vocalizing, such vocalizing would have its necessary choreographic resonances. The knowledge of shouting is the knowledge of hesitance, the knowledge of the very possibility of indistinction, the knowledge of indeterminacy. The distinction, the categorical difference, of choreography and sonicity becomes undone. This is knowledge that is produced through the materiality of dwelling together with others, awaiting sounds and movements as the spirit gives utterance.[27]

The ethnographic scenes that follow in this chapter illustrate the accuracy of Crawley's claims in the realm of sexuality, for the choreosonic in all its vibrant eroticism undoes heterosexism, indeed, an "ethical demand to vary and antagonize" can do nothing less.[28] This chapter attempts to attune the reader to feel the intensities, the energies, the sparks of experience, to feel something unteachable grounded in this entanglement of kinesthesia and sonicity. The choreosonic undoes transcendent power and power in the here and now. Through the choreosonic, Ghanaian queer pneumatic Christians begin to imagine the materiality of the immaterial, the possibilities of the impossible. They feel and move with the impossible and begin to refuse that which seems impossibly overpowering. The divine and demonic cosmos becomes less fearful, less forced, less powerful, and instead pleasure is found in the moving body, in a different sociality.[29]

MOROWA AND KIFAH

On a particularly hot Wednesday morning in March, Emmanuel's deliverance service had a slightly elevated energy even before he arrived. The weekly deliverance service at Emmanuel's church usually lasted from 8 a.m. until 5 p.m. However, you need to arrive early because by 8 a.m. it is difficult to find a seat. The early hours are spent in testimony, song, and prayer. The afternoon is marked by the arrival of Emmanuel who offers guidance, a sermon, and deliverance. On this day, the prophet allowed another pastor to preach and remained home until it was time for deliverance. When I stopped by his compound, I was told he was storing up his spiritual energy to provide a more enhanced deliverance experience. I could not have anticipated that the energy stored would be violently spent on two lesbian women, Morowa and Kifah.

In many ways, this deliverance episode does not stand out as particularly unique among the deliverance rituals of non-heteronormative sexualities. But I cannot unsee or unhear the violence. The sounds and movements of this deliverance have haunted me every day since. They have, in many ways, become my demons. I do not write this event (again) in an exculpatory effort but in an effort to understand more in-depth what I witnessed and how it fits in the spirited experience of my interlocutors.[30] And because I also cannot shake the sense of brave refusal I saw in the choreosonics of Kifah and Morowa.

On this particular day, my own body watched the violent and sexualized deliverance from a position of privilege. Earlier during this deliverance service, I had been identified as "obroni" and called upon by the prophet to account publicly for my presence.[31] I awkwardly stumbled through some answers to the prophet's queries, my voice cracking at one point, and yet was spared bodily contact. Instead of deliverance, the prophet prophesied to the congregation's delight that I would one day write a book—a prophecy I suppose materializing in your very hands. After the prophecy, Emmanuel asked me to watch the remaining deliverance episodes from the comfortable couches on the stage where his acolytes sat. My placement on the stage demarcated my body as subservient to the prophet but also as privileged. I was, admittedly, confused by the whole performance, both my own performance and the feigned ignorance of Emmanuel. The anxiety I experienced, the immediate and unquestioning capitulation to Emmanuel's instructions, and the comfort I felt when moved to a place of honor each left me distressed to varying degrees. I wondered, though, why did Emmanuel purport not to know the reason for my presence? Although I had not met the prophet himself until this very public moment, I had spent a considerable amount of time at his house and had, through his intermediaries, received his approval to conduct research in his church and had been attending his services for some months. My skepticism grew. If Emmanuel knowingly misled his congregants in this minor case, what else traded on deliberate falsehoods? In some ways, this pushed me to pay attention to the stories playing out with congregants rather than the unreliable prophets.

My position at the front of the church also implicated my body in a particular way, one that became increasingly uncomfortable as this deliverance episode began. It would be the only time my body inhabited this specific position, as in quieter moments away from the pandemonium of deliverance, I was able to discuss with Badoe why I preferred to participate as a congregant. Nonetheless, to my significant discomfort, my bodily presence was complicit in what occurred. My quiet, still body among Emmanuel's acolytes—my bodily refusal to intervene—was interpreted as an embodied statement of assent to all that occurred.

For the most part, the deliverance session proceeded as it usually did with many battles against sexual spirits. Not all of the deliverance episodes were sexual—there were demons cast out who were blocking international travel, passport applications, monetary gifts, or job prospects. But sexual spirits were the most frequent and varied. In one example, Emmanuel claimed to deliver a woman from AIDS by making her consume a lime. In another, he delivered a woman from spiritual marriage. As Emmanuel prowled around the congregation picking out unsuspecting persons and delivering them from their demons, he eventually became fixated on Morowa. He asked her in the most oblique terms if she wanted deliverance from "that thing." She answered in the affirmative as if she knew what "that thing" was. This was unique, since Emmanuel usually simply demands, with declarative statements, that people be delivered: "Stand up" or "come here." Emmanuel apologized for calling on her and repeatedly asked if she was sure she wanted deliverance. All the while he continued to move, ambling around the aisles approximately seventy-five feet from Morowa. Morowa stood still, frozen.

From the very beginning, there was unspoken confusion. Morowa later told me that she had a specific issue—not lesbianism—that she thought the prophet was going to solve. She described her joyous thought process in this moment after Emmanuel promised to deliver her from "that thing." She told me, "I was like, which of the spirits is that? I was so happy. I was like my problems are over." Kifah, who will soon appear in the scene, similarly was not present to be delivered from lesbianism but had hoped for a financial windfall from attending Emmanuel's church. The confusion and ambiguity about the deliverance vanished when Emmanuel publicly referred to Morowa's issue as "girl-girl." When the congregation seemed confused by this description, he added other examples to make it clear that he was invoking a categorization of sexuality, girl-on-girl sex.

Morowa's body was discursively made in this moment, in particular by the context of Ghanaian and Pentecostal social attitudes toward lesbianism. The congregation convicted Morowa with their heteronormative sense of rightness. Some of that sense of rightness was constructed via heteronormativity, Ghanaian and Pentecostal attitudes toward lesbianism, and via Emmanuel, who is known to perform frequent and melodramatic deliverances of the demons of gayism and lesbianism. In fact, in the moments before this service, his television station had re-aired him doing a deliverance from lesbianism ten days earlier in Kumasi. But it was these short phrases that made Morowa's body. She was a body among bodies. "Stand up." Then she was a deliverance body. "Girl-girl." Then she was a lesbian deliverance body. These brief phrases punctuated the air and her body, informing the congregation of just how to read Morowa's body. A couple of pastors next to me whispered to each other, and my eavesdropping ear, amidst mostly indecipherable whispers, heard "supi."

A colloquial term, *supi* commonly refers to intimate female same-sex relationships. *Supi* emerged in the early 1990s as a term used to discourage same-sex bonding at boarding schools.[32] Boarding schools hold an essential place in the imagination of both heterosexual and homosexual Ghanaians as a place where homosexuality runs rampant. Accordingly, homosexual relations are often construed as an immature sexuality that can merely be experimentation. However, the fear is that the wily tricks of the devil can turn this sexual existence into something permanent, lesbianism. William Banks cites a newspaper columnist that stated, "The supi in girls' schools and whatever the boys call themselves practiced in our schools is part of the transition to full-blown homosexuality like the pupa to butterfly. The reality is that homosexuality is very rife in this country."[33] It was pneumatic churches that appropriated the term and set the narrative of *supi* relationships as the gateway to the scourge of lesbianism in Ghana.[34] The *supi* threat is also present in Ghallywood films, whereby lesbianism is tied to the spirit world. One film, in particular, invokes Mami Wata cults where the powerful mermaid spirit corrupts women and lures them to lesbianism, which poses a menacing threat to society.[35] These ideas are central to charismatic demonology, and the manner in which pneumatic Christianity has shaped the public discourse on non-heteronormative sexualities is obvious.

Pentecostal public noisemaking has played a significant role in violently wresting same-sex sexualities in Ghana from privacy and discretion and throwing them onto a public stage for enchanted performances. Serena Dankwa argues that lesbianism in Accra has historically been mostly secretive, hidden, and disguised. Nonnormative sexualities were neither condemned nor condoned but existed in "the realm of the unspoken."[36] A Pentecostal cacophony is now overtaking discretion as a sexual mode. Astrid Bochow remarks that Pentecostal churches in Ghana have created "sexuality as a subject of public discourse, if only in its negation."[37] This is the Pentecostal noisemaking to which Kifah and Morowa's sense of the choreosonic responds.

The negation Bochow refers to is one of enchantment via demonization. Deliverance—much more so than discourse—is the public forum that Pentecostals use to construct a demonic homosexuality. For example, before uttering any details concerning Morowa's sexuality, Emmanuel apologized profusely for revealing such a private issue. He even tried to shift the blame to the Holy Spirit, arguing that without the Spirit's prompting he would never have disclosed such information. In the performance there was a clear delineation between what the spirit said and what Emmanuel seemed comfortable with. Before the enactment of the deliverance ritual Emmanuel continued to speak of Morowa's sexuality obliquely, using terms like "the issue," "that thing," and "girl-girl." However, once the ritual of deliverance began, the words "lesbian" and "lesbianism" were thrown around with vitriolic repetition. This strategy of using deliverance to discuss nonnormative sexualities is typical, or as an interlocutor named Solomon put it, "They don't teach about it, it only comes out in prayers and deliverance." Discretion is annihilated by Pentecostal deliverance. Demonizing of homosexuality is primarily accomplished through deliverance and communicated through a sonic combination of speech, sounds, screams, and the embodied reactions that accompany those sounds. Phillip, a gay man in his mid-thirties, told me that in his charismatic church there are no specific teachings on homosexuality. But homosexuality makes a regular appearance through prayers and deliverance. "Prayer, prayer, and prayer," he told me, "because people have characterized people who are engaged in that act as demons, possessed people . . . they pray against the spirit of homosexual acts."

The basic idea consistent across all deliverance services is that non-heteronormative sexualities are demons possessing the human body and using it then to further a satanic agenda. Repeatedly, this was outlined to me by both LGBTQ Christians and anti-queer prophets. Adriaan van Klinken writes, "In this discourse, the issue of homosexuality is enchanted, that is, viewed from a deeply religious worldview characterized by a strong eschatological expectation and by the belief in a cosmic struggle between God and the Devil."[38] As Kwofie said to me plainly, "The natural way is a penis and a vagina, the unnatural equals gay—unnatural sex can put you in contact with spirits, seriously!" Kwofie went on to add a description of exactly how the spirit accesses the gay body: "If you lie with a man, the spirit comes through your anus, a lot of deep, deep demons." Razak is a prophet and is gay, though he likewise thinks that "homosexuality is a spirit." Like Kwofie, he claimed it was a particularly strong spirit that was spread by homosexuals: "Spirits use anything and everything that touches a gay body—a person who is into it—to spread the spirit of gayism. For example, at sports, if you touch a person's towel that has touched the naked gay body, the spirit will enter you." As my friend Solomon told me, "They believe a normal guy wouldn't fuck another guy. So, then there must be an additional something that gives you the interest. Because it is unimaginable, it must be spirits." Michael, a gay activist, told me, "My church sees it as something barbaric, something very bad and demonic." He added, "It is not good to be gay because when you are gay, you are possessed by a spirit," in Michael's case spirits from the marine world.

Since homosexuality is a spirit on assignment from the devil, in this worldview, you have to attack the spirits at the root. Kwofie, having already described how spirits enter the body—deep, deep through the anus—went on to explain how they exit during deliverance. "If a homosexual spirit comes out, it comes out as vomit, or the person urinates seriously, or the person cries," he went on, enumerating the various orifices and fluids that indicated spirits evacuating the body, "and sometimes they ejaculate and discharge in deliverance."[39] These are the signs of deliverance from gayism and lesbianism on the way to the ever-important docile body. This chapter, though, is not about such signs or docility.

Despite the tentativeness in Emmanuel's language, he outed Morowa as a lesbian. Morowa's sexuality immediately became public and problematic, even though she was never consulted about whether she considers herself a lesbian or if she wanted such information to be public. This is an example of thoughtless Pentecostal noisemaking. Morowa does identify as a lesbian, but she did not want this to be public. In being forcibly outed, "lesbian" became Morowa's identity in front of Emmanuel's church in a way that obscures much of her lived life, struggles, and joys.

Morowa lives alone in a run-down hotel in a busy industrial community near Accra. She feels extraordinarily isolated from her family, who remain in Nigeria, but she has found sources of sociality in the city. She is also deeply committed to pneumatic Christianity. Her favorite prophet is the late Nigerian mega-pastor TB Joshua, her "spiritual father." She only became familiar with Emmanuel through a friend, Ethel, and by watching him on his popular television network. Morowa desperately wanted deliverance from something that had been bothering her. Knowing this, Ethel had invited Morowa to this particular service. Ethel and Morowa arrived together and sat side-by-side throughout the service, at least up until the moment when Morowa was singled out.

Morowa had never visited Emmanuel's church previously. This is not unique. At any given deliverance service in Emmanuel's church, approximately one-third of the congregation are first-time attendees seeking some sort of spiritual succor. They are drawn by Emmanuel's prophetic reputation as well as his ubiquitous television presence on his own television network. Unambiguously, this is a battleground of uneven power dynamics. The prophet wields his spiritual authority, which allows him to reign not only over spirits but also the bodies that house those spirits. The excessive and brutal violence of Emmanuel's deliverance rituals—for example, against a couple who conceived outside the bounds of marriage and in another instance, toward a pregnant woman—has received widespread condemnation. But the outrage is selective, and while the deliverance of Morowa and Kifah received no such public condemnation, it was, to my eye, more brutal and sustained in its physical violence. In this case, Emmanuel used the movement of bodies to tell a story about lesbianism as a difficult demon to part with, to vilify lesbianism, and to demonize women's bodies, among a host of other patriarchal scripts. In violently exercising ecclesiastical power, Emmanuel made the body something to be feared, loathed, and ultimately disciplined.

When deliverance began, it was from the first touch an odd haptic experience for Morowa. She had experienced the laying on of hands by many pastors and prophets in the process of healing and deliverance. In the past, she experienced the touch in a particular way: "If a good man of God touches me, I will feel cold, and it will go right from my forehead all the way down, cold!" This is not unique; Pentecostal ritual feelings are often described as sensations of warmth and coolness. What is worth noting in this deliverance, unlike all of her previous experiences, is that Morowa felt differently: "But in this case, I want to tell you the truth, when he touched me, I didn't feel anything cold." Morowa's sense of thermoception reflexively provided clues that this deliverance might not be like anything else she had experienced. She explained that her body sensed and interpreted cues from this world and beyond. Only in hindsight was she able to articulate this fact, curating it as evidence that the deliverance was not real. Her body, though, felt and engaged in a kind of bodily resistance to the touch of the pastors. While it may have remained unconscious, this deeply embodied sensing set off a whole host of embodied reactions toward the force of the pastorate that Morowa exhibited throughout the deliverance episode.

Elsewhere, I have termed this type of bodily knowledge "embodied perception."[40] Embodied perception is the acquiring of knowledge through the moving and feeling body. Embodied perception is not about sudden, cognitive bursts but the oftentimes unconscious ways in which bodies communicate. In this case, through embodied perception Morowa felt resistance. She could not immediately identify the bodily meanings but, over time, reflexively realized that her body had been providing signposts of a narrative far different than the prophetic script.

The area around Morowa was quickly cleared of other congregants and the plastic lawn chairs on which they sat. The fluidity of Pentecostalism is even embraced in the way spaces change and are flexible, eschewing the solidity of church pews for something that can morph at a moment's notice. Two pastors pulled Morowa's arms taut behind her back at an awkward angle while she tried to move forward toward the prophet. As they held her arms and tried to control her body, it became clear that this was an attempt to discipline Morowa's lesbian body. Another pastor held a microphone toward her face to amplify what she was yelling. Morowa repeated into the microphone: "I am a beautiful queen," "I am beautiful," and other similar declarations. Emmanuel responded to the statements about beauty and its irresistibility with "This lady is not for you; she is for Jesus!" emphasizing "Jesus" with a dramatic flair. Emmanuel's verbal cues indicated that it was not Morowa speaking but a spirit. Emmanuel demanded the name of the spirit. Morowa, speaking as the spirit, once, and only once, invoked the name "Creamy," with all of the sexual fluids that it implies.

While Morowa was demanding people pay attention to her beauty, the physical conflict between her and the pastors was ongoing. As they twisted and turned, Morowa yelled that she liked to dance. At first, I interpreted this statement as a joke about how the bodily struggle mimicked a dance. But Emmanuel instructed the pastors to let her go, and he invited Morowa to come to the front and dance. The pastors released her arms and she sauntered up to the front of the church. Emmanuel instructed her to dance, but she did not. She requested music, for her body would not move without accompaniment.

As the band struggled to find a tune that placated Morowa's tastes, she paced back and forth. Her body never stopped moving, but she did not dance. She would walk one direction, turn on her heel and walk back the other way. Eventually, the band gave up and an iPad was secured. A song with a danceable beat began to play, though the lyrics bothered some congregants. Bodies do not just move to any sound, as Morowa's body refused to move until the song that moved her, affectively and physically, began. With the "right sound" Morowa began to dance. Julian Henriques argues that affect is produced and embodied through vibrations. These vibrations are not immaterial but are an example of what he refers to as rhythmic materialism. Through the crush of bodies, the vibrating sound system, and the space itself, affect is materialized.[41] While Morowa waved off song after song, it was not a dismissal of their lyrical content. Instead, she did not like the beat. She did not like the way some of the songs forced her to move. She wanted to move in a particular way, and only a specific soundtrack allowed for that.

Morowa began to dance in a manner that could be described not as provocative but undoubtedly sensual. She enjoyed her body. Her eyes looked up and down her body, and her hands moved around her body. No longer angrily pulling away from the pastors or yelling into a microphone, Morowa smiled. She danced for a few minutes until she shook her backside toward the congregation. They vociferously shouted their disapproval, waved her off with their hands, or turned away in disgust. With a simple hand gesture, Emmanuel had the music cut off. As the music stopped, so did Morowa, but as she slowed her movements, she smiled again—she was pleased, something important had just happened. The joy I saw on her face made me think almost anything was possible. It brought to mind Crawley's description of Blackpentecostal shouters dancing:

> Moving to the rhythm: of the drum, of the clapping hands, of their hearts. Shouting feels good. It is erotic. And that because it is fleshy. Looking at the flesh dance and move and sway prompts otherwise than a sacred possibility. Or, more precisely, sacred possibility is found in what is thought the categorically distinct and pure zone of eros. The gestures, the movements, have within the capacity to destabilize us, watching and becoming destabilized, energized, desirous of the flesh that moves. Such dancing

flesh, such shouting, extends outward and reaches for flesh, for feeling, otherwise.[42]

Her joy in dancing demonstrated otherwise possibility. Only in listening to her later account that "I really enjoyed the dancing so much" were my thoughts confirmed that I had witnessed the choreosonic at work. Morowa had felt affective choreosonic power in her body.

When I remember this experience, I remember most distinctly two dissonant happenings: Morowa's smile as her dance concluded, and the violence that was enacted against her and Kifah. The smile was revealing of an otherwise in the face of heterosexist violence. It screamed out that the churchly script is not the only interpretation at play. There is often this dissonance between the stories told by deliverees and the scripts of deliverers. I often wonder what most congregants saw in that smile, if they noticed it at all. Or did they experience the episode in precisely the way Emmanuel wanted them to, the way he told them to: witnessing his ability to make bodies do some things, stop doing others, and cede to his control.

To dance and touch one's own body did not cross the church's limits of modesty, but when Morowa bent over at the waist at a nearly ninety-degree angle, pushing her backside out in such a way to emphasize the space it occupied and shaking it with the music, the prophet stopped the deliverance body. Dance, for Pentecostals, mediates the immanent and transcendent, the invisible and visible.[43] Katrien Pype has written about Pentecostals and dance in the Congo, and it is instructive here because despite the Pentecostal penchant for dancing in worship, not all dancing is sacred. Pype explores how Congolese Pentecostals negotiate sacred (Christian) and profane (worldly) dances, "although . . . the specific movements and lyrics and the accompanying sounds display much more fuzziness as these fields seem to nourish each other constantly."[44] Dance is either for God or the devil, and in this case, Morowa's dance had been too worldly, a type of refusal of the sounds and movements Pentecostalism tries to impose.

Deliverance is both an act of confession and surveillance—the pastorate and entire church inflict their curious, judgmental, interpretive, and voyeuristic gaze on the moving body—and of control and punishment, as the body is often forced to do or not do exactly as the prophet desires. It is set as a battle between the cosmic forces of good and evil for possession of the body. Still, deliverance is always the attempt to write churchly and cultural scripts—that is, narratives of power, ecclesiastical and otherwise—onto the material bodies of believers. The churchly scripts apply power asymmetrically relying on benevolence and coercion. As the dialectics of confession and punishment have acted as a form of control in some other Christian traditions, deliverance allows for the pastorate to control and discipline the sexual body. Punishment, which will be more clearly performed as this narrative continues, "is the violence to which bodies are subjected when contravening orders."[45] Punishment is enacted to procure docility.

As Althaus-Reid brilliantly defines docility, it is "hetero-hell."[46] Docility, the control and correction of bodies, reinforces hetero-patriarchal ideals and expectations to produce a gendered, heteronormative, and productive citizen.[47] Docility demands appropriate and controlled sexual behavior and is so deeply entwined with the cisheteropatriarchal order of things, it can never be anything other than straight. This all sounds rather hopeless, but the need to produce docility also highlights the fragility of religio-sexual imperialism. Every little movement contravenes the right order of things, producing rebellion. Althaus-Reid captures this when she notes that hell spaces are ripe for ideological rebellions.[48] Hetero-hell and hell spaces are not synonymous in that hell spaces, read: demons, are rich with potential to overthrow the order of things, to refuse docility, and to resist through the movement of flesh.

Confession was part of the modern will to knowledge regarding sexuality. That sexuality is being discussed at all in this scene, as if there is a sexual truth to be discovered, is modern. And yet, as the scene plays out, truth is hard to find. Indefatigable indocility, in the face of punishment, is the refusal to accept a role in hetero-hell, a refusal to acquiesce to the re-presentations and interpretations of the prophet. Instead of the churchly scripts, I was drawn to Morowa's vulnerability, her irreducible openness, as a script that refused Enlightenment's subject. In the verve and noise, in her movement, in her comfortability with co-presences, Morowa's performance rejected the contained subject.[49] This is what Morowa's dancing, and her indocility yet to come, were, not only a refusal to accede to power, but a refusal to accede to sexual hell.

As the episode proceeded, it was interrupted by a sonic disruption. The screams of a woman near the back of the sanctuary pierced through the drama occurring at the front of the church. It quickly became apparent, though, that it was not merely screaming but was primarily a choreosonic disruption. This person was reaching out for a friend, reaching out in a refusal of the scripts being written on Morowa. From the crush of individuals emerged four ushers carrying Kifah's flailing and screaming body. Each usher held a limb so that every time she flailed, her torso bounced up and down, her head hanging dangerously close to the ground.

Kifah came on her own volition, but she knew Morowa because they worked at the same club in their industrial community. They did not coordinate their visits and were not even aware of each other's presence in the church until Kifah witnessed Morowa's deliverance. Kifah's family home is only a few minutes away from Morowa's hotel. She had come to Emmanuel's church on this particular Wednesday not for deliverance, per se, but hoping for a financial windfall. Money was tight in Kifah's family, and Emmanuel occasionally gives away money during his deliverance services. He can be quite generous in this way, and he had been writing checks for congregants quite regularly around the time Kifah visited.

The ushers set Kifah on the ground, and she began rolling around, groaning, all the while rubbing her hands against her lower stomach and occasionally her genital area. For the most part, this is how Kifah's body acted—a repetitive choreosonic loop of groans, screams, rolling, and the rubbing of her abdomen. The introduction of Kifah's deliverance body was very different than Morowa's. Morowa had been selected by Emmanuel and constructed in a particular way: the insatiable lesbian body that must be delivered. Kifah's deliverance body reacted more spontaneously, responding to the stimuli of the experience and the affective atmosphere, rather than the instructions of the prophet and pastors. Exactly what stimuli Kifah's body responded to is unclear. But more than likely, she responded to the sounds of Morowa's deliverance. She was sitting at the very back, and from that vantage point what one can see is severely limited, even if one stands up. I imagine it was the sounds of her friend, and maybe the sight of her friend dancing, that moved Kifah.

Morowa immediately reacted to Kifah's presence, shouting out her approval and proclaiming her affection for Kifah. She bounced from one foot to the other. She repeated how she appreciated the cleanliness of Kifah's body.

This was ironic because the way their discursive bodies were made was the opposite: lesbian bodies are constructed as dirty, sinful bodies. Perhaps it was a phrase of resistance. Thereafter, for a considerable amount of time, the two bodies of Kifah and Morowa were left in their loops while the prophet and pastors presented their scripts as to what they observed. The pastors quickly wrote their discursive sexual script onto Kifah, with one pastor informing me privately before exclaiming to the congregation that she was "a lesbian who liked licking others' vaginas." While the crudeness of his description would shock some church congregations, sexualized and explicit rhetoric is relatively standard fare at Emmanuel's church and is very much in line with the impetus of Evangelical and Pentecostal churches to be as descriptive as possible of all sins that may befall congregants. Each action was interpreted to fit these scripts despite the lack of obvious embodied correlation. In doing so, Emmanuel and his cohorts imposed an affect of disgust on Kifah and Morowa's bodies.

A pastor standing next to me pointed to Kifah's vagina and stated that the "spirit is in there." Another pastor told me there was a snake in her vagina. Without touching Kifah's body, the pastors began yelling "lesbian spirit out," literally requesting the spirit to exit her vagina. The prophet and lead singer, meanwhile, discussed on the microphone that Morowa's love of cleanliness was because lesbians use their tongues to lick vaginas, again invoking Morowa's tongue and Kifah's vagina. The lead singer went to great lengths to describe cunnilingus as excessive homoerotic sexuality. Eventually, the musings about cunnilingus ceased, and the two camps—Emmanuel and his pastors on one side and the possessed women on the other—came into bodily conflict. Most of the pastors began delivering Morowa while Emmanuel focused on Kifah. They attacked both women simultaneously. To say they were attacked is in no way hyperbolic, and the violence that ensued cannot be described as anything else.

Kifah repeatedly touched her genitals and moved her fingers as if she was pleasuring herself. Every time she touched herself, Emmanuel hit her hand. It appeared to have little impact. Emmanuel asked his wife to come and hold Kifah's crotch. The demand for his wife's hand in the process was not viewed as a delivering touch but as a pragmatic way to stop the autoerotic imitation. Her hand formed a barrier so that Kifah could no longer touch herself. Emmanuel replaced his wife's hand with his foot and repeatedly kicked Kifah. With each kick he made a "pfft" sound into the microphone. Kifah continued to wiggle and writhe on the ground, and she never acceded to Emmanuel's desire that she become docile.

While Emmanuel spent all of his time with Kifah, six of his pastors physically tried to rip the demon out of Morowa. As they held her, she managed to drag them around the front of the church. Even amidst the violence, Morowa tried to dance, shaking her backside at the pastors who had her in their grasp. Whenever the pastors' bodies came in contact with Morowa's backside she would determinedly rub her body on theirs. Some of them held her while others punched her in the stomach. One pastor ripped off a bracelet she was wearing. Her face and head were hit repeatedly. One tried stomping on her feet. Another repeatedly pulled her head down toward his crotch, miming a heteronormative oral sex act. She described to me months later that the assault was painfully etched on her body for days: "[I was] feeling headache, pains all over my body, everything. I couldn't even sleep that night because of my headache." While deliverance is always physical and often includes a violent element, this was the most brutal deliverance display I witnessed in my fieldwork. This ritual rending of lesbianism from the body was a bodily beating, yet despite the ferocity, Morowa never spoke of her experience in terms of physical or sexual abuse. She understood all of the physical contact within the context of Pentecostal rituals, namely deliverance. The pastorate may have been wrong in their diagnoses of what plagued her, but in all our conversations, she never condemned or objected to their means.

In her exhaustion, the pastors managed to pull her to the floor and hold her there. Another pastor joined the fray and ripped off her wig. She yelled, "my hair, my hair," to no avail as the wig disappeared into the mad orgasm of bodies and was run out of the church. Devastated, Morowa cried, "my hair, I need my hair" over and over again. She squirmed as much as her tired body allowed. Eventually, they let her stand up while she continued to ask for her hair. She never became docile, and even when held on the ground, her body strained against the weight of the pastors pinning her to the floor. The deliverance service that began at 8:00 a.m. had extended until nearly 7:30 p.m. This saga lasted over two hours, and yet, it ended inconclusively. Docility, that ever-important marker of pastoral victory, never occurred. Morowa and

Kifah never stopped moving, though exhaustion overtook everyone involved, and the movements slowly became less and less determined.

When the service ended, I eschewed the *tro tro* and walked the entire distance to my flat. On my walk, I replayed in my mind the scene over and over again, wondering about my participation and even the viability of the entire project. I rehashed these concerns later that week when a condensed version of the event was replayed on the prophet's television station and there, in the middle of the broadcast, was a clip of me taking notes, a useless look of consternation on my face. I concocted all sorts of reasons—many viable—about why I did not intervene. Although no amount of hindsight absolved me of my embodied complicity, I concluded that I would not have done anything differently given a chance to replay the day's events. It seems to me that these paradoxical tensions often mark ethnographic fieldwork.

Docility is the pastorate's goal in deliverance. The bodily goal of deliverance is to turn a convulsing body into a docile body, and these bodies resisted that effort. To refuse docility is significant and not something I saw often. Docility—silence and stillness—is the antithesis of the choreosonic, whereby sound is felt, and feeling is transposed into embodied movements. Docility (read: hetero-hell) is a lack of options, options limited and curtailed by society and the church. Morowa and Kifah's stories, though, are not stories of docility, literally or metaphorically. I was convinced on that day that there was something more-than, something otherwise beyond these churchly scripts of anti-queer animus operative throughout the whole ordeal. I witnessed an alternative way of being through the bodies of Kifah and Morowa. In their capacious choreosonics I witnessed hints of refusal, especially in Morowa's dancing and in both women's refusal to become docile.

These women resisted by refusing to obey the bodily discipline that was so brutally enacted on them. Perhaps the most prominent way that they resisted those scripts was in their refusal to become docile, rendering Emmanuel's touch, and that of his acolytes, ineffective. Repeatedly throughout this particular deliverance service, and many like it, bodies obeyed the demand for docility. Emmanuel often reserved his touch until the end of the deliverance encounter and then, with a swift slap, watched the bodies fall to the ground. That did not occur in the case of Morowa and Kifah; their bodies refused to acquiesce to the bodily demands of the prophet. Kifah refused to stop touching herself despite persistent efforts by the Prophet Emmanuel and his wife to detach her hand from her genitals. Kifah refused to stop moving even when the pastors and ushers held her body down. Morowa fought back with immense force, at times dragging pastors around the front of the stage. She refused to fall when force was applied, instead applying equal force against the pastors to ensure that she remained standing. Each of their movements, screams, and refusals pushed against the conditioning of the churchly scripts of hetero-hell. Both women, in their commitment to move without ceasing, resisted deliverance and, accordingly, all of its attendant cultural scripts. The commitment to move and to fight in the face of extreme force was an act of radical resistance.

Morowa's dance, to a profane beat, was a refusal. She resisted religious definitions of her body and her sexuality. Sonically and choreographically, she provided an "otherwise possibility, as choreosonic performance—which is another way to say a way of life."[50] That otherwise possibility, that pure zone of eros, is not the hetero-hell of churchly docility. That otherwise possibility is a refusal of the lack of options the church offered, a rejection of limited definitions, movements, and desires. That otherwise possibility is sexuality in all of its possibility, pain, and splendor.

When I discussed the deliverance with Emmanuel afterward, his answers were evasive and short, abnormal for our conversations. Perhaps his answers lacked specificity because he knew that his deliverance had failed. Morowa and Kifah—despite the insistence of these churchly scripts—were not delivered from their "lesbianism." Ecclesiastical power was not the end of the narrative; it did not possess the story. This story demonstrates that there exists at least the possibility that power, though dominant, can be refused—sonically and kinesthetically.

Morowa and Kifah's responses were slow in coming, as initially they were unsure of how to process the pandemonium and madness of the deliverance event. Still, after three months of conversation with Kifah and Morowa, the two women explicitly rejected their deliverance. Or, as Morowa stated, "Nothing really happened." Yet, it strikes me that unconsciously this conclusion might have been drawn first from the movements and sounds during the deliverance encounter. Importantly, their bodily movements and their shouts, their screams, and their physical responses were a form of resistance that need not necessarily be accompanied by a discourse of assent to be powerful. Refusal is not something that necessarily happens immediately or consciously, but instead through the perpetual moving of the human body, each determined breath, and every resistant shout.

Of the three women we met at the beginning of this chapter, only Ethel continues to attend Emmanuel's church. The other two avoid it as a mode of rejection. "I am not going there again," Morowa told me, adding, "I told Ethel, 'I am not going to your church again' . . . [it is] not as if the church is a bad church or a fake church because no, it's not fake, it's good, very good but me I don't like the church." That ambivalent denunciation is solely centered on rejecting the deliverance event that they were part of. Morowa and Kifah do not deny the office of the prophet, or even necessarily the efficaciousness of Prophet Emmanuel. Morowa, in particular, believes that prophets hold the answers to all of her issues in life. She just does not think lesbianism is the issue—or an issue—that Emmanuel should have been worried about. To be clear, she does identify as a lesbian: "Yes, I am a lesbian. I am a lesbian, no doubt. I enjoy making love to a girl." Note the present tense, as part of her rejection of the deliverance is to continue making love to women. She added, "Lesbian spirit is not my problem. I have a bigger problem that is after my life, what is lesbian then? Lesbian is nothing. I have a bigger problem that is after my life. What are we talking about? When there is a bigger thing in front of the prophet? What is lesbian?" This question reverberates as an incredible challenge to Emmanuel's scripts. What is lesbian? Lesbian is not a limiting factor in Morowa's life despite Emmanuel's best effort to demonize it. Lesbian is a form of pleasure, something enjoyed, flesh in flesh. Lesbian is not a problem to be solved. She described it as such: "I cannot see a difference. Because if the Holy Spirit has healed me, what has gone from my life [lesbianism] wouldn't have come back. I am not saying there is no Holy Spirit in his [Emmanuel's] church. But if the Holy Spirit was used on me, what left my life [lesbianism] would not have come back."

Disappointed, Ethel admitted the deliverance did not work: "She [Morowa] isn't ready to change. She has made up her mind about that act [lesbianism]; she still does it." She added, "Morowa doesn't want to stop it [lesbianism], so she has closed the doors of her heart not to be delivered. You can't force someone to be delivered." This statement is ironic, as deliverance is defined by the imposition of force—physically and spiritually. It is the attempt, often violent, to force a body to abide by the prophet's worldview. Nonetheless, Ethel's statement indicates that both Kifah's and Morowa's movements and sounds have cracked open—at least for Ethel—the power of deliverance, revealing a gap in its efficaciousness. Looking back on the deliverance, Ethel wishes she had realized earlier that the deliverance was not taking hold. She said that the extraordinary length of time the deliverance took was not a sign of a stubborn spirit that would eventually be ousted (as the prophet rescripted it) but instead that "it took hours because she [Morowa] was not ready to be delivered."

Kifah and Morowa ultimately rejected and resisted deliverance consciously by (re)claiming their lesbianism. Still, the argument here is that the rejection and resistance existed long before Morowa said that "nothing happened" and long before Kifah rejected Emmanuel's church. Instead, that resistance occurred within the experience of deliverance. The refusal was in their choreosonic sense: to yell and shout and move. They cultivated choreosonics, a moving sound of refusal. I do not, however, want to overextend this claim about the movement from affect to consciousness to imply that such a development is necessary for resistance. Morowa and Kifah's bodies resisted in meaningful ways without conscious assent: their pushing, yelling, dancing, denouncing, and unyielding bodily choices were resistance in and of themselves.

ADJO

The story of Morowa and Kifah is unique and yet common. Many in the Ghanaian queer community attend Pentecostal churches that ritualize the deliverance of gayism and lesbianism. And because of this they have either encountered deliverance or have very purposefully developed strategies to avoid being outed by deliverance. Many in the LGBTQ community in Ghana shared with me their stories of sexual deliverance that did not alter their sexual identities, practices, or worldviews. They told me of prophets unsuccessfully trying to push them to the ground, prophetesses attempting desperately to deliver them, and prayerful exhortations being screamed at them. In the end they always rejected the deliverance. The ultimate proof of that rejection was almost always participation in non-heteronormative sex, but along the way they found evidence in their sounds and in their movements that indicated the deliverance would not take.

Adjo, for example, told me how in his charismatic church he repeatedly heard admonishments against homosexuality. He recounts, "I noticed I had attraction to people of the same sex but then again I couldn't practice because I kept hearing in the church, 'no that's not the right thing to do, that's not the right way to go, this is the way to go.'" Words like abomination, punishment, and hell were thrown around in combination with invectives against homosexuals and men with "feminine mannerisms." Adjo remains closeted in many ways but is proudly effeminate, a refusal to accept his prophetess's pronouncements.

Adjo, though, worries that sounds could out him to his prophetess. He worries that she might hear something. Adjo sings in church. He sings both as a chorister and is often a featured soloist. He is very good. He does not get nervous singing unless he has had sex recently. "I get nervous all the time. Even when I do it on Tuesday and sing a song on Friday," he said. He added, "Every single Sunday I get nervous because she could just pick up the microphone and say sit down and reveal things—you indulged in immoral practices yesterday and today you are singing to God. Go sit down I don't want you to sing again." If he has had sex recently he will come up with a bevy of excuses to avoid singing in church rather than risk sonically communicating his transgressions. Adjo does not want to hear his sex life outed by the prophetess, and he does not want her to hear it in his songs. There is a corollary, though. As much as Adjo fears being outed by his choreosonics, Pentecostal leaders fear its possibility. They fear its power of contagion. They fear its ability to communicate an otherwise that is a threat to the orders they have invested their lives in. Their fears reveal the power of queer choreosonics.

Nimi Wariboko, in *The Pentecostal Principle*, argues that sound is excess, moving toward and between people with no definitive teleology.[51] Because of this, sound refuses to be ordered which is why Pentecostal leaders fear the choreosonics of their queer congregants. This idea of a sexually compromised choir or chorister is prominent in Victoria Eto's work. She writes that evil spirits spread sexual pollution throughout church choirs: "For this reason, wherever I go to preach I advise pastors to screen their choirs. The choir attracts them because they are snakes and fishes. Music attracts these creatures. Some of them may be the best singers." She continues with specific advice, "Screen your choir and your fellowship occasionally. Hold intensive Bible Study revivals. Above all encourage everyone to be sincere. Any member who runs away from such revivals should be removed from the group. Christian music is very important and it must come from sanctified lips."[52] Sanctified lips, for deliverance ministries, are straight lips. But this empowers those queer individuals who sing and move differently; it acknowledges the sacred power of the choreosonic and its ability to undo. Those perpetuating hetero-hell are afraid of the otherwise.

Adjo is unsure about the efficacy of deliverance. "The truth is I don't know [if I believe the prophetess]. She is in a position to see more things than you can," he said. And sometimes she is right. "She has revealed certain things that were really true. So, you are tempted to believe. You want to believe it, but . . ." The "but" exited his mouth and hung over the conversation. He added nothing and did not need to. He simply was not sure of everything that the prophetess said. The "but" largely hinged on what Adjo deemed ineffective deliverance.

Adjo's ambivalence toward deliverance hinged not only on his own sexuality, but his brother's. Adjo's brother Nicholas is also gay, and the prophetess regularly launches spiritual assaults on the spirit of gayism coursing through Nicholas's body. She repeatedly rebukes the spirit of gayism, demanding it exit Nicholas's body. "She says a lot of things," Adjo told me, "and then my brother keeps rolling on the floor and jumping around." Watching the deliverance, Adjo was convinced that the spirit of gayism was real and had afflicted his brother. As his brother moved to and fro he saw "the spirit of homosexuality manifesting." It happened several times. But he was unsure that deliverance worked. Adjo continued, "When they do this deliverance so often and it does not work that is when you begin to ask questions like 'are they fake prophets?' Because my brother wasn't really delivered from anything. He wasn't rehabilitated. After each deliverance he comes back and it is even more than it was before." While Adjo never stated as such, the poignant question from Morowa could be appropriated here: what is gayism? Because of his brother's choreosonic refusal Adjo continues to question his religious leaders and his sexuality.

———

Solomon, a young man in his early twenties with a deep gravelly voice, avoids prophetic public outing by simply avoiding any church where discretion is not valued. But this strategy is not foolproof. Solomon's mother told his pastor that Solomon was gay. Solomon recounts that his pastor was shocked: "He was surprised and started weeping and was like are you serious because he can sing so well." Again, the complicated dance between sound and sexual spirits emerges from behind the choral curtain. Homosexuality—or more aptly for this pastor, the spirit of homosexuality—was so monstrous, so grotesque that it should make sweet sounds impossible.

Solomon was sent for deliverance. Like Adjo, he simply did not see any results in deliverance: "They would tell me you are supposed to fast from this time to this time and when in that state meet some pastors and pray but I didn't see anything." If anything, the fasting and prayers had the opposite effect, and "After a fast, I always want more sex than I did before. If it was two times per week, it'll now be four times per week." And no matter what they tried, he heard nothing that convinced him it was wrong or a spirit: "They prayed for me but I didn't fall under dramatic powers . . . I stand there still." The pastor could not come to terms with what he saw as a contradiction— superlative singing and sinful sex. He kept saying, "If that act is so unclean why should he sing so well and he touches people?" He turned his office into a courtroom, making Solomon swear on a Bible and answer questions such as: Have you had sex with a man before? How many times? Who becomes the female? Who becomes the male? You do both? They removed the sim card from Solomon's phone and surveilled his contacts. Solomon left and attended another church, an act of refusal. He accepts his pastor's logic, saying, "If it is wrong, I'll no longer be able to sing." But he can still sing, sweetly, so what is gayism?

The stories repeat themselves over and over again. Michael, a gay activist, could not avoid deliverance. He came to church late one Sunday and tried to sneak into the back unnoticed. Unfortunately, he was noticed. A prophetess approached him and shared a dream she had about him. In the dream

Michael was gay but kept denying his sexuality, adamantly pleading that he was in fact straight. The prophetess went on explaining the dream. She demanded that he be straightforward with the truth and tell her everything. She began asking questions that are all too familiar. "Do you have gay friends?" Michael answered yes. "Are you gay?" No. She added, "Do you know it is bad to be a homosexual?" Michael questioned why, to which she responded, "it is barbaric, it is demonic, and it is satanic." She and another pastor initiated deliverance, and after reading some verses from the Bible and providing the popular but inaccurate animalistic anecdote that animals do not engage sexually with the same sex, the prophetess and pastor laid hands and started shouting for deliverance.[53] Eventually Michael gave up, fell down, and was briefly convinced that he was delivered, "and I thought that would be okay for me, like, I won't be gay anymore." But the deliverance did not hold: "I realized I am still the same person I used to be and there is nothing they can do about it."

After another deliverance episode, Andrew, a young gay man, concluded similarly, "There was a time I would cry and plead with God to make me change, but I've realized it is an orientation, it is not spiritual, it's a feeling." Similarly, Michael recently saw another attempted deliverance of a particularly "flamboyant" man. They laid hands on him and started praying loudly. As soon as they started "it was like he was possessed, he started crawling on the floor." But it did not work. Michael explained, "Deliverance is not good. It does not work out because he is gay. There is nothing deliverance can do about it." These are all examples of bodies that refuse docility, bodies not seduced by Pentecostal noisemaking but instead by a choreosonic sense that constructs a clamoring resistance toward exclusionary Pentecostal sexual mores.

FIVE

SPOUSAL SCENES

The week-long deliverance event at the prayer camp heralded the end of all spiritual marriages. Prophet Ofori dressed entirely in white, his tunic pulled tightly around his stomach, shouted the invective with more gusto than his usual remarkably sedate instructions: "Pray against your spiritual husband or wife. The husband or wife that you see in your dream!" Not far from the front of the church sat a woman wearing a sports jersey with the word "Pervert" printed on top of the number 17. The whole week—and indeed many, many moments throughout my research—combined both spirits and humans in a kind of pneumatic perversity known as spiritual marriage. For Pentecostals, spiritual marriage, a kind of spectrophilia in which demons have sex with humans, is an ever-present threat that needs to be destroyed. Phillip, one of Nikoi's acolytes, defined spiritual marriage as "a covenant between a deity, a spirit, with a human being who have come to an agreement and have sworn an oath that binds them to be lovers." Many sermons, prayers, deliverances, and healings were aimed at breaking spiritual marriages. Sexual relations between demons and humans are an essential part of deliverance belief and practice.

According to pneumatic Christians, spiritual marriages affect everyone—every human being—and they believe that it is one of the most pervasive problems haunting humanity. Phillip was one of my primary guides through the world of spiritual marriage. He had thought a lot about it, prayed a lot about it, and delivered a lot of people from it. He claimed that every Saturday morning, as we gathered in the humble tent, up to 70 percent of those seek-ing deliverance were afflicted with spiritual marriage. Even prophets are not immune to the sexual wiles of demons. Prophet Ofori, for example, appealed to his own experience in order to articulate the gravity of this sexual threat. Ofori often sextified as a kind of apocalyptic warning about the severity of the problem of sex with spirits. The implicit logic was that if even this man of God could end up sexually involved with demons, then so could you! Before becoming a pneumatic prophet, Ofori had dabbled in other religions, which exposed him to the demonic. He said that through his contact with other religions he had married a demon. To encounter non-pneumatic religions is not merely to weaken the body's defenses against demonic intrusion, it is to invite the demonic into a sexual relationship. It should be obvious how such a theology demonizes other religions as sexually deviant, for even the slightest contact can contaminate. In this way, common spirits from several African cosmologies are integrated into Pentecostal demonology as evil spirits, reen-acting "the broader historical translation process of African cosmologies into Christian discourses by missionaries."[1]

While Ofori said he became married through non-Christian religions, there are a plethora of alternative ways in which one can become spiritually married, and the possibilities are so varied that nearly nobody can avoid it; vulnerabilities include but are not limited to immorality, dancing, mastur-bation, or bathing. Or, as my friend Phillip informed me, spiritual marriage is also contracted through physical sex outside the bounds of heteronorma-tive marriage. Phillip was an unpaid assistant to Nikoi, always trailing him around but receiving no recompense for his efforts. As he described it: "If one person is possessed with a demon, then it will transfer [to the sexual partner]. The same way you get HIV through blood you can transfer spirits and curses, sexually transmitted demons." Sleeping with a prostitute is even worse, ac-cording to Phillip, as you receive the demons of the last seven men with whom she slept. Accordingly, the threat of spiritual marriage looms in all sorts of quotidian acts, sexual or otherwise.

In Ofori's oft-repeated narrative, he was married to a mad spiritual hus-band. The husband—note that already we are in areas of sexual deviance for this pneumatic church—was a woman with "a man's organ." Prophet Ofori continued to sextify by describing the curse of spiritual marriage. He explained he had sex with his spiritual husband in his dreams, and correspondingly the mad husband accompanied him everywhere, day and night. This kind of dreamlike sexual encounter is how spiritual marriages are consummated; the truest sign that one has an apparitional paramour is intercourse in dreams or something like dreams. Spirits consummate the relationships with acts as diverse as fellatio, cunnilingus, and vaginal or anal sex. This sex is damning because, for pneumatic Christians, spiritual marriage is a covenant, a lifelong promise, between a demon and a human. It extends far beyond the frequent and vociferous sexual encounters but is concretized in those experiences. And the consequence is the unending, consistent accompaniment by a demon. As Solomon, a published expert on spiritual marriage, told me, "The word married is used to show you are not alone."

Solomon's warning about not being alone is an important point for Pentecostals. There is a subtle transition between chapters 4 and 5 in *Seductive Spirits* in that queer sexualities and masturbation are very material, embodied sexualities while the spirit spouses in chapters 5 and 6 largely emanate from dreams. However, it would be a mistake to assume that much changes in the transition to dreaming as if it were a solitary individual existence embedded in one's subconsciousness. For Pentecostals, dreaming is the mingling of real co-presences, real entities, and the consequences are far-reaching and material. In the words of Amira Mittermaier, writing about the dreams of Muslims in Egypt, dreams "matter in the sense of having significance in people's lives and, more literally, in the sense of having an impact on the visible, material world."[2] Further, in deliverance rituals, these dreams become public, social, and shared. In these ways dreaming is social and intersubjective, a slightly different milieu than waking but no less real.

For Pentecostals dreams are a ubiquitous and quotidian social reality, simultaneously fantastic and of grave concern. As Phillip stated, spiritual marriage is "when a person sees himself or herself sleeping with somebody like a physical act of sex but in a dream." Admittedly, at times in my interviews it was difficult to discern when interlocutors were discussing events that occurred in dreams or in waking. The possibility of such indistinguishability haunted Enlightenment thinkers like Descartes leading him to dismiss the senses and assert the primacy of rationality.[3] But *Seductive Spirits* relies on the senses, and if one is to take Pentecostals seriously, one must become comfortable with dreams as reality and embrace all the ontological, epistemological, and ethical possibilities such an embrace posits.

Ofori later returned to add more details to the testimony of his own spiritual marriage. He said that the woman's penis was abnormally large. He repeatedly emphasized the seemingly supernatural size of the spirit's member; it was "as big as the prophet's arm." This outsized penis stood erect and held a knife. I was never able to receive an explanation for how this erect member held a knife—whether the penis had something akin to hands or if the blade was grafted onto the penis. Nonetheless, we have a template that is in many ways familiar among those with whom I spoke: they described a sexual experience with a spirit that transcended human sexual norms (as in the monumentally sized penis with a knife), that was equally pleasurable and problematic, desired and abhorred, summoned and resisted, and that supposedly left one in an inescapable relationship with a demon.

Spiritual marriages are experienced as a kind of sixth sense, extending the boundaries and barriers of the body in fantastic ways. As Chimaraoke Izugbara notes, "Ethnographic literature on witchcraft and the occult in Africa also regularly makes references to exotic and perverse sexual practices and the sexualization of the paranormal."[4] However one wants to describe it—paranormal, supernatural, or spiritual world—humans are believed to have an extraordinary sense that allows them to feel certain forms of sex that transcend while also implicating the material world. Or, as Phillip stated, spiritual marriage is "when a person sees himself or herself sleeping with somebody like a physical act of sex but in a dream." In spiritual marriage this sixth sense bridges the gap between spiritual and material. This sense allows for the experience of something immaterial in tangible ways.

Metakinesis is the theoretical lens through which I will consider this sixth sense.[5] In her work on Evangelicals in America, Tanya Luhrmann draws out the Evangelical desire for intense spiritual experiences.[6] In particular, Evangelicals valued trance and other "out-of-the-ordinary experiences" in order to "develop a remarkably intimate, personal God."[7] These out-of-the-ordinary experiences were felt in "intensely bodily ways."[8] That is, intimacy with God is simultaneously experienced through moments of altered consciousness and deeply embodied sensations. Luhrmann describes this process as "metakinesis," a term co-opted from dance theory. As opposed to linguistic or cognitive states, bodily states are recognized as a way to know and feel. Bodily states are primarily a way to know God intimately, to be in an interpersonal relationship with a deity.[9] As Luhrmann states, "I use the term metakinesis to refer to mind-body states that are both identified within the group as the way of recognizing God's personal presence in your life and are subjectively and idiosyncratically experienced."[10] Bodily phenomena are seen as evidence of God's love for and intimate involvement in believers' lives, providing a new lens through which to view the cosmos. Or, as Luhrmann writes, "As a result of these phenomena, congregants literally perceive the world differently and they attribute that difference to the presence of God."[11]

Luhrmann's use of metakinesis riffs on the musings of John Martin, a dance theorist. John Martin's theory of metakinesis is simply that the physical and the psychical are merely two aspects of a single underlying reality."[12] If metakinesis is movement with psychical overtones, I want to explore those psychical overtones in the realm of extrasensory perception. David Howes, in *The Sixth Sense Reader*, points out the traditional five senses all correspond with bodily organs.[13] A sixth sense, especially one that looks at extrasensory perception, does not have a corresponding sense organ. In fact, as a psychic sense it is thought to operate only from a distance.[14] Metakinesis, then, offers the possibility of closing the gap by making the psychical also intimately embodied.

As with the choreosonic, I argue that the metakinetic is often erotic. Pamela Thurschwell has argued that the Victorian obsession with the séance and investigating mediumship included a sense of the erotic.[15] As Thurschwell writes, "When spirits materialized they were touched, embraced, kissed, in the name of testing the limits of their materiality, and they in turn touched, embraced and kissed their investigators."[16] The erotics of metakinesis reach into the cosmos, feeling the materiality of the spirits. But these erotics went beyond touching and kissing. The search for spirited materiality also involved an extrasensory erotic. Thurschwell calls this an "erotics of mind melding," which she goes on to argue is based on the desire for absolute knowledge and melding with another.[17] There is something erotic about the metakinetic; something revealing that immediately renders the experience erotic. In spiritual marriage, the erotics of the metakinetic are always present with the potent combination of the physical and psychical, the combination of out-of-the-ordinary erotic experiences that are felt in intensely sensual and embodied ways and a deep desire to know through these experiences. In this combination pneumatic Christians feel demons intimately.

Ofori's story of a spiritual marriage is not meant to be unique. It was a strategic performance to normalize demonic sex dreams as real sex with demons. Among Ghanaian pneumatics, such sextimonies are standard. Accordingly, every deliverance ministry is inundated with people seeking deliverance from spiritual marriage or sextifying about their deliverance from a determined spiritual spouse. The idea of spiritual marriage, however, is not universal for all pneumatic Christians. It is most dominant in the West African hotbeds of charismatic Christianity (primarily Nigeria and Ghana) and Central Africa, and also can be found in many non-African locales, including the United States.[18] However, spiritual marriage is mostly unfamiliar to non-African-diasporic congregations in Europe and North America.[19]

Demonic sexual partners in this belief system manifest in various and unique ways. Ofori pointed out, "At times, spirits come in human form, in your dreams you see them like normal human beings like a nice lady coming to you. You can even see in that situation that you are in the hotel, and you have to do something with the woman, and before you realize it you will have done it." But also, "At times they come as a snake, they come in different forms. Even some people it will come like a wind physically. You are there, and then an unusual wind will blow under you, meaning the spirit has come and had sex with you." The real star of spiritual marriage, though, is Mami Wata. Pneumatic Christians in Ghana are greatly afraid of Mami Wata in large part because they understand or are sympathetic to her charms and seduction. They simultaneously despise her and are fascinated by her.[20] In fact, she symbolizes something of an insult, as at one church I saw a shirt that said in large block lettering: "Don't be such a Mermaid!" Ofori clearly stated, "Mami Wata's function is spiritual marriage. That is the key." All of those who have long documented Ghanaian Pentecostalism, including Onyinah and Asamoah-Gyadu, have articulated Mami Wata's centrality. As part of the covenant with Mami Wata, people are rendered impotent and infertile on Earth because they instead procreate spiritually with this goddess. From his own fieldwork, Onyinah cites the story of Bobby, who had sex with a woman who later revealed herself as Mami Wata. As per the laws of spirited sex,

Bobby was then spiritually married to Mami Wata. In Bobby's case, sex with Mami Wata was not experienced through a dream but in the real, human, fleshy connection to a woman who trans-mogrified back into the guise of Mami Wata.[21] Asamoah-Gyadu has also published cases of spiritual marriage to Mami Wata, such as a woman named Felicia, where the sexual romping happened in both sleeping and waking.[22] This ambivalence—dreamlike and physical—constantly haunts the stories of Mami Wata. Mami Wata is imagined as simultaneously having a body and being ethereal.

Mami Wata opens up metakinetic possibilities. Joseph, Kwofie's longtime and most trusted assistant, was previously married to Mami Wata, whom he described as the "ultimate perpetrator of spiritual marriage." As he described his marriage, Joseph revealed to me this physical and psychical sense that mediated between dreams and embodiment. He told me: "You will do everything with Mami Wata, sleep with her, you will sometimes even see her physical in a body and form you like. It is not just a dream, but sometimes it appears physically. I had a spiritual marriage with Mami Wata. So, any time I would sleep, the spirit would come. When she came, sometimes she manifested as a very beautiful woman. I was with her for about two years."

Joseph was not immediately conscious that his spiritual marriage was to Mami Wata herself. But he went to Ofori's prayer camp, just one of many examples of how intertwined all of these individual ministries are, and was instructed to do a forty-day residential fast on-site. As he was fasting and praying, Mami Wata—or the physical manifestation of Mami Wata—began to behave strangely. The moment of apprehension though, could not be any more explicit: "I detected that this lady had something with Mami Wata. And lo and behold, I was with this lady on the bed, and suddenly the lady changed to a fish from the waist downwards." Immediately Joseph "sacked her," sending her away. I asked how such a thing is possible, how does a woman and then a mermaid manifest on one's bed? He stated that "though physically you see her as a woman but her spirit is from Mami Wata. The spirit cannot live without a body, so they use our bodies as a chamber or habitat and dwell in that body." In this case, Joseph believed Mami Wata used both Joseph's body and the woman he was sleeping with.

Solomon was my most confident guide through the world of spiritual marriages. I called Solomon unexpectedly one Saturday when the *tro tro* returning me from grocery shopping drove by an old banner hanging sadly off of a fence. The only elements that were still visible on the faded fabric heralded Solomon's expertise in fighting spiritual marriage and a barely legible phone number. I dialed the phone number and arranged a meeting with Solomon. The next day I was sitting with him at a nice hotel. He brought with him all the books and pamphlets he had written about spiritual marriage. He was an expert in spiritual marriage, and unlike most of my other interlocutors who dashed this way and that in the ever-expanding and creative demonic cosmos, Solomon never strayed from his focus on spiritual marriage. He repeatedly warned that "sexual affairs in your dreams is one of the most poisonous infusions you can ever have in life. Until you stay without sex in your dreams, you will always be a victim of marine slavery."

When I told Solomon that Phillip is convinced that everyone is or has been spiritually married but that most people are simply unaware of the sexual curse on their lives, he quickly interjected. Solomon mostly agreed with Phillip, but he added, "Not all evil spiritual marriages are unconscious. Many are very much aware of the fact that they are married in the spirit. They know when it started! They can tell the perfumery of their spiritual spouse. They have the details of the marriage. They enjoy that relationship more than any form of marriage." As Eto states, "The victims fall in love with the demons and have sex with them. They know they are demons but they don't mind."[23] In many ways the persistence and acceptance of spirit spouses confirms my suspicion that many Pentecostals are not solely interested in banishing demons, but embracing them in a relationality thought impossible.

Even when those involved in a spiritual marriage describe being tormented, for they know it is considered sinful, they also enjoy the intense sexual ecstasy demons are capable of causing. The pleasure is so intensely enjoyable that it often is described as feeling not normal or not natural, which is an important distinction. The intensity of the physical, sexual sensation is not normal because they are supernatural; however, the sensations bear enough resemblance to the natural world to still be recognizable as sexual. The sensations are metakinetic.

As I explained above, for my informants, sex with spirits often appears dreamlike, happening in the hazy, lusty moments between waking and sleeping. In those libidinous moments, spirits usually take on the appearance of someone familiar, for example, an old lover or a mother, and fulfill human lascivious desires. But these dreams are genuinely metakinetic, psychical yet accompanied by physical sensations and movements. Dreams for Ghanaian pneumatics move through the material world; they are not interior but events in the objective world. The way it was described to me is that dreams happen exterior to people wherever they find themselves. To dream of sex with a spirit is for that spirit to exist exterior to the body and interact with that body in the place where it lies.

Dreams in this view are not fanciful but material. Joseph had thought a lot about spiritual marriage in his arduous journey from being Mami Wata's lover to a deliverance minister. He had particularly thought about the sort of lusty, hazy dream state that spirits utilize. He said, "Dreams are a point where they [demons] normally manipulate people and control their body. Dreams are a place where spirit and body meet. Dreamland is where unclean spirits come in the body." Those I spoke with described being awakened by various physical sensations from their spirit spouse: hands fondling genitalia, lips caressing breasts, tongues stroking vaginas, or burning hot seminal fluid. Despite the dreamlike qualities, such encounters are considered real, existential experiences. The word that kept repeating in descriptions of spiritual marriage was "real." "Spiritual marriage is real" was an oft-repeated refrain. Solomon took it a step further and said, "There is nothing as real as spiritual marriage."

If there was anything Solomon wanted to impress upon me, it was the severity of spiritual marriage and the immense powers of Mami Wata as real. He said, "Mami Wata is like a mermaid. Mami Wata is real; I want to be emphatic to you. Mermaid spirits are real. What do you mean by real? Real means that they live and are affecting people. I know people who serve tables for their spiritual husbands; they serve them food to come and eat." This realness was a point to which he returned frequently. One of the ways he tried to impress upon me the reality of Mami Wata's existence was biblical, citing Zechariah 9:4 as an incontrovertible truth: "But the Lord will take away her possessions and destroy her power on the sea, and she will be consumed by fire." Until that day, the Queen of the Coast's "very, very, deep" power has been released onto the earth. He added to this fearful warning, "My humble advice to you is that you never doubt the existence of spiritual marriage. You might not be experiencing one. That does not make it unreal."

Nobody I interviewed questioned the realness of spiritual marriages. Nikoi prayed, "Any spirit that claims me as a wife and makes love to me from the marine world, your stronghold catch fire! Any seed they've deposited in me, I take it out! Any spirit that sleeps with me for sex. Die! Die! Perish!" He immediately followed this up with a related thought: "Anything that gives you orgasm outside of God's plan for sex is a spirit." One of the points of "realness" in descriptions of spiritual marriage is the fact that almost every sexual encounter with a spirit induces ejaculation. The human actors explain that they experience supernaturally caused orgasms that are said to be more pleasurable than humanly initiated orgasms. One woman who has had sex with a demon for decades told me how, when she wakes up wet with vaginal secretions, she knows her spirit spouse has visited her. She believed that the sexual intensity of her demonically induced orgasms left her wet. Alternatively, if she wakes up from a sex dream and is not wet, she told me she knows that it was merely a sex dream about her human husband, who currently resides on another continent. The distinction is striking. Her spirit spouse, a demon from whom she has tried for many years to be delivered, is experienced in her body as more real, more physical, and causing greater sexual pleasure than her human husband. At the same time, her spirit spouse cannot materialize in the same way her husband can. The materiality of the spirit is complicated, as it supposedly causes humans to feel real physical experiences while only possessing an ambiguous, temporary materiality of its own.

Spirited semen was also the focus of a video sent to me in February 2018 by a friend and pastor from Emmanuel's church. The content was a young woman, her voice cracking, sextifying to Emmanuel about the power of his deliverance. As she told her story, the crowd repeatedly reacted with disgust, but Emmanuel kept comforting her with the promise to protect her with the blood of Jesus. She admitted to being married to Mami Wata for over fifteen years. This claim received no reaction from the crowd due to its commonness. It was what Mami Wata required of her that drew out the gasps and groans of the congregation. She explained that Mami Wata requested that she collect men's semen. She would fondle and tug at the men's penises until ejaculation and then collect the sperm in condoms. She then claimed that she would relay that semen to Mami Wata, who would immediately drink it to receive power. She professed to have fed Mami Wata the semen of more than forty-five men.

Sometimes, she pointed out through tears, if the semen amounted to too little, Mami Wata would punish her and demand more semen. Paul Gifford cited similar examples. In the testimony he witnessed, male sperm was allegedly "collected in sperm banks under the sea and used to create havoc in a man's finances."[24] Describing what I am terming as the metakinetic, Gifford states, "The physical aspects of sexuality have especially mystical properties."[25]

Badoe wanted to drive home a similar point as he told me about the scourge of spiritual marriage. First, he repeated that spiritual marriage is about sex, or as he said, "Spiritual marriage is about sex, sex, sex, sex!" When I asked Badoe why spirits used sex, he told me that he had once posed the same question to a sexual spirit, and the spirit responded by saying that sex is utilized because sex is potent. Then he went on what appeared to be a tangent about spirits drinking human semen as a covenant. "Sex," he said, "is the easiest way to get something from your body to create that covenant." And then it became clear what he was trying to communicate; he wanted to make it explicit that in sex with spirits there is this flimsy relationship between the spiritual and the physical. "Spirits take sperm physically," he stated, "It happens spiritually but has a physical component." This is metakinesis. The sex happens physically with all its attendant fluids. Still, it is also spiritual in the Pentecostal imagination, with the spirited partner hailing from another realm, and the physical fluids being taken between realms to concretize the interpenetration of multiple orders.

Linda van de Kamp has written about spirit spouses and "marido espiritual" in Maputo, Mozambique, and, similar to the argument here, notes that the spirit spouses have a complicated materiality. She spoke with women in spiritual marriages who were regularly visited in bed "by a man at midnight who has sexual intercourse with her."[26] Of course, she was not referring to a man but a spirit. In fact, the women and pastors made it a point to emphasize that "there was no physical person involved but that women experience real sexual intercourse with their spirit spouse and that this is visible and can be proved, for example, by marks on the body."[27] One woman she spoke with was divorced by her earthly husband because of nightly visits from her spiritual husband. Her mortal husband was apparently disturbed by watching his wife having sexual intercourse with a spirit that he could not see. He was disturbed by the metakinesis—the movement inspired by the psychical. But van de Kamp writes that it was not only in the privacy of this woman's home and the cover of darkness that the spirit spouse satiated its sexual needs; sometimes it was in public such as on public transport.[28]

Materiality in spirit marriages extends beyond semen to the demons themselves. One prophet I spoke with shared the story of one of his parishioners whom he had been attempting to deliver for a long time. He forbade me from talking to his parishioner because he feared the tenuousness of her deliverance. He said that the woman had been initiated and taken to live under the sea as a marine spirit. While under the sea Mami Wata commissioned the woman to go to the churches of Ghana to sleep with pastors and foil their ministries. At one particular church, she accomplished her goal, having intercourse with a senior pastor under the mango tree next to the church. The sex, though, was not what the pastor thought it was: "She confessed that the pastor didn't have sex with her as an individual, but actually as a marine, with a ring as her private parts. You as the human will think that you are having sex with her private parts, but actually, it's a ring and that ring pulls the semen. The moment the spirit takes your semen, the spirit controls you."

For the most part, though, apparitional paramours are described differently, understood to be something other than a facsimile of the human body but something akin to bodily materiality. Sometimes this temporary materiality is witnessed as a ghostly figure, but I was told that for some lovers nothing at all appears while the demon ravages their body. The experience—dreamt or otherwise—is defined by all the physical sensations of whatever sex act is occurring. The sensations are embodied, the spirits are felt, and the marriages are permanent. Whether informants were describing sex with a spirit that was an animal (dogs, roosters, and fish being the most common), a human body they recognized, a body they did not recognize, or an invisible being, they always described how it felt in their bodies through a sort of extrasensory perception. It was the spirits' touch in the night, the hazy view of a spiritual being leaving a room, pleasurable and painful penetration, or secretions left on or in the body by the spirit that revealed these spiritual marriages.

Despite the commonness of the sexual sensations, each of my interlocutors was absolutely certain that their sexual liaisons had taken place with a being that belonged to another realm. Throughout this book, a variety of senses have been enumerated that reached into and toward something more—the "more." We need to develop a way in which to talk about the manner in which senses are entangled, controlled, and manipulated by personalities of a different dimension. Metakinesis, with its emphasis on the physical and psychical—that relating to faculties that are inexplicable by natural laws— offers a way to talk about this "more." In deliverance-dominant Pentecostalism, there is a spiritual sense that is in tune with the spiritual forces that fill the cosmos. It is not merely some ethereal sense but one that simultaneously senses both the supernatural and the natural, while erasing any demarcation between those two realms.[29]

Spiritual marriage only ends through deliverance. Though they are not always used, most deliverance services include questionnaires that require the faithful to detail their own and their families' religious history, their sexual history, and their dream history. In other cases, the spirit does the revealing. At each deliverance service, Phillip has a particular method to determine which congregants are in a spiritual marriage. The most obvious cases present when the deliveree admits to sexual dreams. Secondly, congregants who complain about their frustrated life opportunities are usually describing the symptoms of a spiritual marriage. Phillip believes his real gift, though, is deduction through manifestation. Spiritually married people react in identifiable ways to deliverance. Often those who are spiritually married will scream statements such as "I won't leave her," "I won't go," "Who are you to come to take her?" or the least subtle, "I've been married to her for so many years." Such phrases were prominent in Esther's deliverance in the introduction to this book. These declarative statements are, of course, understood as the utterances of their jealous spirit spouses. There are a plethora of nonverbal cues as well: "The person might twist at the waist and talk about lust, they might act sexy with dancing, so you know it is a spiritual marriage. They might play with the ring their spiritual spouse gave them." I witnessed the ring finger manifestation regularly across all locales. Phillip was quick to point out that such manifestations do not happen by accident but are caused by the anointing of the deliverer. People manifest in spiritual marriages around him because of his high level of anointing. Badoe added that he was so adept at identifying spiritual marriages he could smell them: "Because you slept with a spirit, you smell like a spirit." Clearly, then, the Pentecostal sensorium is believed to reach beyond this world.

Once possession is identified, the pastor prays for the possessed person. One prominent pastor described such prayers as a way of "penetrating the veil between two worlds." Prayer is an analog to the sexual act with demons that penetrated the human body, bridging the gap between the supernatural and natural. Prayer attempts to separate both worlds that are sexually entwined. After prayer, the pastor enacts the very physical rituals of deliverance. As described in previous chapters, often the pastor will lay their hands on the person being delivered, pushing against their forehead, lightly stroking their stomach, and sometimes even applying pressure to the genitals. The pastor then physically acts out the divorce and murder of the spirit spouse by removing the spiritual wedding rings and slaying the spouse with imagined swords. In this deliverance process the spirit often will speak to the pastor, outlining lurid details of sexual liaisons, and adamantly refuse to depart their lover. In one case of deliverance that I watched, a female spirit married to a woman defiantly screamed "I love her" again and again. Other common refrains were "she is my wife" or "she is my husband." The deliverance only ends successfully once the spasming body is rendered docile and silent. The body under control is deemed free of its dastardly spiritual spouse.

OFORI

Returning to Ofori's spiritual marriage to the mad spirit that inaugurated this chapter, it is noteworthy how closely his description follows the ideas and practices described above. To begin with, Ofori said he had sexual dreams from which he would wake up every morning and notice that he had "physically discharged." He described the sensuous ambiguity, saying, "It happens in the spiritual, but it is also physical, so my situation was the worst situation. The worst type is when you have the thing in the spirit, and then physically you see yourself discharged." Spiritual marriage develops what Ofori calls a soul tie—a deep, spiritual connection to the body. The idea of a soul tie as tied to sexuality is a common feature of Evangelical and Pentecostal circles.[30] Ofori shared with me that as his spiritual marriage and attendant soul tie developed, the spirits manifested physically; the same spirits he saw in his dreams were taking physical form and enjoying carnal relations with him. It was only through deliverance that he was eventually freed from his mad spiritual spouse. Ofori said that through deliverance he was able to cease having sex with this mad woman with a large penis: "I had to get delivered from spiritual marriage through prayer, fasting, and learning the word of God and then living for Christ."

After he concluded his testimony about his spiritual marriage, Ofori began to preach about the curse. His testimony was not merely an anecdote but served as a form of authentication: Ofori's knowledge of spiritual marriage could be trusted because he had experienced it. Ultimately what he wanted for his congregants was what he said he had already received, deliverance from wretched spiritual spouses. In a series of short sentences, he stated, "May God release you this morning from any spiritual marriage. God proves himself in our midst by demonstration of his power. The power of God can destroy every spirit married to you." Beyond his hopes to deliver everyone from their spiritual marriages, he also pointed out several interesting characteristics of spirits to help his congregants identify their spirit spouses. Unsurprisingly, "the primary way to know spiritual marriages is through sex in a dream." But more interestingly, "In spiritual marriage dreams, men perform the same as women and women same as men." Here, we see the kind of gender-bending among demons that renders binaries incomprehensible.

The real climax of Ofori's service was not his sextifying nor his preaching. Most of the people present already knew precisely all the facts Ofori was sharing about spirits being married to humans. Instead, what really mattered, or what would prove the prophet's worth, would be his ability to deliver people from this sexual curse. As such, Ofori moved to a time of deliverance. As the prophet began to pray, people began to react to the power of the spirit. The first woman to come up screaming, dressed in a grey dress, was immediately wrapped in a sheet and placed on the broad swath of floor that is reserved for people reacting in the spirit. She screamed and writhed, the contortions of her body making a zig-zagging pattern across the ceramic floor tiles. The prophet let her scream for a few moments as three other women jumped and flailed toward the front, creating a cacophony of high-pitched screams. The prophet then walked down from his platform and addressed the spirit in a now-familiar manner: "Who are you? Who are you?"

Two ushers helped the woman to her knees, from where she continued screaming. She interrupted her screams to provide some information, but she steadfastly refused to answer the prophet's question. "Leave her alone," she pleaded.

The prophet continued to implore her, "who are you?" while lightly hitting her chest.

Again, the woman refused to answer but made it clear what the nature of the relationship was between spirit and human: "She is my wife! My wife! My wife!"

The other three women at the front of the sanctuary continued to writhe and scream in repetitive loops, making it difficult to hear the interactions between the prophet and woman. Because of this, the prophet tried repeating what she said, only further confusing who was speaking: the woman, the spirit, the prophet, the prophet repeating the spirit, or the prophet repeating the woman. The woman petitioned the prophet: "You will leave her to me. I am telling you to leave her alone."

Neither the woman nor the prophet would move on in the conversation, with the prophet demanding the name of the spirit and the spirit responding incongruously with claims about marital status. Eventually, the prophet tried to break the loop by tapping her on the head and demanding, "Identify yourself." She responded, "Leave her alone. She is mine. I love her." The prophet had seen enough and walked away. As he ambled toward the front row of the congregation, he informed everyone in an unaffected manner, "She has a spiritual marriage. It stems from the fact that her mother is a witch."

This episode with the first woman was interrupted by one of the other women, clad in a purple dress, rising to her feet and aggressively trying to confront the prophet. She was thwarted by the swift actions of the ushers and the prophet's bodyguard. They did not put the microphone anywhere near her face, robbing her of the opportunity to speak. Instead, she screamed loudly and unceasingly. "Pow," the prophet yelled back as he hit her forehead with some force. Her body immediately became docile and was lowered to the ground by two ushers. The triumphant prophet turned to the congregation and, in a matter-of-fact tone, said, "She was married in the spirit because her mother and father belonged to a shrine for childbirth." Perhaps most prominent among the reasons given for spirit marriage is an encounter with non-Pentecostal religions either experienced personally or somewhere in one's family history. A conventional possession narrative is that one's parents may have visited a shrine to offer up prayers and gifts to assure the birth of a healthy child. That child is then contaminated with the religion of the shrine, married to the shrine's inhabiting spirit. Many have written about how Pentecostalism emphasizes a complete break with the past, and this certainly constitutes an example of that.[31] Or sort of. Pentecostalism also performs and reiterates the other, bringing the past forward and the present backward.

Ofori demanded that the congregation raise their hands. "Anticipate. Anticipate. Anticipate!" he yelled slowly and methodically, warning the congregation that deliverance was about to start en masse. He stretched his hand out toward the congregation and yelled, "Power of the Spirit! Power!" The volume of his shouting was overwhelming, and the sound system screeched in response. He continued yelling about the power of the Spirit: "The power is coming to you. Power. Receive power! Receive power! The power to deliver you!" With Ofori having sent the power of the spirit into the ether, people began to react. People started falling out and screaming all over the expansive church building, followed by the mad rush of ushers running to catch those falling out. Usually, people bounce, jump, or move in a frenetic manner before falling to the floor, which gives the ushers just enough time to catch those moved by the spirit(s). However, sometimes they do not always arrive on time, and earlier on this day a woman fell hard to the floor, cracking her head open on the ceramic tiles. There was a brief commotion around her as the puddle of blood pooled on the floor. She was carried out, dripping blood across the sanctuary, mops were quickly procured to clean up the mess. All the while, the prophet continued yelling, "receive the power" as if nothing out of the ordinary had occurred.

The number of bodies at the front of the church doubled and then tripled as the prophet blew into the microphone, making a tornado-like wind sound that filled the sanctuary. "Power. Receive the power. The power in Jesus's name!" One woman sprinted toward the front, bouncing high off the bodies that lay on the floor. Another tried to run away, racing toward the back until ushers could catch up to her and drag her back. The chaos only intensified when the prophet moved down from the platform to begin treating people on a one-on-one basis, moving quickly from person to person. As he ran down the row, he yelled in the faces of each person, "POWER! You are delivered!" or "Your marriage is over. You are delivered" or "Your marriage is destroyed.

You are delivered!" He interspersed these deliverance claims by blowing right into people's faces. As he did so a woman in a black shawl confronted him. He screamed, "power!" and stomped his left foot. He blew on her face, which caused her to scream, lean backward and then forward, at which point the ushers adroitly lowered her to the ground. "Your marriage is broken," Ofori celebrated as she lay docile on the ground.

Eventually, the number of people at the front of the church dwindled. Ofori yelled a slow, sonorous "A-men," which marked the conclusion of deliverance. The crowd responded by clapping politely. The last few deliverees stood up, wiped themselves off, and returned to their seats, their first few steps often unsteady. The whole deliverance event took approximately forty minutes, and hundreds of spiritual marriages were believed to be broken.

When I spoke with Ofori about this deliverance session, he presented a vast amount of material that further elaborates this connection between the physical and psychical. He described in particular one case where he identified a person as being married to an ancestral spirit:

> So, when the Holy Spirit is present the Holy Spirit comes to deliver. So, when I stand there to minister he can reveal to me that there is someone here with an ancestral spirit that is worrying him. Immediately, I speak about it you see the person will fall down. That is a struggle between the ancestral spirit and the Holy Spirit that is coming to cast it out, that is why the people fall. There is like two elephants fighting. So, the power of God comes to bring deliverance then Satan will try to resist and then there is a battle and after the battle the person is set free. So that is why you see people screaming and falling.

Ofori added, "The spirits come and stay in the physical body, so if the spirit is being ejected, the body will react. And the body will feel it too. The spirit and the body will feel it." In these quotes, we see the metakinetic. There are sensing spirits sensed in the bodies of participants that are fighting like elephants, resulting in dramatic physical manifestations, the psychic and physical intertwined.

Ofori continued to describe why, with a messianic flourish, he could deliver people: "The presence of God is on me because at the day of Pentecost when you read the scripture it says 'the Spirit came on them and then the

Spirit filled them.' So once the Spirit has come on you and filled you, you are God." But what was interesting as Ofori talked about deliverance was his description of his own deliverance techniques. Again, in his description, he points toward a sixth sense, a sense that is able to perceive something more. He said:

> When I blow, use my eyes, touch them, it is the same results but different methods. You understand me. I believe that when I blow air I am blowing fire into the person. And because the presence of God is with me and I believe in the presence of God, the power of God, the fire of God . . . So, if I blow the air the air enters the person as fire and the fire works in the person. The person feels fire in the body.

The metakinetic works on several levels here. First, there are the prophetic metakinetic actions. He blows, he looks, he touches, and when he does these things, he believes something psychical happens. From his perspective, he sees into peoples' lives, identifies their problems, and then deals with them by applying something supernatural such as blowing fire. Then there are the metakinetic sensations of the deliveree, who I am told actually experiences this supernatural fire as a fire in the body. Bruno Reinhardt, writing in the Ghanaian Pentecostal context, has pointed out that "the evocation of 'fire' is not gratuitous . . . the grammar of sensation embedding experience revolved around passionate and violent burning."[32] And finally, Ofori sees the demon who more than feels the heat but is burned by the flames until it departs. Each spoken word is not merely cerebral but powerful spiritually and materially. In this worldview there is no distinction between discursive and nondiscursive; each word is multisensory.

ORFORI'S CONGREGANTS

One of the women who was delivered in Ofori's crush of bodies was Dorcas, who shared with me her admiration and love for one of the foremost African American Pentecostal preachers on sex, Juanita Bynum. Bynum's work has global appeal, and her works can be found throughout Accra in most spaces that sell Pentecostal literature. Dorcas, in particular, found great appeal in Bynum's message. Dorcas told me that she had an insatiable appetite for fornication. She simply could not stop. But one day with a friend she listened to Juanita Bynum's famous 1997 "No More Sheets" sermon given at a packed Dallas Convention Center.[33] Of the famed sermon, Dorcas said, "What she was talking about was what I was experiencing." But not exactly. Bynum's sermon is about her licentious sexuality before finding God.[34] Dorcas was talking about spiritual marriage—it was sex with spirits that she could not stop, sex with spirits that she used to try to fill her longings, sex with spirits in which she tried to find a partner. But she found in Bynum's oft-repeated refrain "No more sheets" the freedom that she desired. About that same time, she heard a voice directing her to Ofori's prayer camp. She immediately went to the camp and started a fast. During deliverance, she realized that her family was cursed and that though she was a virgin physically, "even a virgin can have a spiritual marriage." Ofori freed her from the last vestiges of her marriage.

Another woman delivered in this dramatic service was Abigail. Abigail came to Ofori's prayer camp because of a spiritual marriage to what she described as a woman whose face was concealed. This woman demon, as Abigail said, was an old woman with a man's penis whom Abigail did not recognize and repeatedly visited her dreams and had sex with her. Abigail told me, "The only way spirits can get me is through sex. I don't know why they use sex. I don't know why." She did not wait long after the appearance of this old woman before racing up the mountain from Accra to Ofori's camp, desperate for these experiences to stop. Upon arrival, she met with Prophet Ofori, and he instructed her to partake in a twenty-one-day fast. As he does with every visitor, he provided her with a sheet filled with deliverance prayers. One of the instructions reads: "Pray against your spiritual husband or wife and destroy the strange children or babies you've seen in your dreams."[35] She did so. But it was the prophet's prayers during the deliverance service that finally broke the marriage: "And now when she tries to come to sleep with me, the angel of the Lord hits her and she goes back and is not able to have sex with me."

Gifty, too, said she had been under spiritual attack through a spiritual marriage and had spent years at Ofori's camp before being delivered. She was adamant that "it [sex with a spirit] was not normal. As I am saying it, somebody might think it is just a dream or a nightmare, but I am talking about reality, what I experienced personally." She knew she was in a spiritual marriage even though she could not see the spirit sleeping with her. She could not see the spirit, "but you'll feel something." Most notably, she said "I felt something going on in this thing" while pointing to her vagina. The spirit taunted her by reminding her how much she enjoyed it. Anxious about the repeated experience of sleeping with this bodiless spirit, she prayed that God would reveal the spirit. After this prayer, she dreamed that she was in a car with a driver who "was not a normal human being." Eventually, she said, this being told her that she was his wife. That was when she realized that this was her spiritual husband from whom she needed to be delivered. Shortly thereafter, she was delivered from this spirit spouse when Ofori tapped her on the head and told her she was delivered. When we spoke, she had not had sex in her dreams since Ofori touched her. When I asked her why spirits use sex to access humans she said, "I think spirits use sex because when a man and a woman have sex spiritually they are connected. So, they use sex so that they become one with you because as you have sex, something goes out of you and enters the person. So, they use that to pollute you so they can delay you in life." Her statement is rich in metakinesis, materiality and spirit comingled in sexual encounters.

EMMANUEL'S CONGREGANTS

In many ways, spiritual marriages among Emmanuel's congregants mirror some of the elements we have already seen from Ofori's deliverance service. Emmanuel's episodes, though, tend to provide more narrative shape than some of the other prophets, and for that reason, I will include a couple of exemplary scripts from deliverance sessions for analysis. About sixteen minutes into one of his marathon deliverance sessions, Emmanuel identified a woman as having a relentless spiritual marriage. Immediately after Emmanuel identified the problem, the spirit began to speak through the woman: "I made her have children with different fathers, and she worries. She keeps crying, and I'm the one who enters her when she cries. She has been running around for solutions, and here she's got it . . . You are unburdening her, and why do you do that to me? Bishop, why are you disturbing my peace? She is married to me."

As is typical, Emmanuel demanded the identity of the spirit: "Who are you?"

She replied: "I'm an idol spirit from Akuapem, her hometown."

Emmanuel continued his line of questioning: "What have you done?"

She responded with an excellent description of how spiritual marriage works: "I've married her . . . I keep sacking her suitors, and no man will ever marry her. I keep putting scary masks on her face to scare away her suitors . . . I make her suffer. Why are you disturbing my peace? Leave me to see clearly! Ah. Why? I am getting tired. Just leave me alone." The statement was followed by extremely labored breathing; her whole body heaved with each breath. The unnamed spirit that was haunting the woman bragged about their prolific virility and how it made the woman unable to marry a human man. In these interactions between the body and spirit there emerges the idea of a plastic body, a body that can be changed and distorted in appearance. In this case, the spirit claimed to have altered the woman's face with a variety of masks, making her unknowable and grotesque.

Emmanuel was unimpressed by the speech. "Are you done talking?" he asked, while leaning against Prophet Badoe's shoulder, his forearm resting heavily on his second-in-command.

The spirit was not done talking: "I've really destroyed her. All her sisters are beautiful yet not married. No one marries in the family."

Emmanuel asked again, "Who are you?" Supposedly this question must be asked repeatedly because of the spirits' unwillingness to give up their identity, as such a revelation leads to their death.

She responded with a lengthy diatribe: "I do not mention my name. She's been to many prophets, but yet I do not mention my name to them. I'm from her hometown. No one marries in the family, yet she wants to. When she marries, she'll travel abroad and I do not want her to go. I want her to stay back here and struggle to death." The crowd gasped audibly at the forthrightness of the spirit.

I've vowed not to allow her to marry, and she's been going around until now. She comes from a family of idols and no one is to marry from there. She's more glorious than all others in the family, so she can't marry. She's a hard worker and ought to have made it in life, but I drag her behind.

I keep putting scary masks on her face to scare away her helpers. Leave me and let me sit. Why are you bothering me like this? Leave me. Why are you disturbing me like this? Why have you surrounded me as if I'm in some fire? Allow me some space to think.

Emmanuel and the women went back and forth until Emmanuel asserted himself, "Listen to me. With the power vested in me by Jesus, my father, I dissolve your marriage." The pastors around him chimed in with an "Amen." Emmanuel continued, "I restore whatever you have destroyed back to her." Again, followed by a chorus of amens.

Finally, Emmanuel warned the spirit, "Do not come back to her again in the name of our Lord Jesus." Following this he moved toward her, hit her, and made a "poof" sound into the microphone. She immediately fell down crying, claiming, "I am gone, and I will come to her no more. You have put a blazing fire around her!" Out of fear the woman sitting next to the delivered woman jumped up and moved away. Emmanuel again pushed her face and said, "Poof! Do not come again." She was left lying on the ground in tears.

Another day, eschewing his standard vibrant suit and opting instead for a white shirt and bowtie combination, the prophet stared over the center section of the congregation and then to the back. Pointing at a mass of people assembled at the back he said, "That beautiful sister at the back; the fat one with the round earrings." From the throng emerged a woman wearing green pants, a white t-shirt, and large hoop earrings. She walked toward Emmanuel.

"Your time has come," Emmanuel said, repeating an oft-used phrase. She reacted by clenching her eyes and teeth, scrunching up her face and raising her right hand. "Your time has come," Emmanuel repeated himself. "I am praying to God to help you, so you can abandon certain things you do for your family to know that you serve a living God," he added in Twi before recognizing the confused look on her face. "Do you understand Twi?" he asked. After ascertaining that she spoke English he had another prophet translate his Twi phrases to her.

He declared, "Tell her there is a beast before her and also another behind her. If she wants to quit her spiritual marriage, the beasts are there to stop her, so she'll never quit. So, I'm going to take off the beasts for God's purpose for her to work!" "Lift up your two hands," he instructed her. She lifted up her two hands, and as soon as they were raised to the height of her face, Emmanuel moved toward her, yelled "Pooof!" into the microphone while hitting her on the forehead. Her neck snapped back dramatically. Her body followed the trajectory of her neck, falling toward the ground where it was caught at the last second by the ushers and gently placed on the ground. This was not the end, though. Emmanuel continued: "Today, fire must eat up this body and free it from Satan and his spirits." "Out of this body!" he demanded of the spirits.

As Emmanuel spoke, the woman sat up with a pained expression on her face. Emmanuel appeared perturbed and said to nearby congregants, "You should move away from her. Her claws are beastly and can hurt you." She stood to her feet and Emmanuel panicked, yelling, "Move, move, move!" Quickly the ushers sprung into action, pushing people up and out of their seats and away from the threatening claws of the woman. She dramatically shook her head at the commotion.

"Who are you?" Emmanuel queried—a question that is now a familiar tactic at drawing the spirit out.

"Ah! You are asking me, why?" she responded.

"Who are you?" Emmanuel repeated.

"No," she responded defiantly. "I am not in the mood. Asking me who I am, for what? You know what, this girl . . . okay . . . okay . . . let me explain something. As you can see her, she is my wife."

"She is your wife?" Emmanuel asked.

"Yeah. I love her," she confirmed.

Emmanuel, as is his custom, sought more information, "How many years have you been married?"

"Oh, I've been married to her since she was a baby. Yeah. Yeah. Yeah." she said.

"What is your name?"

She refused to answer. "I am a giant man."

Emmanuel implored her with extraordinary politeness, "Can you please mention your name."

She remained steadfast in her refusal. "My name. Why? You people like to disturb." She laughed deeply, pivoted toward the back of the sanctuary, and began walking away from the prophet.

"Look at me!" Emmanuel yelled, retracting the previous civility. She continued to try to walk away, but the ushers turned her around and dragged her back to Emmanuel. As they did, Emmanuel continued to warn, "Be careful of her claws because she's turned into a beast." This beastly narrative quickly disappeared; the beasts went from surrounding her, then she was a beast, and then the beasts were never mentioned again.

Emmanuel turned to the woman and, with prophetic confidence, asked, "Do you know the person you are talking to?"

She summarily dismissed him. "Who are you? Hmmm. Ha! Now I am looking at you. What? You can't do anything to me!" Again, she laughed derisively.

Emmanuel turned to the congregation and said, "I don't want to give you details of what the spirit uses her for." As he often does, Emmanuel skillfully used the guise of discretion to titillate. Even though Emmanuel would not be specific, one could begin to imagine the lurid sexual depths of this woman's interaction with her spirit spouse. If most sexual acts are easily shared in deliverance and testimony, how base must this woman's marriage to the demon be?

The woman responded by saying, "She has been my own for a long time. Can you deliver her?"

Emmanuel did not waver. Always confident, he said, "I can deliver her."

"No!" she shouted. "The last time your junior pastor tried and then I entered her. For like two weeks she was delivered, and then I entered her," she said, pointing her thumb at her genital area and gyrating. Despite the discretion in the discourse, there was no doubt among the congregants that this woman was involved sexually with this demon. She continued, "She is my wife. She likes to bathe outside in the night and then I enter her. You don't know if you've delivered these people sometimes because they like to bathe outside in the night and then we will enter them. You don't know; we always possess them at night!" Emmanuel took her soliloquy as an opportunity to jump in and lecture the congregation: "You cannot bathe in the open because when you do so, any passing spirit can marry you by lust." He returned to the woman in need of deliverance. "Listen to me."

"Listen? What? I don't have time for you. Please, please, please," she responded.

"The Lord has said; her time has come," Emmanuel repeated the promise that inaugurated the whole episode.

The woman speaking as the spirit spit out a sexual threat, "When this girl gets back to her place, she has no idea what I will do to her. She will never forget me. Stupid girl." After a brief pause, she added, "I possess her to destroy her."

Emmanuel was ready for this to be over, tired of the threats and dismissive remarks of the spirit. "Leave her," he instructed the ushers. The ushers dropped her arms, and she immediately ran toward the front of the sanctuary. Near the front she fell backward screaming. On the ground, her legs and arms were outstretched, creating a star shape. "It is done," Emmanuel announced confidently with a smirk.

When she stood up and continued to manifest, Emmanuel continued the deliverance. "She is delivered by Jesus. Buh-bye. You will go. You will go! I send Holy Ghost fire to burn you. I will send Holy Ghost fire to burn you. Leave this body! Out!"

"I will not go. I married her," she said, with less conviction and force than she had previously.

"Out of this body! Out of this body! Jesus!"

She began spinning. "I will go," she repeated four times. She spun faster and faster and then fell to the ground, unmoving, delivered.

As she slowly got to her feet, Emmanuel asked her, "What happened to you?"

She could only recall part of the story, stating that "I was sitting there and you asked me out."

"Then what?" Emmanuel pressed.

Flummoxed, she replied with, "I can't remember."

Proudly and yet casually, Emmanuel announced, "That is deliverance." As he suggested, this inability to remember what happened in deliverance is further evidence that there is some sort of sixth sense involved. The whole possession scene in this way is described as inexplicable, as inaccessible to the human imagination or memory, as beyond our sensory capacity. Demons are part of the human experience and yet clearly impinge on humans in ways that are not simply captured through modern modes of thought and analysis. Demons are only understood through the psychical and the physical.

In another example, I spoke with Richard. Richard received deliverance from Emmanuel one Wednesday morning, but we met at Ofori's prayer camp since he lived nearby. Talking over the din of the prayer camp—people going about their daily rituals—we discussed his spiritual marriage. His sex dreams were varied. Sometimes he would be making love to a person without seeing the person's face. Sometimes he would be visited sexually by a "small boy, sometimes an old man." Sometimes it was an older woman with male genitals. And sometimes it was Mami Wata, "I don't know the lady, but I'll have sex with that spiritual marine." Sometimes it was a dream, but sometimes "the dream became real." As he described it, it was "normal sex, they ejaculate, and it's pleasurable . . . more pleasurable than physical sex, and then they leave." Marianne said something similar about the sex with spirits that she had and enjoyed: "Mine was always normal with ejaculations and everything. Just like having sex with your boyfriend." And while the spirits manifest in different forms, Richard always wakes up "all wet." He was confused as to why spirits use sex to access humans, saying, "Why do spirits use sex? I don't know, only God knows."

On this particular Wednesday, Emmanuel chose Richard from the crowd. He was sitting near the front on the right-hand side. That is all that he remembered of deliverance. He was only aware of his own deliverance because he had watched the service replayed on Emmanuel's TV station. From my perspective, it was not a particularly dramatic deliverance moment, which illustrates just how quickly the fantastic becomes mundane and quotidian, and my own reaction in some ways explains the logic of prophets' behavior becoming more and more outlandish. Emmanuel asked Richard, "How many times have you slept with women spiritually?" Richard answered, "Many, oh, many." Emmanuel quickly touched him, and Richard fell to the ground. As Richard lay on the ground, Emmanuel prayed that "every fetish priest who is married to him, get out." Emmanuel turned to the audience and said, "This man is delivered." With that, Richard stood up and said, "Thank you, Jesus." However, Richard did not remember any of these events; he had only become aware by replaying the scene many times on his television. That is how deliverance works, though. The metakinetic sense does not necessarily reveal everything, but is always operative as exemplified by Richard's body falling to the floor in this deep spiritual haze. The psychical is physical and the physical is psychical.

SERPENTINE SCENES

A woman slithered one way, causing a mini-stampede as people rushed to get out of her way. She then slithered the other way, sending a whole new group of congregants spilling out of their seats. "Look at the snake in motion," Emmanuel instructed the congregation. Everyone watched, staring intently, terrified by the women's movements. But what were they watching? What were they seeing? As we will learn throughout this chapter, Emmanuel was not speaking metaphorically. He did not instruct the congregation to look at the woman moving *like* a snake. He instructed them to look *at* the snake. He redoubled his efforts when he rhetorically asked, "Have you seen the snake?" Eventually, Emmanuel detailed the simple plan for his pastors to defeat this spirit: "Cut off her head." The pastors sprang into action, swinging wildly at the throat and neck of the woman. Again, what did they see? They saw a snake and held machetes as they enacted this violence against the ser-pentine spirit. As an outsider, I was not seeing what they were seeing, as their eyes bulged with intent, never straying from the slithering spirit.

Emmanuel later that week described to me the events of the day in very literal terms. He said that snake spirits always want to appear physically. On that day when he delivered the woman, "a snake appeared, physical." But what does that mean, when all I saw was a woman acting like a snake? He explained, "You will see the deliverer as a human person there, but as a prophet or pastor, the Lord God will open your eyes so that you will see that the one lying there is not human, you will see the snake. I see it in a snake form. That is why when I say I'll cut off your head, I see the head cut off." I realized in that moment that I did not have demonologeyes, my neologism for the kind of vision that sees bodies trans-mogrify, the type of haptic visionary sense at the very core of deliverance. Others have noted the haptic vision of Pentecostalism and assumed that this is merely another manifestation of visual supremacy in Pentecostal culture.[1] And yet, Pentecostal demonologeyes challenge visuality by seeing that which cannot be seen by mere human eyes.

During a conversation that followed shortly after the alleged deliverance of Morowa and Kifah, I asked Emmanuel how he was confident that the women had been delivered. Without ever referring specifically to Morowa or Kifah, he provided a generic answer about what he sees with his "open vision" or "spiritual eyes"—what I am calling demonologeyes. He said, "When I see in the spirit that you are having gay, I see that spirit in you. I see that lesbian in you. So, when I deliver you, I see that it has vanished. It is not by faith that I say 'I have delivered you, go.' I see that it is no longer there." This is done not by faith but by sight, sight that unveils the supernatural. With open vision, Emmanuel already knows everything about everyone; he sees it. However, he waits for God's instruction and direction for whom to deliver, "so that day was for those particular people, the lesbians." According to Emmanuel, the difference between what I saw and what he saw—be it the serpent or the demons in Morowa and Kifah—is that my lack of faith means I simply have normal sight. His deep faith in God gives him demonologeyes, a sense of sight that sees things thought impossible. Phillip concurred and warned that my not being sufficiently in tune with God to have such a sense put me at grave risk of spiritual marriage.

To the uninitiated eye, the whole performance of deliverance has an absurdist feeling to it, as if one is watching actors with a green screen before the special effects are added. In my eyes, I witnessed people pretending to throw something, acting as though they were chopping and slicing something, and addressing something unseen. Demonologeyes see not the human arm and hand slicing through the air but a machete slicing through the head of a stubborn snake that refuses to die. Demonologeyes see that head actually fall to the ground, detached from its serpentine body. In this context I could not help but think of Michael Taussig's discussion of the eyeball as "an extension of the moving, sensate body," except for pneumatic Christians, while sight is necessarily haptic, it also extends well beyond the visible universe.[2]

The sense of sight is undeniably central to deliverance. It is so entwined that all the preceding chapters have, to varying degrees, been unable to describe the primacy of other senses without significant reliance on sight. That is certainly not to imply occularcentrism, as sight has not been privileged over other senses, but various senses are deeply entwined with sight. However, the sense of sight in deliverance is not the same as the detached Enlightenment gaze; in deliverance the sense of sight is an enchanted one that can make people see and feel fantastic things, and even change the way their body moves and occupies space.

There are a variety of explanations for the appearance of spirits as animals. First, Kwofie explained to me that demons struggle to maintain the human form for very long. When Satan and the angels were cast out of heaven, they lost the ability to maintain the human form. The animal form is much easier to maintain. Additionally, Kwofie went on to explain, animal spirits are connected to an ancestral element. He pointed out, "In Ghana, some believe that the dog is their ancestor, so they [the spirits] come as a dog. Some believe that a bird is their ancestor, so they come as a bird." For Badoe, every person has a spirit animal: "If the evil spirit wants to get connected to you, he will look at you and see the kind of your spiritual animal that it will be easier to get connected to you. Then he will turn into that animal." The spirits are attendant to one's personal beliefs and use that to their advantage.

Snakes, in particular, are common because, in Kwofie's estimation, "90 percent of the deities in Africa are represented by serpents." Nikoi also concluded, "Most of the time if the family worships snake—as a symbol of their god—any time the spirits come, it can come in that appearance of a snake." Kwofie went on to explain why snakes appeared specifically to him, and the reasons were even more varied. First, his family believed that the snake was their ancestor. Accordingly, when he was born, a large snake appeared and placed saliva in his mouth, a sign of things to come. Of course, once converted these serpentine experiences were recast in a Christian narrative, and Kwofie always returned to the snake as a part of Christian history: "Satan is a serpent, he appeared in the Garden of Eden as a serpent, so that is how it is." Nikoi agreed with Kwofie, "The snake is right from the Garden of Eden."

Further, based on a particular interpretation of Genesis, Nikoi believed that "the snake is a very carnal animal." Meyer captures this ambivalence of the snake symbolism:

> Traditionally, at least for the Ewe, the snake symbolizes fertility. A woman who dreams that she has been bitten by a snake is said to soon become pregnant . . . Alongside these positive associations the snake has also been imagined as one of the animal shapes a witch might take. This negative image has been strengthened with the introduction of the Christian account of the Fall, which depicts the reptile as a representation of the Devil. Hence the snake has developed into a highly ambivalent creature linked alike with the positive value of the continuity of life and the destructiveness of witchcraft and the Devil.[3]

As such, Kwofie, Badoe, and Nikoi's descriptions of the snake as coming both from the Garden of Eden and from traditional beliefs are perfectly emblematic of the symbolic power the snake now possesses in Ghana.

Deliverance manuals tend to emphasize biblical precedents for spirit animals. Peter Horrobin cites both Genesis 3 and Luke 10 as exemplars of demonic manifestations in the form of animals. But there is no biblical precedent for the scope of animals represented in deliverance:

> Certainly we have seen many demons manifest during deliverance as snakes or scorpions. People have finished up slithering across the floor in an incredibly snake-like manner, or with their backs bent so far over that the tail of their spine resembled the sting of a scorpion. It seems as though these are the commonest animalistic manifestations, being part of the basic character of the demonic. In addition to these we have experienced almost every possible animalistic manifestation you can think of. Innocent looking girls have suddenly become fierce tigers as the Holy Spirit has exposed hidden demonic power. Demonic lions, bulls, dogs, rams, goats, cockerels and many, many more have surfaced and been dispatched in the name of Jesus.[4]

Horrobin's enumeration of animal spirits emphasizes that for pneumatics, textual exegesis is deemed superfluous and direct experience is the ultimate arbiter of truth.

In traditional Akan beliefs about animals there is often a supernatural or sacred element, but not all of those beliefs easily map onto the deliverance cosmos.[5] For example, there is a tradition of fear of supernatural animal forces among the Akan, in particular when northerners are able to trans-mogrify into hyenas and werewolves.[6] The Akan were quite afraid of this power of shapeshifting, which they linked to witchcraft and the practice of *bayi*, or soul-eating.[7] While I did not encounter this particular belief or any hyenas or werewolves, John Parker correctly notes that in Ghana and greater West Africa "the ontological boundary between people and animals was highly porous."[8] The boundary between animal and human is ambiguous, unstable, and volatile, which necessarily shapes notions of the body and spirit. As we interrogate the boundary between animal and human, we must keep this kind of fluidity in mind and discard bounded concepts.[9]

More appropriate to the cases in this chapter is the widespread belief that witches can turn into any animal that suits their environment and desires, including but not limited to poisonous snakes, fish, lizards, cocks, dogs, soldier ants, antelopes, tigers, and lions.[10] Onyinah refers to these witch-spirit animals as *nahomoa*.[11] For example, Hans Debrunner cites a Ga story in which a witch trans-mogrified from owl to a snake and then was defeated by a medicine man and changed back into a naked woman.[12] The snake is the most frequent choice and is intimately involved in the witch's initiation. The prophets interviewed for this text saw trans-mogrification of witches and wizards as emulating Satan in temporarily taking on animal forms to carry out diabolical acts. According to Debrunner, to become a witch you "go into the bush together with a witch who has become tired of her witchcraft. You both strip yourselves naked, bow down and let anus touch anus. Then a snake will leave her body and enter yours, and you have become a witch."[13] In an understated sentence, Debrunner articulates that "there are all sorts of connections between man and animals."[14] Those connections, importantly, blur the very distinction between the categories of human and animal.

As with much of the material throughout *Seductive Spirits*, there is considerable colonial baggage when relating humans and animals that cannot simply be ignored. During colonial expansion the categories of human and animal were primary in constructing a model of universal humanity. Within this enduring Enlightenment construction of the human, " 'the African' does not symbolize 'the animal'; 'the African' is 'the animal.'"[15] Achille Mbembe, in *On the Postcolony*, similarly observes that Africa is treated as "a meta-text about the animal—to be exact, about the beast: its experience, its world, and its spectacle."[16] Africans, the argument holds, are assumed to be animals occupying the human form. But instead of focusing on a humanist recovery project, sex with animal spirits and trans-mogrification into those animals demonstrate the provisional nature of the human as a category. It is certainly difficult to render an argument that Pentecostal bestializing is an effort to be recognized as normatively human. What if Pentecostals, instead of reifying the human, are actually nullifying it? What does this Pentecostal rupture of the human by bestializing (sexually and trans-mogrifying) accomplish?

SANDRA

Returning to the scene that inaugurated this chapter, Emmanuel called all those struggling with spiritual marriage to the front of the church. There was a dramatic and immediate crush of people rushing toward the stage. Hundreds of people filled the area in front of the platform and spilled into the aisles like overflowing tributaries. That this is unremarkable is actually remarkable. By moving forward, hundreds of people, a significant portion of the congregation, were marking themselves as sexually involved with a spirit or spirits. As people continued to spill into the aisles, eager to confess their sexual liaisons with spirits, the prophet asked them to raise their hands. Everyone raised their hands, swaying to the music as the worship band belted out a heartfelt worship song with the flimsiest of lyrics. Before the pastors were set loose to do battle with these sexual spirits, Emmanuel engaged in a repeat-after-me prayer. Prophet Emmanuel stalked back and forth along the top stair of the stage, scanning the crowd, his eyes darting back and forth. It appeared as if he was looking for something or someone in particular. In stunted sentences, short enough to be repeated, the prophet led the congregation through a prayer of deliverance, the responses of those possessed of spiritual marriage created the droning buzz of a crowd trying but failing to speak in unison.

"Raise your hands and say Jesus."

"Jesus," the crowd yelled.

"Say Jesus," he repeated.

"Jesus!" the crowd yelled louder than their first effort.

The rest of the prayer followed that pattern with the possessed repeating everything the prophet said: "Spiritual sex and marriage. Has tormented me for a long time. It has brought to me much evil. And blocked my fortunes. Today. If Prophet Emmanuel. And his pastors. Touch me. Let that spirit. Vanish! Vanish! In Jesus's name." The prophet's final instruction to those in sexual relationships with demons was "tell Jesus to touch you as we pray." He promised, "You'll be free." Here Emmanuel emphasized tactile touch as freeing, a familiar sensation.

With the prayer-filled niceties over, the pastors sprung upon the crowd, starting from the front. As the pastors pushed on foreheads, struck stomachs, and engaged in all sorts of other physical exchanges for the sake of deliverance, the prophet stood abeyant on the stage. From time to time he would participate, but only ever from a distance releasing a piercing scream of *apue*—come out or release—or imitating throwing something with his left hand. His eyes continued to scan the proceedings, observing the reactions as they occurred.

As some in the front row started to spin out of control, knocking over those near them and causing the crowd to sway and swell in various directions, the prophet pleaded for "strong men sitting idle" to help restrain the excessive and exuberant bodies because "some of the manifesting spirits are very strong." And while some bodies continued to spill out, fall, and swing wildly, most people were touched by a pastor and returned to their seats without an extreme reaction, though returning to their places was an arduous journey through hundreds of bodies. As the crowd thinned, the excessive bodies were left with more room to spin, jump, and run.

The prophet, still observing the commotion from his perch, urged the crowd to join in with clapping and prayers. The clapping added a sort of syncopation to the intricate deliverance dance happening at the front. On top of the disjointed beats of the congregation, the prophet repeatedly whispered "spiritual marriage, spiritual sex" in such a way that it took on the sonic hook of a mantra, the nine syllables taking on their own rhythm: "Spiritual marriage-spiritual sex, spiritual marriage-spiritual sex, spiritual marriage-spiritual sex." He kept chanting all the while clearly perturbed by the persistence of the chaos and refusal of so many bodies to respond with docility. When the deliverance extended beyond what Emmanuel had imagined, he exhorted his pastors to discipline and punish the spirits, "Pastors, try and punish the stronger spirits that are manifesting. Such spirits are stubborn and deserve to be punished." The punishment of the spirits manifested in the discipline of human bodies, as the pastors responded with more violent means of pulling wildly at congregants' hair, open palm slapping, and closed fist punching. Of course, in stating that human bodies were punished I am admitting that I do not have the demonologeyes capable of witnessing the spiritual impact of such violence.

The violence, though, did not necessarily procure the desired results, so Emmanuel became more explicit in his instructions: "Torment them with fire, spiritual sex out!" Fire, an obvious symbol of the Holy Spirit, is supposed to torment the offending demons without torturing the human body. Badoe described to me that "the moment you throw fire on it, the spirit will identify itself. The moment you mention the fire, the spirit wants to run away to avoid the fire." But again, fire is not merely a metaphor for Prophet Badoe, Emmanuel, or any other deliverance minister. Badoe told me, "You yell 'Holy Ghost FIRE!' Spiritually the moment you open your mouth to throw the fire and the fire goes straight to the spirit . . . you will see the fire. You yourself, you will see the fire from your mouth." It should already be clear that in this chapter we are dealing with a heightened or peculiar sense of sight. In this case, the enhanced sense of sight identifies an exchange differently than the one witnessed by merely watching the bodies as they occupy space and time. This enhanced sense of sight included seeing the spirit, the fire leaving the mouth, and the fire burning the spirit. This is an enchanted deliverance sight.

Demonologeyes see things thought to be invisible. Gregory Delaplace writes that Mongolians refer to a wide variety of entities as "invisible things." However, invisibility "does not mean that nobody can ever see them— otherwise they would cause little trouble—but that their encounter is subject to specific perceptual modality."[17] These entities, demons in the case of deliverance ministries, are not experienced in precisely the same way that living people or cattle are experienced, for they are only perceivable by those with this enhanced, enchanted sense of sight—they are seen only "by some people, in certain contexts, and in a particular way."[18] Kirstina Wirtz has used the term "perspicience" for this enhanced, enchanted sense of sight. In contemporary usage, the term connotes keen or clear perception and insight. However, in a now obsolete definition it described the ability to see all things, or infinite vision. Wirtz refers to perspicience as "knowing awareness of the spirits."[19] Perspicience operates, for Wirtz, much the same way demonologeyes operate here, as the special sensory orientation that recognizes spirits in the material world, or knowledgeable seeing. It is the ability to know through the senses, to see, and sense that which others cannot see. In so opening up oneself to these supernatural powers, one exceeds their sense of self and the world in which one finds themselves.

Meanwhile, as his pastors swung wildly with the madness of street fighters, Emmanuel moved in a calm and controlled manner. He touched outstretched hand after outstretched hand—open-palm-on-open-palm high fives—and with each touch, the congregant turned and moved deliberately back to their seats. There were no excessive reactions or extravagant spirits, just a gentle high five and the promise that the "spiritual marriage is broken, in Jesus's name. As I've touched you, I've set the demon ablaze. It is broken from you." With his demonologeyes, Emmanuel told me he witnessed the scorching of spirits.

As all of this happened, a woman named Sandra slithered across the back of the assembled masses of people. Lying on her stomach, she slowly made her way across the width of the church. Obscured by the many people still seeking deliverance from their own sexual demons, she went unnoticed. Sandra moved slowly, deliberately, unconcerned, and unresponsive to all the bodies moving around her, which were stepping over her and jumping out of her way. Only the prophet, from his elevated vantage point, noticed. "Which spirit is behaving so poorly?" he asked of one of his pastors. "Apostle," he continued to implore, "which spirit is that? Which spirit is being that stubborn?"

The angriest of Emmanuel's acolytes, Apostle, moved toward Sandra, who was still lazily slithering across the dusty floor. Apostle moved indignantly toward Sandra. He adjusted his plaid suit jacket in its purple, white, and pink sartorial splendor and tugged at his pink bowtie before commencing to deliver her. Four ushers met him at the site of Sandra's slithering body and stood her up, ending her snake reenactment. Two ushers pulled at her arms but were clearly out of their element, lacking the control and unison that more skilled ushers execute. As the ushers tugged her arms, Sandra's body flailed and jerked. Apostle, with his characteristic rage, buried his hands in Sandra's short afro.

As he yanked her hair upward, he rotated his wrists, painting vicious circles in the air with her head. Around and around her head turned, her neck bending so that her head fell behind her shoulder blades and back around so her chin met her chest. Apostle removed one hand from her hair and used it to hit Sandra on the top of her head repeatedly. She began to fall to the floor until Apostle grabbed her again by her hair, holding it tightly until she hit the ground. The ushers immediately restrained her, pinning her to the ground on her right side before she could recommence snaking across the floor. Apostle changed his course of action but not his violent means, swinging his arms like a rapid pendulum so that his left arm hit her back, and his right arm hit her stomach in quick succession. As she tried to slither away from the rapacious and repetitious blows, another pastor grabbed her hair and pinned her head to the ground. The attention of all the pastors, the prophet, and the congregation was now concentrated on the pile of bodies immobilizing Sandra, fastening her to the chalky ground. The last woman beside Sandra to be delivered got up from the ground wearing only one sandal. Realizing that the other shoe was next to Sandra, she deftly stuck her foot amidst the pile of bodies and retrieved her footwear, returning to her seat. It was now everyone against Sandra, or against the spirit that was making her slink around in such a serpentine manner—depending on what kind of vision one enacted.

For a few moments, this played itself on loop, the group of bodies pinning Sandra to the ground, heaving with Apostle's deliverance movements. Everyone else watched, transfixed. Without any warning, everyone left the body alone as if it had been successfully rendered docile. But as everyone backed away from the snake, Sandra quickly rolled onto her front and redoubled her slithering. As she wriggled and writhed, inching her way along, people started jumping out of her way. The prophet confirmed the embodied fears of everyone by describing what was happening. He yelled, "Heh, heh, that is a snake creeping. If you put your leg in her way, she'll bite you." The warning ensured that everyone else she encountered would continue the pattern of leaping out of her way. The prophets and pastors parted as she moved. At the risk of repetition, as they jumped, they leaped not out of Sandra's way but out of the way of the snake. It was not Sandra's bite they feared but the fangs of a snake. They saw a snake slithering across the floor, not a human body moving like a snake.

At this point, it is perhaps unclear why this woman sliding across the floor is part of this book. In many ways, this account reads like most of the other deliverance episodes already discussed with a similar soundscape, similar kinesthetics, and the ever-familiar centrality of touch. Most notably, it lacks the explicit sexual content that has loosely tied the other scenes together. But indeed, this woman sliding across the floor emulating a snake is another example of sexual deliverance. Animalistic manifestations are often associated with spiritual marriage or spiritual sex. As Emmanuel told me, "If they manifest as an animal, it means they were spiritually married to that animal. In the supernatural realm, the easiest way to contact you is sexual. They have to marry that person." The second claim—that the most accessible link between the human and supernatural is sexual—is worth emphasizing; in fact, it is the central premise of this whole book that sex is used by Pentecostals to make spirits immanent, embodied, and sensuous. The first claim, though, is a potent one, indicating that spirit animals and humans have sexual liaisons.

Badoe made the connection between animality and sexuality explicit, "The spirit will turn into that animal and pursue you sexually." Phillip, who was always very forthcoming, described to me that spiritually marrying an animal was a particularly evil experience. He said that Mami Wata will use any "vessel" she can be it human, animal, or even something immaterial like the wind. Phillip enumerated a sort of ranking system about the attendant evil with each different form. Sleeping with a spirit disguised as a human was the least serious. Sleeping with a spirit disguised as an animal was much worse. "Animal means serious," Phillip said, and he explained that sex with a hermaphrodite was somewhere in between those two options. The zenith—or nadir, depending on your perspective—was sleeping with an invisible spirit. But, Phillip told me, animals are serious as they mount humans with oversized genitals, causing incredible sexual pleasure, and leaving behind a wet, sticky aftermath to remind humans of what has occurred.

Kwofie confirmed that he had long taught about the possibility—the probability even—of being married to a spirit animal as a basic tenet of deliverance. Kwofie explained, if someone is being delivered and an animal manifests—it could be moving like a fish, barking like a dog, or slithering like a snake—then that person is married to an animalistic spirit. The animal that appears is the spirit to whom they are spiritually married, which is to say that pneumatics believe that the person is sexually involved with that particular type of animalistic spirit. When an animal manifests, as it did in Sandra's case, it means that a spirit animal has had sex with the human body, and in this way, the spirit has taken control of the body. As Badoe said, "When the animal is in the person, it is in the whole body."

To return to the snake imagery, participants see not merely the transmogrification of a human body into a snake but a body that has undoubtedly engaged in sexual liaisons with a spirit in the form of a snake. Victoria Eto wrote extensively about the presence of sexual snakes and the need to treat them seriously in the deliverance cosmos. Of the many people who are possessed by spirits disguised as snakes, she writes,

> Some of the snakes are for sex. These girls tie the snakes round their waist. Then when they want to sleep with anybody they will put the head of the snake in their private part while the boys will use the tails of the snake. The extra sensual nature of the snake tongue and snake skin will make people think these are wonderful bedmates. When you have sexual affairs with such a person different kinds of problems start coming into your life. This is because anybody who sleeps with them is possessed by evil spirits. Some possessed people can turn into snakes.[20]

In another example, Eto wrote of a specific young man, a Christian young man, whose faith was threatened by spiritual marriage to marine spirits who provided snakes and dogs to satisfy him sexually. He entered into a marriage contract with these marine spirits by drinking water. While he drank, "they rubbed every part of his body to evoke sensual feelings—thus soaking his blood and skin with sensuality."[21] This young man then washed his eyes and face. It was his eyes that gave away possession as they carried "a decidedly unchristian look." As we have seen in all spiritual marriages, the terms of the contract were sexual fidelity to the spirit and total abstinence from human sexual intercourse. In exchange, the young man was provided with a "dog which comes to lick him and satisfy his sexual cravings. They also gave him a snake which resided in his penis. They taught various sexual arts including painful and advanced forms of masturbation."[22]

Paul Gifford cited several animal-based sexual experiences at Prophet Salifu Amoako's deliverance services. In the first description, Gifford explains that there was a rat spirit. The prophet said you could be confident that "not everyone in a skirt or blouse in the street is a human being."[23] In this case, the man had sex with a woman and awoke the following morning to find not a woman but a large white rat wearing human clothes.[24] The man had not slept with a human being but with a bestialized spirit, with an animal. The most graphic tales Gifford shares, though, were serpentine in nature. For example, in one story, a man was accused of being a witch. The evidence of his being a witch was an allegation that he had slept with eight spirit wives, all different animals. Not only had he slept with these different animalistic spirits, but he had impregnated each of them. When the rat spirit the man had been sexually betrothed to was cast out of him, it reputedly immediately possessed a woman in the front row. Returning to the man, Prophet Amoako—perhaps the most confident prophet I have ever encountered, which is impressive considering Pentecostal prophet is a rather cocksure profession—declared that the man's penis was a snake. The snake was threatening not only to the man but especially to all the women with whom he had sex. Supposedly the snake penis would bite any and all women that it touched. For deliverance, Gifford writes, his penis "had to be treated, and while he lay on the stage his trousers were loosened and oil was poured on his penis."[25]

The penis is often imagined in various ways during deliverance. Recall Prophet Ofori's description of his spiritual marriage in the previous chapter where his penis held a knife. In another deliverance, one of my informants blamed a Mallam—an honorific title for Islamic scholars often associated with miracle workers—for shrinking his penis until it disappeared. By acceding to the magic of the Mallam, my informant believed that he had sacrificed his "manhood." It was only the deliverance power of a particular pneumatic prophet who was able to restore his penis. Most frequently, though, possessed penises are imagined as snakes. Deviant possessed penises are said to threaten vaginas. As Salifu Amoako's example warns, snake penises bite and enter vaginas, taking possession of the vagina and blocking the ability for the possessed to marry humans.[26]

Theoretically, the predominance of animals—as both sexual partners and that into which humans trans-mogrify—allows us to consider the category of the human entirely differently. In fact, we must rethink the human and the animal. As Jackson writes, "'The animal' as symbol, as trope, as locus of possibility, must be *rethought and transformed*; otherwise, it will continue to animate antiblack discourse and institute itself biopolitically."[27] In order to consider this possibility, I turn to Mel Y. Chen's *Animacies: Biopolitics, Racial Mattering, and Queer Affect*.[28] Chen explores how matter is animated, pointing out how pieces of animate matter are necessarily and always consequential to each other. Animacy forces a rethinking of the relationship between human animals and nonhuman animals and brings a new awareness of the many connections between both forms of being. Animacy violates proper intimacies as a "craft of the senses."[29]

The "animacy hierarchy"—which defines human life over and against the animal or the object—flows from white, able-bodied humans down through animals to inanimate objects. Chen wants to disrupt this hierarchy by exploring encounters between bodies of varying levels of animacy, including a reconsideration of the relationship between humans and animals: "For it is animality that has been treated as a primary mediator, or crux (though not the only one), for the definition of 'human,' and, at the same moment, of 'animal.'"[30] African Pentecostalism fundamentally upsets this hierarchy with inspirited animals; trans-species boundaries between humans and animals are quite porous and indeed are connected by "animate affinities" that bring bodies into contact.[31] That is to say that "the 'stuff' of animal nature . . . sometimes bleeds back onto textures of humanness."[32] This bleeding into one another—something that is occurring in the spiritual marriages examined in this chapter—should be less surprising than it is, as the boundedness of the human being is artificial and arbitrary. That is, in deliverance, the body is no longer viewed as autonomous, bounded, and contained. As difference disappears when the human animals and nonhuman animals bleed into each other, the body becomes quite dynamic. In deliverance, the body is seen as unstable, always at risk of becoming something other, something animalistic.

In particular, I utilize the prefixal *trans* and the hyphen in the same way that Chen does. Chen writes, "trans- is not a linear space of mediation between two monolithic, autonomous poles . . . not least because the norms by which these poles are often defined by too easily conceal, or forget, their interests and contingencies."[33] *Trans-* in this chapter is not simply about gender but about the relationality of human, animal, and spirit. In particular, *trans-* refuses the fixed rigidity of those categories and resists foreclosure by emphasizing the open-endedness and fluidity between animal, spirit, and human.

The hyphen is also decolonial in the same way that Christina Sharpe's use of the asterisk is. Sharpe uses *trans** in multiple ways for possible trans*formation by black bodies. The asterisk is a wildcard that dismantles Euro-Western forms, demonstrating the inability of categories like gender to describe and control the black embodied experience. Sharpe writes, "The asterisk speaks to range of configurations of Black being that take the form of translation, transatlantic, transgression, transgender, transformation, transmogrification, transcontinental, transfixed, trans-Mediterranean, transubstantiation, transmigration, and more."[34] In this chapter, we will explore two of those related trans- actions for Pentecostals: trans-mogrification and trans-substantiation. Trans-mogrification, the changing into fantastic and grotesque forms, is important in that it demonstrates the plasticity of the human form for Ghanaian Pentecostals. The sensuous human body gives form and receives form and is always trans-. But the Pentecostal experience with spirited animals, especially the sex with animal spirits, is not completely captured in trans-mogrification. As Chen argues, the nonhuman animal "transubstantiates beyond the borders of our insistent human ontologies."[35] Trans-substantiation is a religious term and pushes us beyond changing form into a changing and sharing of substance.

While deliverance ministries expel the figure of the animal, or more accurately, they intimately embrace them even while they dismiss them, we must ask how they matter sexually. In doing so we discover the trans-ness of animal figures. That is to say that animals violate borders.[36] Chen writes, "If human substantiation enduringly depends on the expulsion of animals—then it is imperative that we ask questions not only about how animals matter, but how they matter sexually."[37] Chen directs this trans-ness toward trans-substantiation, the "relational exchanges between animals and humans can be coded at the level of ontological mediation, or alchemical transformation, one that goes beyond vitalism that infuses given boundaries with life-lines."[38] This trans-substantiation is a form of ontological mediation between the human animal and nonhuman animal. The possessed actually become animals in a substitutional form, and they are of the same substance.[39] The blurring of the boundary between the human animal and nonhuman animal happens at the point of the human becoming-animal.

Spiritual marriage to animals trans-substantiates in unthinkable ways: the animal becomes human, or the human becomes animal; the spirit takes on human form; and the human and animal have sex. The last example, the combination of the human animal and nonhuman animal in the realm of sexuality, is not that unique. As Chen points out, analogies have often been made between nonhuman animal and human animal sexualities. She observes, "Humans and nonhuman animals recombine sexually within the same ontological fold in which they are sometimes admitted to belong."[40] This is a crucial point; it denudes human exceptionalism, self-control, and bounded individualism, performing something that is distinctly neither. In the words of Jackson, "it also illustrates the animal potential of the human."[41] Animals are powerful, and their physical and psychical powers offer something beyond the human. Embracing the animal potential destroys the manichean distinctions of human-animal, psychical and physical, good and bad. There is no absolute human autonomy, instead, trans-substantiation relies on mutual accommodation.

Returning to Sandra's story, in which Sandra is a snake, the participants in the deliverance assumed that the snake was Sandra's spiritual spouse. They believed that Sandra was manifesting as a snake because she had sex with a spirit in the guise of a snake.[42] That is to say that the logic of Pentecostalism dictated that congregants believe that Sandra had not only trans-mogrified into a snake, but had trans-substantiated with the snake to share substance and form.

With Emmanuel's warning about Sandra's ability to bite, her unimpeded movement turned toward the congregation. She skulked toward the center aisle and then turned down it. She slithered slightly to the left, then slightly to the right as she slowly made her way toward the congregation. Her head rolled gently from side to side, her face so close to the ground that the sides of her afro became tinged with the light dirt and dust that layered the concrete slabs on which the church's tents were erected. Her legs dragged behind her, shoulder-width apart. Clad in a blue and white dress, she never lifted her body off of the ground, using her forearms to propel herself forward. Large beads of sweat visibly rolled down her face. The entire time her face was contorted, her eyes stayed rolled back and her mouth never closed, staying slightly ajar.

Emmanuel announced that Sandra was a "snake in motion" and asked those in the congregation—who were already looking—to "look at the snake in motion." Emmanuel asked again, rhetorically this time, "Have you seen the snake?" Commands to look, to see, were reiterated throughout the whole performance simultaneously embracing and exploding occularcentrism with demonologeyes.

Sandra squirmed ten meters down the center aisle and then veered into the chairs to her right. People bolted from their plastic chairs and cleared everything from her path. Chairs, bags, children, adults all split left and right to clear a route for Sandra. Sandra's slow, deliberate movements ensured that everyone had ample time to scatter. She slid slowly, which was further dramatized by a plodding song from the worship musicians. It was as if the whole scene was unfolding in slow motion. Since deliverance was the only option to stop Sandra from slithering, Emmanuel encouraged his pastors to deliver her. Emmanuel yelled from the stage, "Pastors, behead the snake." He repeated the last part of the sentence three times as if there were an echo or reverberation throughout the church: "Behead the snake. Behead the snake. Behead the snake." As the first pastor reached Sandra and touched her shoulder, she spun 180 degrees, rising to her knees. As the second pastor arrived, Sandra exploded from her knees and leaped at him, her arms flailed in an attempt to grab him. He jumped backward to avoid her grasp. At the same time, a third pastor tackled her from behind, toppling to the ground. Sandra tried to get up but was forcefully pushed back to the ground.

A fourth pastor started to enact the slicing off of Sandra's head, running his hand across her neck as if it were a knife. This cutting off of the head motion is a ubiquitous action in deliverance. The junior pastor only sliced at Sandra's neck a couple of times before the prophet halted the effort. Emmanuel yelled, the concern in his voice palpable, "Leave her, or else she'll bite you!" Emmanuel seemed more excited than usual; his voice went higher in pitch as he added, "Even if she bites you physically, the venom will make your hand swell. It will swell until it becomes a sore and needs to get amputated." The pastors backed off and left Sandra on all fours, the front of her dress filthy from all the dust it had accumulated during her lengthy serpentine journey. As she started to crawl away, some pastors cleared a path, while others continued the slicing motion with their hands to perform the beheading, all while keeping their distance from her for fear of her venom. These slicing motions did not touch Sandra as the first two did, instead they were cutting through the air. Or they appeared to be cutting through the air, but with demonologeyes they were making direct contact and cutting at her head.

Without waiting for Emmanuel's sanction, a group of three pastors took it upon themselves to end this charade. Each of them put their hands near Sandra's neck and sawed away. When one of the pastors grabbed her shoulders from behind, the other two pastors transitioned from sawing to large, dramatic slicing motions. They took turns, one after another, perfectly choreographed, with each slice appearing to come closer and closer to her neck. Eventually, one of the exaggerated slicing motions contacted her neck. As soon as contact was made, Sandra bolted up into a standing position by using her outstretched arms in a propeller motion to push the pastors out of the way and push herself forward toward the stage. Sandra walked briskly toward the stage, her eyes still rolling backward. On the stage, watching everything transpire, the prophet waited for her. Before she reached Emmanuel, a pastor known as Doc interrupted her movement and began throwing imaginary things at her, one hand after another. She responded by doing the same so that they were engaged in a dramatic battle that played out with the drama of Neo dodging bullets in *The Matrix*. Doc threw with his left hand, her body bent backward avoiding whatever was being hurled at her. Then she snapped forward, throwing with her right hand. His body responded by leaning back and then, likewise, snapped forward as he threw with his right hand. She bent and then threw with her left hand. It all happened quickly. They went back and forth, stopping only when the prophet told Doc to cease.

Throwing imaginary objects with her appendages and standing on her two legs with her own volition seemed to move her out of the realm of performing the role of the serpent. I began to wonder what demonologeyes were seeing now. Did demonologeyes rely on the nature of her physical movement? She put her hand on her waist and stalked the stage while Emmanuel answered some of my questions by describing Sandra's further trans-mogrification: "She has turned into a hippopotamus." While there was continuity between her material performance and the prophet's narrative about seeing the serpent, the hippopotamus required a more liberal imagination. Or perhaps it merely required a different type of vision. She responded to his announcement of her new identity by patting her chest and walking backward, never taking her eyes off of the prophet.

Emmanuel moved toward Sandra. His movement caused her to speak, but nobody put a microphone to her mouth, so her verbal responses and outbursts remained inaudible. "Look at me," demanded the prophet, "Hey, look at my face." "Look at me" was a familiar refrain. In this case, the prophet demanded that she return his deliverance look; that she see him with demonologeyes. She averted her attention to Pastor Leo, the prophet's personal assistant, who quickly tried to divert her gaze by pointing back to the prophet. Emmanuel grew impatient and continued to demand her sight: "Hey. Look at the prophet . . . Look at me!" *Look at me*; the command seemed to suggest that sight can deliver from something both unseen and seen.

Sandra walked away, refusing to abide by Emmanuel's commands. Emmanuel took two steps and grabbed Sandra's afro, which jerked her head back toward him and stopped her forward momentum. Emmanuel, still holding tightly to her hair, pulled her head so that they were facing each other separated only by his arms-length. He had physically forced her to come face to face with his eyes, his piercing gaze, which elicited a shrill "aaahhhhh" from Sandra. Emmanuel responded with "pooof." Emmanuel does not employ the airy "poofs" with the same ubiquity as Prophet Ofori, who uses them in nearly every deliverance scenario, but when he utilizes "poofs" he does so generously. The only sound he made for the rest of the deliverance was "poof" and "Jesus." "Poof." He grabbed Sandra's hair. "Poof. Jesus." He swung her around in a circle. "Poof." He again swung her in a circle. "Poof. Jesus." She slipped to her knees. "Poof." He pulled her hair until she was lying prone on the ground. "Poof. Jesus." She rolled over, but he continued to pin her head to the ground.

With his hand on her face covering her eyes, he uttered instructions to the spirit: "I crush your head, do not come again. Out of this body in the

name of Jesus, out of this body! Out of this body in the name of Jesus. Amen."
The whole time he was uttering his instructions to the spirit, Sandra was
muttering and mumbling, but he pretended not to notice. At the completion
of his prayer, the prophet left his hand pushing down on her face, his fingers
extending down her chin onto her throat. He quietly made one final sound, a
sort of "chewwww." He took his hand off, stood up, and told her, "Go and sit."

There was a moment of silence, the congregation uncertain if the deliverance was complete or not. When the prophet strode confidently for a few more
steps, the still, quiet, and rapt attention of the congregation exploded into
celebratory commotion. The musicians launched into an upbeat song. Frozen
and silent viewers were trans-formed into participants. Over the lively song,
Emmanuel implored the congregation, "if you believe what you saw, clap,"
which was met with raucous clapping, assent to a sense of sight that captures
the materiality of the immaterial. Discontinuous with everything happening
around her, Sandra sat still for a while, gathered herself, and then left.

EMMANUEL'S TRANS-SUBSTANTIATION

Emmanuel has a complicated connection to animality. Emmanuel received
a rather vociferous backlash from the Ghanaian pneumatic community—
where his antics are often pilloried and parodied in internet postings and
memes—when he claimed that he had become a snake himself. He claimed
that he could, and does, become various animals as it suits his ministry. Emmanuel says he utilizes animal spirits to combat animal spirits. He claimed
to possess supernatural powers that allowed him to trans-mogrify into any
animal. I could not help but wonder what Sandra saw when he forced her to
look at him.

His wife endorsed the magnitude of his magical ability to metamorpho-
size, primarily but not limited to trans-mogrification into a snake. Emmanuel
claimed that he once trans-mogrified into a snake while at the same time Jesus
transformed into a lion, and they jointly visited one of his congregants. When
his comments, believed heartily by his followers, were met with some public
derision, he said: "You don't touch the anointed. Even Angels in Heaven do
not have the same powers. Some are more powerful than others. When you
sleep, you sleep deep; but I don't sleep. I lay down and work for the children

of Jesus in the spiritual realm." He remains adamant that most people simply do not understand the enhanced sense of sight and being that his spiritual powers allow. In other words, most people do not have demonologeyes.

Prophet Badoe not only endorsed Emmanuel's claims, but added that he too changed into animals. He was incredulous when I asked about animality, smirked and said, "I can turn into an animal, definitely." He described why a prophet would ever want or need to turn into an animal: if a person is being pursued by a spirit animal then an incredibly effective way to attack that spirit is to submit to the animal kingdom yourself: "If you want to go there you have to also turn into that animal." Here he suggests that in the same way that the spirit is disguised as an animal, the prophet must also work with disguises. In typical Pentecostal parlance, Badoe said, "It is a gift . . . the gift is there, so there is no incantation where you have to cite words." Not to belabor the point, but this commitment to inhabit the spirit world demonstrates a desire to play, create, destruct, and experiment with spirits and demons rather than a desire to banish them. Badoe told me he has turned into a snake, spider, lion, and a dog. These are all familiar animal spirits with whom people claim to have had sexual experiences. He told the story of one time when he turned into a spider. In this story, a woman looking to become pregnant was being pursued by an evil spirit disguised as a giant spider. Badoe recounted, "The spider opened its mouth to swallow her . . . she shouted [and] I quickly turned into a bigger spider and I swallowed the spider."

Long before he acquired this spiritual skill, Badoe said that his encounter with animal spirits had been one of spiritual marriage. Badoe would regularly wake up and realize that he had engaged in sex with a dog spirit. "I slept with dogs!" he proclaimed, "what I would see was a dog. Dog, dog, dog." But one day, he explained, his sexual dreams—or sexual experiences with spirits—became physical. He told me he woke up and realized he was physically fighting the dog. The same dog that had been his sexual partner apparently manifested physically and was only thwarted when Badoe picked up a rock and hurled it at him. Only after the physical manifestation of his canine sex partner had been chased away did Badoe claim to have experienced deliverance.

Others I spoke with were dubious of Emmanuel's claim about changing into animals. Nikoi told me, "That is a false man of God." But Nikoi had never been a fan of Emmanuel and had always implied that his work was that of someone summoning evil powers. Kwofie, who earlier tried to claim Emmanuel as one of his disciples and often spoke admiringly of Emmanuel, said, "No true man of God can turn into a snake." Kwofie, in his previous life as a traditional priest, said that he had been able to turn into five different animals: a snake, crocodile, butterfly, lizard, and a crab. But for him, that ability marked ungodly powers. He writes of a conversation between himself and a demon about the power of trans-mogrification:

> "I can change humans to the forms of animals," the demon replied. "I can change humans into animals or vice versa!" I laughed, and suddenly, he changed me into a snake. I got so excited and wanted to leave the room and go and play in this new body. I looked at the door, but it was locked. I wanted to open it, but Satan told me to just think about it, and it would happen. So I thought about going through the door, and I did! Without realizing that I had the same mind, just a different body, my changed body began to slither on the ground like a snake.

These powers of trans-mogrification, sanctioned or not, manifest in a porous, unstable body.

KWOFIE, ETHEL, AND ROSEMARY

It is not only serpents but also a host of animal spirits that visit humans sexually. Kwofie told me he has seen a variety of animals—snakes, dogs, cows, bulls, lizards, birds—in deliverance, and after the animal spirits manifested, he sent them back to the bottomless pit of hell. For Kwofie, the deliverance of animal spirits is considered something of a specialty, and he proudly told me the stories of the two most obstinate animal spirits he had successfully delivered. The first was a kangaroo, which is notable for its distinctly un-Ghanaian character. This kangaroo was embodied to perfection with the person disguising their limbs to match the short upper limbs of a kangaroo. As the person-as-kangaroo hopped around, it kept gyrating at the waist and loudly proclaiming how pleasurable the sexual experiences with humans had been. The way Kwofie dramatized the pleasure it seemed that the human and kangaroo were still in the throes of sex: "Oh, oh, this is so pleasant. Oh, oh, this is so wonderful. Oh, oh, my love!" What is noteworthy in Kwofie's account is that in these stories, the spirits are very clearly seen to be receiving sexual pleasure as they manifest as animals, which indicates a level of trans-substantiation whereby it is not merely the taking on of fantastic forms but the sharing of substance and pleasure.

In another deliverance session, Kwofie said that he had struggled against a gorilla. It supposedly had a tremendous voice and kept shouting out claims of sexual pleasure: "Oh, my husband, you are so good, don't take anybody else." As Kwofie shared this story I was admittedly uncomfortable. As he re-enacted the scene, bouncing around his office as a gorilla, I could not ignore the connection to the hoary colonial claims that Africans and apes shared libidinous sexual characteristics or were sexually linked.[43] In fact, even the dog of Badoe's dreams and reality could be linked to colonial stereotypes of African religion. Paul Christopher Johnson has noted that black dogs were a standard seventeenth-century European mise-en-scène to demonize West Africans.[44] The trans-ness of spirits, animals and humans, threatened the en-lightenment project, and sexuality in particular was used to define boundar-ies. But I remain convinced that embracing such a stereotype in ritual is not an attempt to reenliven the stereotype but to demonstrate that the very proj-ect that made these animalistic comparisons, colonialism and Eurocentric human exceptionalism, is untenable. It was a distinct moment in fieldwork where as an ethnographer I began doing theoretical flips and turns trying to understand my discomfort but also, and more importantly, the profundity of Pentecostal rituals and experiences that reference a stereotype to express potential liberation.

We have encountered Ethel before at Emmanuel's church, but in a sec-ondary role. Ethel was the friend who invited Morowa, who experienced the violent deliverance—or perhaps more accurately, non-deliverance—from the spirit of lesbianism. During the proceedings, Ethel stood demurely up front, making it transparent that she did not identify with the spirit of lesbianism. But that is not to say that Ethel did not struggle with her own sexual spirits. Sitting outside her house, Ethel confessed to me that she was spiritually mar-ried to a fish. Often in her dreams, she found herself sleeping with a fish. She said, "We have this fish, we call it madfish . . . At times I dream that fish is sleeping with me." She added with a sense of levity, "I've never dreamt that I slept with tilapia. It is madfish. It is always a madfish."

Knowing this, I was unsurprised when during Badoe's weeklong crusade against spiritual sex, Ethel was caught up in the deliverance. When I asked Ethel what she was delivered from, she referred to the madfish, only the mad-fish were multiplying. Her sexual experiences with madfish were not only more constant but also, "At first it was just one fish, but now I'll be playing with many madfish in the boat." The experiences were also becoming more frightening. In her own words, she woke up "with my legs splayed and wet. I can't move my legs. I had to yell Jesus, and only after I yelled, Jesus, could I move my legs." Sometimes people are uninterested in finding out much about the spirits that plague them, but Ethel was curious and asked a lot of questions. She was sure it was a marine spirit, that the fish "in reality stands for marine spirit, Mami Wata, and stuff." She still had not figured out how she contracted the marine spirit, but she believed that the dreams meant she must be married to that spirit.

While his own ability to trans-mogrify into animals is hotly contested and unique among prophets, the idea of animal spirits having sex with humans is not unique to Emmanuel's ministry. It is quite widespread. I am loathe to call my informants friends, it always reads so artificially, but there is no other way to describe my relationship with Rosemary but as one of friendship. I was invited to her wedding, and she was an ever-present guide for me through the world of Ghanaian Pentecostalism. She was a believer and a skeptic, a prophetess, and an academic. But of all the things in this book, if there is one thing she believed fully, it was spiritual marriage to animals. Sex between humans and spirit animals was undeniable to her. A prominent bishop in one of Ghana's foremost Pentecostal churches told me something similar, "That one, I can confirm it does exist because I've been involved in deliverance and I've met believers who have perennial experiences where animal spirits come and sleep with them."

There are many reasons why Rosemary believed so firmly in the insa-tiable sexuality of animal spirits. To begin, there was the story of Cindy, a woman who occupied a prominent place in Rosemary's cosmos. Cindy was caught and accused of witchcraft, though Cindy herself claimed to be a prin-cipality above a witch, "a little closer to Satan." This caused Rosemary to go off on a tangent: "I don't believe demons are only angels cast out of heaven, I am tempted to believe that humans can become his [Satan's] angels." Cindy was a human who had superseded the boundaries of witchcraft and become close to Satan. As Rosemary said, "She couldn't have lied! It was really scary for me. I believe demons and witches have sex; if Satan himself sleeps with them as Cindy said, then it must be true." The logic for Rosemary, a logic that helped her understand her own experiences, follows that if people like Cindy have sex with Satan, then, of course, Satan's minions in the form of demons and witches must have sex with humans.

Spiritual marriage to animals "has something to do with witchcraft," and Cindy and others were evidence that spirits can take many forms. Rosemary stated definitively that

> when you study witchcraft, you realize that most of the people who fly in the night or go in so many forms, you understand they change, some come as male even though they are female, some go as snakes, in fact, there were times when we had the opportunity to interview some witches who were delivered, and some of them said they turn into birds, some said they turn into snakes, some tortoise and all of that.

Expanding on these examples, Rosemary added, "Spirits come in so many forms. One lady used to see her dad, you can be a female, yet you see a female having sex with you or with a female with male genitalia, so many forms." One of those animal forms was an ant. I mentioned that Rosemary was a prophetess. She does not have a church per se but does practice deliverance, and she said she once delivered a woman from a sexual relationship with an ant. Slightly different than those we have been considering, this one blurred the line between animal spirit sex and human sex. This woman would "physically feel a bite in her vagina from an ant, excuse me for saying," Rosemary told me with her own discretionary flourish. After each bite, the woman would become insatiable sexually until she had slept with someone. The number of bites equaled the number of men she would sleep with. Rosemary helped deliver her from this ant spirit who demonstrated that the sexual veil between human and spirit was thin and penetrable.

Rosemary ardently believed in human-cum-spirit-animal sexual experiences not only because she had heard about others' experiences, but also because she herself had long been plagued by a spirit animal. Well aware of the risks of spirit animals, Sandra developed all sorts of rituals to try to fight off the possibility of them sleeping with her. But it did not matter. She recounts, "During my time, I could pray much, I could see so well, you know, but then I was encountering all of that." Here she invokes her enchanted, enhanced demonologeyes—she could see the things happening that are beyond the material body. She could see peoples' problems and prophesy about them and deliver them. But she could not stop from having sexual experiences with animal spirits. This confused her greatly—how could she have such clear deliverance sight and not be able to shake the sexual animal spirits? How could she deliver others and not deliver herself? Every time she encountered a spirit animal sexually, she questioned God, "because we always see that spiritual marriage thing as coming from the devil, so how can . . ." Her sentence just trailed off. She added:

> There would be times when you are fasting, even when you haven't gone out, you haven't sinned . . . because normally we say when you compromise, when you sin, the devil gets the chance to get into you and use you to do all sorts of things. So, in a situation where I personally had asked for forgiveness of sins and was fasting and then I'd been in my room, I had not gone out throughout the day, I had not sinned, I had not thought about anything bad yet I sleep and a spirit animal comes to sleep with me. It was something else to me, it was a question I posed to god.

Amidst her jumble of thoughts, the question is: how could such a faithful Christian and powerful prophetess with deliverance sight be prone to sex with spirit animals? How, and why? When her prayers and pleadings with God failed her, she resorted to more extreme material efforts. She,

> would put my Bible on my private parts trying to prevent that spirit, but still you wake up and the Bible is somewhere and it looks like the devil is not even afraid of the Bible in your pants. And I've encountered other people who put the Bible in their pants and the spirit would still sleep with them. The Bible will still be there but the spirit has slept with them. I remember once I got wet because of that . . . and because I put it there that particular one was a New Testament, those small Gideon's translations, when I put it there, I mean, when I woke up it was wet because the spirit came to sleep with me. I said, "Oh!"

This fantastic image indicates the depth of the anxiety that plagues those visited by these spirits. And yet, despite her desperate efforts, the spirits still visited her, still slept with her, and still left her wet and satisfied.

When I asked Rosemary why spirits use animals, she had an interesting response. At first, she claimed she did not know. If it was only dogs, Rosemary said she would understand. Dogs are carnal and sexually lascivious. She cited Revelation 22:1 and said the "Bible has helped us understand who dogs are." It is unclear how Revelation 22:1 addresses dogs, but she also cited a Ghanaian tradition, saying, "dogs are seen as immoral because they can have sex all the time."[45] To call someone a dog is to imply they are a "fuckboy." Nikoi similarly emphasized that the dog was an obvious choice for the spirits because "their lifestyle is lust-filled." He added,

> Normally if it comes in the form of an animal the spirit is trying to hide its identity because Satan doesn't want to be identified in a particular way because the moment you expose the spirit it won't work and manifest itself any more. If you have sex, let's say you see a dog making love with you in the dream, that's the spirit of lust. Physically we see dogs having sex outside and that is why the person can't control their sexual appetite. You can be stuck in a dog's vagina for a long time.

But spirits manifest in animal forms less obviously lascivious than dogs, and so Rosemary was stumped.

Rosemary hummed and hawed and then finally stumbled upon an answer. "God reveals these things to us. It is God, for me, that causes us to see the spirits [as animals]. God covers them in the form of animals so that there is no confusion." God causes the spirits to take animal forms so that the believer becomes acutely aware that "something happened and it is devilish." This was not the only time I heard this theology espoused. God is in the business of animality and bestiality. God causes humans to see the spirits, to see animals; God gifts demonologeyes: "If you see it in your dream, at least God has given you a clue of what you are dealing with. So, when you see it, it means God is really talking to you because Job 33:15 says God speaks to us in our dreams." Phillip went on to quote part of the verse stating, "For God speaketh in a dream, in a vision of the night, when sound sleep falleth upon men, in slumberings, upon the bed." In many ways, Phillip believes it should be a relief that one receives sexual experiences with spirits because then all that is left is deliverance and counseling. As he says, "So when you see it in a dream, it means about 50 percent of the problem is solved because God reveals to redeem. So, when God reveals something, it means God wants to do something about it." While I am not concerned with theological rightness, what I love about Rosemary's explanation is the way it disorganizes the world and those within it. There is no great chain of being in this universe where God, demons, animals, and humans are so interconnected and so fluid that being itself is unmoored.

Nikoi, in his prayerful assertiveness, yelled, "Any animal that represents sexual immorality perish! I locate the head of that animal and cut it off!" The point of the prayer was that any manifestation of animals is real and must be killed. As if his own prayer had sparked something inside of him, he turned to the assembled mass and transitioned to a mini-sermon on Exodus 22:19.[46] The verse condemns to death anyone who has sexual relations with an animal. The point of the sermon was that these fleeting nocturnal encounters were not merely phantasmagoric. The half-glimpsed, shadowy figures of animals were not illusions but real animals, and sexual relations with these animals meant certain death. In his prayer-sermon Nikoi captured the realness that deliverance ministries ascribed to visions that were only captured by enhanced demonologeyes, realities not legible in colonial constructs of the human or the animal, and a sense-ability that "operates or becomes manifest as an ability in the realities from which this other realm or mode is excluded."[47]

DECOLONIAL DEMONS

I have tried to conclude this book many times in many disparate ways, traipsing far afield and then returning to the thick description of field-work. Having presented these materials to many audiences over the years, I am acutely aware that no conclusion will satisfy all. Sex with spirits and deliverance are messy—from the spilled fluids to theoretical conundrums. And yet, as should be apparent throughout, from my earliest moments in the field I have had an inkling that there is something more to these materials, that there is something profound and revelatory in the sensual and sexual world-ings of Ghanaian Pentecostalism. I am convinced that these embodied erotic experiences and rituals forge something new.

Many have attempted to articulate the wide-ranging possibilities embedded in deliverance and the Pentecostal fascination with the demonic. Some have argued that engagement with diabolic spirits embodies the contradictions of modernity.[1] Meyer, whose work has featured prominently throughout this book, has argued that ambiguous African Pentecostal ideas of evil are fundamental to, among other categories, conversion, individualism, family ties, approaches to African traditional religions, and global politics and economics.[2] Gifford and others argue that diabolic resistance and deception are logical responses to the failure of the prosperity gospel.[3] Lindhart, meanwhile, offers multiple answers for the appeal to diabologies, including their ability to address intra-church tension and as a way to articulate the difficulty of fleeing sin.[4] Each such conclusion is compelling in its own way because these theories are rooted in the reality that for many Pentecostals, nothing is more fundamental to their worldview than the demonic.

Meyer, though, gets closest to my own conclusions when she writes, "By creating room for the expression of the satanic in the context of deliverance, Pentecostalists are allowed to enact otherwise forbidden or muted aspects of themselves."[5] She continues in one of my favorite descriptions of deliverance-dominant Pentecostals: "Though allegedly born again. . . ."[6] The ambivalence multiplies in "though" and "allegedly" but not as a pejorative dismissal or judgment of their salvation. Instead, the ambivalence is deeply related to deliverance practice, which is relatively unconcerned with salvation and instead captivated by that which is "allegedly" disallowed. In the case of *Seductive Spirits*, that disallowed content that is repeatedly revisited is sex. More specifically, sex with demons is recursively performed. Meyer concludes that the demons "enable believers to thematize their problems with modernity."[7] Similarly, I'd like to conclude *Seductive Spirits* with an argument for the decoloniality of the demons in this book. That is to say, in its sensuous eroticism, in the historico-embodied movements, sex with spirits perceives the wound of modernity/coloniality and rejects its concomitant rhetoric of salvation. Instead of salvation, new worlds are found in that which modernity/coloniality defines as evil and demonic.

Cavorting with sexual demons is decolonial in that it unveils the religio-sexual foundation of modernity/coloniality, delinks sexuality from binaries, good and evil, hetero- and homo-, and constructs new sexual worlds. In many ways, this argument is very much in line with Greg Thomas's goals and hopes in *The Sexual Demon of Colonial Power*. Thomas writes,

> The world put in place by colonialists is not the only world that has ever been. It is not even necessarily the only world that is. It is most assuredly not the only world that can be. To contest this world, it is nonetheless necessary to criticize and contextualize it in ways which it could or would never envision . . . The movement from one world order to another, more desirable one must involve a spirited movement of bodies and minds. These movements must move against an order of knowledge that articulates and organizes minds and bodies in a fundamentally colonialist fashion.[8]

The argument I will develop herein is perhaps an overly literal reading of Thomas's claim that decolonization requires "a spirited movement of bodies and minds." More specifically, the movement of bodies in manifestations and performances of demonic sex can be decolonial. In spirit-rich language similar to Thomas's, Walter Mignolo writes, "The hope of the present towards the future is the growing decolonial Spirit of delinking to re-exist (a basic decolonial move), accepting that Eurocentric fictions in all spheres of life, but above all, racial and sexual fictions embedded in the economy (capitalism), politics (the State), epistemology (the university, museums, schools, the church), and authority (the army and the police) manage and control emotions and sensing of the world."[9] Here, like *Seductive Spirits*, Mignolo ties together an idea of spirit, sexual fictions embedded in the church, and the senses. This growing decolonial spirit may need to be demonic, decolonial demons.

At first blush, this may seem like an unlikely conclusion, though there have been many hints along the way. Its unlikeliness is rooted in two realities. The first is that African Pentecostalism has, in many ways, been defined by its close relationship to modernity.[10] Secondly, any such decolonial conclusion depends largely on where one's attention is drawn in the many scenes depicted throughout. In reading the scenes throughout *Seductive Spirits*, perhaps you have been left with the impression that Ghanaian Pentecostalism is singularly shaped by modernity/coloniality. Perhaps it appears that sexually Ghanaian Pentecostalism is merely a facsimile of modern/colonial cisheteropatriarchy, with its male leaders disciplining any sex that does not worship the phallus. It is easy to come to such a conclusion because we have been inculcated by what Marcella Althaus-Reid calls Christianity's obsessive cloning desires, that is to say that there is only one way to be human that must repeatedly be emulated.[11] These obsessive cloning desires are an essential element of modernity/coloniality. If one only focuses on the acts of the pastorate, it would seem cloning desires are also a vital element of Ghanaian Pentecostalism. However, I have and want to continue to read against that pastorate-centric trend. Instead of reading deliverance-dominant Pentecostalism as a way to navigate or come to peace with modernity/coloniality, I want to explore sex with demons as pushing against some of the most central tenets of modernity/coloniality. In order to do so, we must divert our attention beyond the pastorate, beyond the desire for docility, and focus on the sexualities performed so extravagantly in deliverance-dominant Pentecostalism.

To be clear, assuming the modernity/coloniality of deliverance and its demons is not entirely misguided. Demonization, in many forms, indeed is intrinsically modern/colonial and has long been a primary ordering tool of modernity/coloniality. Modernity/coloniality orders the world so that that which does not fit its definition of civilization—racially, religiously, culturally, and sexually—is demonic under and against that which is reified (white cis-heteropatriarchy). To claim that demons are decolonial inherently runs the risk of reengaging or reanimating these meanings. Similarly, writing about extravagant African sexualities runs the risk of melding liberation and domination, possibility and pathology.[12] Nonetheless, exploring the worldings of sexually decolonial demons is worth such a risk because thinking decolonially with demons offers a substantial critique of the universality of modernity/coloniality, the possibility of unmaking modern/colonial orders, and replacing such orders with worlds anew.

Reading sex with demons as decolonial requires dispensing with a variety of assumptions. At different times in the field and in analyzing sexual deliverances, I myself have fallen prey to some of these assumptions. For example, I must admit that, at times, my lines of questioning failed to consider the expansive definition of sex at play in sex with demons and spent too much time looking for penetration rather than hearing the broad descriptions of the erotic. I must admit that I sometimes watched deliverance only looking for that moment of acquiescent docility rather than reveling in the expansive sexual worlds unfolding in front of me. In particular, there are three assumptions that I wish I had dispensed with earlier. In removing these assumptions, there is much to learn from what might be termed subjugated knowledge, which official knowledge represses, disqualifies, and marginalizes. The first assumption to be abolished is treating judgment as fact. For example, anti-queer scripts spewed by a particular prophet are one piece of data. Still, they should not overpower the many other data points that include queer congregants, resistance to deliverance, and how anti-queer animus is often followed up by tarrying in queer possibilities. Similarly, any equating of deliverance with salvation is misguided. Deliverance recursively tarries in that which is disallowed. Salvation is a telos that orders everything in past-present-future, with salvation being the progress that moves believers confidently into that future. Salvation fits the modern/colonial sense of time as forward moving. Deliverance visits and revisits sexual experiences, so that time itself is destabilized, progress is unstable, and conclusions are never final. Finally, we must dispense with the assumption that demons act as reminders or signposts of that which is bad or evil. Demons in Pentecostalism provide so much more possibility than being limited by simple good/bad binaries.

The key to moving beyond these assumptions is rooted in the practice of tarrying. Tarrying flies in the face of teleology. Tarrying, traditionally, in Pentecostalism implies the active bodily work of waiting for, upon, with, and within the spirit of God in community. But tarrying need not be limited to Christianity's undifferentiated and undefined spirit, the Clean Ghost. Tarrying is the act of staying longer than intended, to delay leaving a place, situation, milieu, or experience. In deliverance, Pentecostals tarry with demons. The goal of deliverance is to soak in, elongate, to enhance the encounter with the demonic rather than race to the terminus of that relationship. Meyer asks the appropriate question of such tarrying when she writes, "If people try to get rid of demons, why do they first choose to attend churches in which these demons are rendered real?"[13] Tarrying is an embodied demonstration of desire for supernatural presences. By staying down with their demons, Pentecostals demonstrate a desire to be ordered otherwise than the God(s) or Spirit (singular and holy) of modernity/coloniality. At its core, deliverance-dominant Pentecostalism is about worldlings that tarry amidst that which is disallowed by modernity/coloniality. If instead of capitulating to Pentecostal theological self-descriptions, instead of allowing Pentecostals to say "we visit this often, we tarry with it, but it is bad, trust us," we follow their senses, their bodies, and their practices, then we find that deliverance-dominant Pentecostals actually use hell-spaces and demons to practice ideological rebellions.[14] The ideological rebellions of Ghanaian Pentecostalism's intimacy with the demonic are decolonial, flying in the face of modernity/coloniality. This, then, is my answer to Meyer's question in the context of *Seductive Spirits*: significantly, deliverance Pentecostals reiterate and tarry with the demonic, especially sexually, as a realm of invention whereby alternative ways of being, sensing, and having sex are dreamed, practiced, and performed.

Accordingly, in the words of Althaus-Reid, "It is in this context that we claim the right of demonologies, that is the right to listen to rebellious spirits which have rejected the light for the darkness. The transparency of light which carries with it the clarity of imperial logics and the white axis of its racial supremacy gives a global identity to demons."[15] To perform and have sex with demons is to embrace rebellion in the face of damning imperial logics. It is a refusal of global racial supremacy which demands a sexual order rooted in modern/colonial heteronormativity. This conclusion is an attempt to listen to the rebellious spirits.

MODERN/COLONIAL DEMONIZATION

While demons offer the possibility of fleeing modernity/coloniality, it is essential to understand how demonization has been a fundamental tool of modernity/coloniality in defining Africa. Demonization is different than demon-talk. As Lincoln defines it, demonization is "the rhetorical construction of those from whom one feels radically estranged, not just as different kinds of people, but as outside the pale of the human and the moral: a polemic act of (re-)classification that legitimates subsequent violence against the demonized other."[16] Demonization is an act of signifying. Signifying is a modern/colonial will to power rooted in Enlightenment methods and epistemologies applied to the Other. Such signification, as demonstrated by the preeminent historian of religions Charles Long, "paved the ground for historical evolutionary thinking, racial theories and forms of color symbolism that made the economic and military conquest of various cultures and peoples justifiable and defensible."[17] Signifying then is not simply naming but naming to objectify and other. The signifiers constructed categories, forcefully applying new names onto the signified. I think a case can be made that the most illuminating form of signification is demonization. It is among the most prevalent textures of colonial relations, utilizing a euphemism to objectify and dismiss an entire continent.

Long defines signification as "the verbal art which obscures and obfuscates a discourse without taking responsibility for doing so."[18] Such a definition would appear to eliminate demonization as a form of signifying, for surely to demonize is such an explicit act of othering that it neither obfuscates nor obscures. Demonization in its very definition seems to admit that which it attempts to accomplish. However, demonization does obscure. What is ostensibly a religious designation does not take responsibility for the way in which it paved the way for comprehensive economic and military conquest.

Instead of constructing a genealogical history of demonization, I will mark three manners in which modernity/coloniality has demonized Africa.[19] I rely on loosely connected ideas, practices, and claims to explain the demonization via modernity/coloniality. I do not claim that there is some cause-and-effect unidirectional linear history to be traced here. The expectation of a unidirectional linear history is the very modern/colonial imposition that demonizes in the first place. Hegel, famously and problematically, wrote, "What we properly understand by Africa, is the Unhistorical, Undeveloped Spirit, still involved in the conditions of mere nature, and which had to be presented here only as on the threshold of the World's History."[20] Hegel excludes Africa from the progress of history. And acutely for *Seductive Spirits*, he uses the phrase "Unhistorical, Undeveloped Spirit." While not his intention, Hegel, in using such language, sets up the potency of the demon to speak to modernity/coloniality, which can, at least in Pentecostalism, be considered a spirit that is unhistorical or ahistorical (no concrete or consistent answer to where they came from) and always undeveloped (at least in the sense of their lack of systematization and ever-present creative plasticity). The demon and the African are Other in nearly everything about modernity/coloniality, including history itself. As such, instead of constructing a genealogy, I want to demonstrate how demonization carries with it assumptions, ideas, and principles of modernity/coloniality and how demons might be able to challenge or rebel against modernity/coloniality. I want to outline these modern/colonial inheritances not to dismiss the category of demons. Instead, I want to use these inheritances to point toward a creative capacity in demonology that remembers, revises, and potentially reverses those impositions. Demons, now so entrenched in the African Pentecostal cosmos, may offer a discursive path.

The evidence of demonization relative to Africa is manifest throughout various historical epochs and a myriad of mediums. Herein, I wish to demonstrate three primary ways that modernity/coloniality demonizes Africa: metonymic demonization, possessive demonization, and manichean demonization. To be clear from the outset, these are not concrete categories; they are malleable and bleed into one another in sometimes indistinguishable ways.

The reason for this malleability is rooted in the relentless demonization by modernity/coloniality; in modernity/coloniality, the means of demonization are ever-shifting, sometimes incongruent and contrary, while the function remains static as it suits and aids in domination.

The first manner of demonization is not merely allegorical but metonymic. As O'Donnell has accurately articulated, colonialism is founded on "a theopolitical archive that long equated Africa and blackness with the Satanic."[21] African identity was associated with the devil, and demonic rituals were cited to justify oppression, conversion, and exploitation. For example, David Brakke has done extensive work demonstrating the ways in which Ethiopians were demonized and demons Ethiopianized.[22] Two elements of Brakke's work are relevant to this conclusion. The first is that the demon's blackness was considered a demonstrable and unmistakable sign of evil.[23] To paraphrase a quote from Abdul JanMohamed, once black skin is categorized as demonic, black individuals become interchangeable units of demons.[24] Secondly, Greco-Roman culture associated black Ethiopian bodies with hypersexuality, and accordingly, black demons inherited the stereotype that equated blackness with eroticism and hypersexuality.[25]

Two examples that demonstrate the association of blackness with evil and, in particular, the evil of hypersexuality are found in *The Life of Antony* and Didymus the Blind. The black demon in *The Life of Antony* (ca. 357, the earliest monastic citation of such a demon) is sexual. The black demon is the apex of sexual temptation, "fornication's lover" or "the spirit of fornication," whose titillations foiled many but not Antony.[26] In another example, Didymus the Blind eroticizes salvation setting Ethiopians as macrophallic children of the devil, black from sin and ignorance, and desperately in need of salvation.[27] Salvation, or being "wounded by the choice shaft," divinely discards the Ethiopians demonic and black traits.[28] Blackness is the fleshy embodiment, against the Spirit, of devilish or demonically disordered sexuality.

These types of stereotypes persist in modernity/coloniality. Europeans attempted to concretize the location of demons in Africa by intimately connecting the demonic with blackness and sometimes implanting demons "in the skin-color of Africans themselves."[29] Greg Thomas notes, "Positing scientific reason as the gift of classical Greece to modern Europe has entailed conceptualizing Black people, in particular, as an undisciplined mass of sexual savages."[30] In modernity/coloniality, sexual shame and dehumanization de-monize Africa. There is a kind of symbiotic metonym in which sexual savagery is evil, a sensory nature is evil, and Africa is the heart of darkness or hell.[31]

Any list of signifying via demonization in Africa must also include a dis-cussion of spirit possession, for this is what demons are imagined as doing throughout the continent, whether possessing land or human bodies. As Paul Christopher Johnson has eloquently articulated, "The category 'spirit posses-sion' is native to Europe and its colonial appendages," rooted in early modern demonology.[32] The transfer and translation of European demon possession to spirit possession phenomena encountered on faraway shores was a com-plex operation of colonial semiotics.[33] Possession, a "proto-anthropological comparative class," was "most eagerly applied" to Africans and African reli-gious practices at the same time it was decreasingly applied to Europeans.[34] In particular, modern/colonial Christianity deemed the religious Other as evil. The pervasiveness of demons was an import of modernity/coloniality. Any attempt to locate the devil in traditional religions is an imperial imposi-tion distorting traditional religions. Possession, then, stands as an important marker of comparison and Euro-American self-representations. The differen-tiation was purposeful, marking African bodies as "unfree, nonautonomous, irrational, even possibly dangerous" in comparison to the free, autonomous, rational European body.[35] This purposefully marked Africans as demonic, as incorrectly or incompletely human individuals over and against the proper personhood of the Euro-American, which was deemed rational and auton-omous. Possession was a colonial signification of the opaque, irrational, and evil Other. These proto-anthropological descriptions usually marked total alterity. Demons were part of the racist enlightenment apparatus as other—irrational, unnatural, and aesthetically abominable. The figure of the demon was the marker of the Other, par excellence.[36] Often this was coded as black; demonic blackness was possession. The lens through which possession as a pillar of modernity/coloniality was viewed was Christianity, marking Africa and Africans as possessed of demons.[37] The figure of the demon emerged from its native European Christianity and throughout the globe via colonial-ism. Signifying Africans as possessed or demonic is not simply a game of semiotics; it is a pernicious colonial effort to create the conditions to own or occupy African bodies and African territory.[38]

It is important that while outlining the demonic horrors of modernity/coloniality, we never lose sight that such demonization holds within it the seeds of its own demise. Thomas uses the trope of possession to challenge modernity/coloniality, for possession requires attention to the mental, bodily, and spiritual in a way that modernity/coloniality simply cannot with its mind-body-spirit schisms. Thomas argues that rethinking possession as embodying mind-body-spirit simultaneously erases "the erotic schemes of empire" and offers Africa, where possession is meaningful, revolutionary potential.[39]

Another way of thinking about the otherness of demonization is through the manicheanism of modernity/coloniality, everything is compartmentalized and delineated as good or evil. Fanon says it directly: "The colonial world is a Manichean world."[40] In this manichean structure, Africa is evil. Fanon says this most clearly when he writes that colonialism/modernity sees "Africa as a literal repository of evil."[41] Africans are "a sort of quintessence of evil," "the depository of maleficent powers," or more pointedly, "absolute evil."[42] Further, Fanon writes, "This world divided into compartments, this world cut in two is inhabited by two different species."[43] Another way of stating this: in the colonial/modern worldview, Africa is demonized, another species. In the modern/colonial manichean view, one species is praiseworthy and one is vile; one is human and one is not.

Modern/colonial manicheanism has many ways of painting the African as evil. JanMohamed states, "In fact, the colonial mentality is dominated by a Manichean allegory of white and black, good and evil, salvation and damnation, civilization and savagery, superiority and inferiority, intelligence and emotion, self and other, subject and object."[44] All of these manichean splits are interchangeable ways of stating that Africa and Africans are evil. Jan-Mohamed notes this in the various modern/colonial stereotypes and tropes of Africans as children, savages, and uncivilized. Each trope feeds into an archetype of Africans as "demonic parodies of civilized whites."[45] A whole signifying system is reduced to the manichean split between good and evil, demon and human, which is the underlying logic of modernity/coloniality.

JanMohamed calls the purchase of this manichean order not "a logic of sexuality and power but an allegorical coding or a mytho-logic of sexuality, race, and power."[46] Sexuality is a fundamental pillar of modern/colonial demonization. The obsessive cloning desires of modernity/coloniality in the

form of cisheteropatriarchal monotheism demanded that the colonized resemble the universal Man. Such resemblance, and Homi Bhabha has exqui-
sitely demonstrated that any attempt of the colonized to clone oneself is only
ever an incomplete resemblance, is rooted in the cloning of a cisheteropatriarchal sexuality, a dismissal of sensory natures, and demonization of all that
falls outside the human always and only rooted in modernity/coloniality.[47]

Modernity/coloniality is a "sexually hegemonic theological project" that
attenuates erotic diversity.[48] As Keguro Macharia notes, "Managing intimate
life was central to colonialism."[49] This was especially true of missionization,
which was "more sexual than Christian."[50] Christianity impels modernity/
coloniality by imbuing cisheteropatriarchal sexuality with sacredness, evan-
gelizing Man, and demanding heterosexual people and cultures. Redemption
or salvation, always sexual, then is the disruption of all sexualities that do
not fit the universal cisheteropatriarchial model of Man and the cloning of
a predefined heterosexual order. The relentlessness of modernity/coloniality
simply demonized any sexuality contrary to an assumed natural and proper
order of men desiring women and women desiring men.[51] Thomas has called
cisheteropatriarchy empire's "normative genealogy of desire, indeed a colonial telos for all individuals and human beings."[52] Unsurprisingly, the racialized sexuality of modernity/coloniality is manichean, and anything that
falls outside the colonial telos is evil.[53] Accordingly, modernity/coloniality sets
Africa as evil, illicit, and disordered in its "unchecked libidinal desires."[54] Jack
Halberstam writes of how in the eighteenth and nineteenth centuries, the
colonial missionary ethos set "savage sexualities . . . as evidence of backsliding into heathendom."[55] Backsliding assumes a world ordered by the colonial
telos of cisheteropatriarchy. Irrational sexual savages are distinguished from
rational humans, and their sexual savagery is used as evidence that Africans
are evil and need all that modernity/coloniality offers in its rather limited
cisheteropatriarchal order.

Sexuality is a central component of definitions of the demonic, which
is what makes the decolonial possibilities of sex with spirits so compelling.
Thomas writes, "The very notion of Western civilization is therefore founded
on a primary opposition between white and non-white persons that is graphically sexualized."[56] This, though, gives power to the sexual worldings of Pentecostalism, which tarry in all sorts of sexualities not imagined by modernity/

coloniality. Despite being graphically sexualized, modernity/coloniality actually revolves around limited sexual worlds. Modernity/coloniality cannot comprehend the expansive and extravagant sexual worldings of demonic sexualities. To embrace such an "evil" by the order of modernity/coloniality produces entirely different outcomes.

Others have noted that the manicheanism of modernity/coloniality provides the demonic with "a special mystical power to the underdog."[57] By invoking the devil and a manichean split, modernity/coloniality invested the demonic with power. If analysis of African Pentecostal demonology begins with the demonization of Africans in modernity/coloniality, it becomes evident that demons hold latent decolonial power and possibility. That is to say that demons countersignify.[58] In Long's study of colonial signifying he illuminates that the arbitrariness of signifying lends itself to the religious creativity of the oppressed as resistance; signification is "both a potent form of oppression and a potent form of resistance to oppression."[59] To be signified does not eliminate recourse, but recourse often occurs via religiously inflected worldmaking which demonstrates the fiction (or lie) of signification. The rupture in signification reveals alternative possibilities. Countersignification is the creative force of signified persons to play with the very signs of their being signified in such a manner that imagines a world freed of the modern/colonial order. In so doing, modernity/coloniality is subverted and resisted. For Long this was most obvious in Cargo Cults which, in the face of cultural contact and hegemony, created new languages and sacred forms to oppose Westernization.[60] But countersignification can and does happen around sexualities. For example, in a line that perfectly captures countersignification, Lamonda Horton-Stallings writes that black sexualities, or funky erotixx, reject "the Western will to truth, or the quest to produce a truth about sexuality, and underscores such truth as a con and a joke."[61] But countersignification is not simply about revealing the lie, but also creating worlds anew.

Analysis of African Pentecostal demonology must begin with the possibility of countersignification. It is impossible to watch the practical demonology of sexual deliverances and not acknowledge its ability to respond to the inheritances of demonization from modernity/coloniality. In so doing, analysis of demons shifts. Absent the relevant context of being signified through modernity/coloniality, the demons of deliverance sexuality appear to be about personal behavioral transformations. That is to say, deliverance seems to be discipline for unruly sexualities. Demons, though, are not primarily about such transformation; otherwise, more time would be spent tarrying in docility. And this is why the inheritances of modernity/coloniality are vital to interpreting the demons with whom Ghanaian Pentecostals tarry. Taking the demonization via modernity/coloniality into account moves the demonic toward the crucial task of transforming orders of knowledge, being, and senses. My approach herein understands demonology as coding a new collective identity beyond modernity/coloniality, as embracing a countersignifying identity as "les damnes de la terre" not in the sense of inferiority but unfolding alternative ways of being primarily through alternative sexualities.

Demons, especially sexual demons, exceed the manner in which they are pillars of modernity/coloniality. It is not enough to historicize the demonizing of sexuality in the colonial enterprise. The complex of Pentecostal sexual demons offers tools to imagine a way beyond modernity/coloniality. The rigidity of modern/colonial manicheanism establishes clear and powerful boundaries. But as O'Donnell, relying on Derrida, demonstrates, such rigid public truths are susceptible to contravention and inherently rely on the possibility of contravention. O'Donnell writes, "Demons here come to operate deconstructively, operating within and against sovereign power, destabilizing the very structures that require them for consolidation."[62] Modernity/coloniality relied on demonization, but demons can and do transcend demonization.

To embrace a demonic model is not simply oppositional resistance to demonization. Demonization signifies Man versus Other or Demon. Versus is a comparative technique of modernity/coloniality that assumes an identifiable hierarchy in such comparison. Demonology or the demonic model is about creating something new, something unimaginable in the order of modernity/coloniality, not simply the opposite. Sex with spirits, in the words of Marcella Althaus-Reid, is the "beginning of a rupture with that Colonial Theology, which is at the same time to mark the origins of something new."[63] A rupture is not strictly, simply, or exclusively oppositional in its refusal of the world modernity/coloniality has put in place. A rupture leads to new ways of being, not a way of being relative to or marginal to the classifications of modernity/coloniality.[64] Sex with demons is decolonial, but that decoloniality is not simply reactionary in an attempt to replace the demonization of modernity/coloniality but offers new ways of being for those onto whom demonization was imposed. Disruption of modernity/coloniality happens by offering radical alternatives.

Now to be clear, Ghanaian Pentecostals have responded to modernity/coloniality in a variety of ways. One path was mapped out by Mensa Otabil of the International Central Gospel Church.[65] Otabil, compared to most Ghanaian Pentecostal leaders, is wary of an overemphasis on the demonic and instead writes of total African liberation from the ravages of colonialism through a rejection of myths of inferiority.[66] In his book *Beyond the Rivers of Ethiopia*, Otabil writes that reclaiming the truth of Africans being made in God's image can combat colonialism's stereotyping.[67] There are two important strands to this argument. The first is a rejection of the demonization of all things African by modernity/coloniality.[68] The second is to reject the obsessive cloning desires of missionary Christianity which imposed a Christianity "so much clothed with European cultural norms that it became difficult to separate the wheat from the chaff."[69] The demonic, for Otabil, is the message from modernity/coloniality through Christianity that Africans are inferior and the West superior, that Africans are demonic and the West is human. He writes, "You have to ask yourself why is it although the black people are supposed to be weak everyone attacks them. They are supposed to be weak, poor and not have anything but it seems that everything is being done to suppress them. Both on the home continent and away there is a demonic attack from hell to stop Africans from executing their spiritual office."[70] Otabil's argument resignifies demonization. It articulates modernity/coloniality as "a demonic attack from hell." The solution is Africans reclaiming their rightful spiritual and material mantle. And while Otabil's argument—and, in fact, his relatively muted engagement with demons overall—is very different from the argument herein, it is at least evidence that the decolonial possibilities of Pentecostalism are front and center for Ghanaian Pentecostals.

The weakness of Otabil's efforts is rooted in the difference between resignifying and countersignifying. Resignifying challenges the original significations but does so rooted in the order and language of the original signification. Resignifying provides a new meaning to something. In other words, resignification may alter the content of the original act of signification—in this case, the demonized shifts from African traditions to colonialism—but it fails to challenge the language, structure, style or the order of signifying. While

Otabil signifies upon signifying, demonstrating the arbitrariness of the original signification, he continues to use the language of demonization. Otabil's resignifying is an act of recovery and does little to imagine worlds otherwise. Countersignifying, alternatively, does not traffic in demonization but plays with demons to "create a new form of humanity."[71] Resignifying simply does not create new worlds the way that countersignifying does.

A. Christian van Gorder, who has analyzed the persistence of Otabil's decolonial work, writes that "most Pentecostals in Africa, however are far more interested in navigating through the spiritual realms of demons, witches, and angels that float freely though this world than deal with issues of social justice."[72] This kind of critique assumes that the world of demons is radically detached from political hopes of transformation. While I obviously disagree, it is necessary to note that there are significant critiques of religion's and ritual's ability to respond to modernity/coloniality. Specifically, since Fanon has been invoked above, Fanon dismisses the potential of the "outlandish phantoms" of myth and the "muscular orgy" of ritual to fight modernity/coloniality.[73] Worse, he thinks that myth and ritual have acted as a distraction from the real decolonial work required.[74] Fanon writes specifically of possession and exorcism that they fulfill "a primordial function in the organism of the colonial world."[75] That function is placation and alienation; possession and exorcism act as an emotional and physical release placating the aggressivity, frustration, and impatience with colonialism and alienating the colonized from the true source of frustration and impatience. He writes, "We no longer really need to fight against them since what counts is the frightening enemy created by myths. We perceive that all is settled by a permanent confrontation on the phantasmic plane."[76] Fanon also writes, "In most cases, the black man cannot take advantage of this descent into a veritable hell."[77] But *Seductive Spirits* makes the case that taking advantage of this descent is exactly what Pentecostals do when they tarry sexually with the demonic—they countersignify.

Obviously, I think the phantasmic plane might offer more than Fanon or van Gorder allows because of its plasticity in countersignifying. As Abdul JanMohamed writes, "The transference of political reactions to religious activity is common."[78] Specifically, many before me have argued for the political potential of spirit possession, or countersignifying in their own terms, in the colonial context. Perhaps most powerfully, Paul Stoller demonstrated that the Hauka enacted mimetic characters of white colonial agents within their spirit possession rituals.[79] The tragicomedic mimesis evoked colonial history but also demonstrated postcolonial possibility and power. Raquel Romberg has referred to this as "ritual piracy," in which symbols of power are used in transgressive and power-shifting ways.[80] The key for Stoller and Romberg is that such acts are not merely mimetic in the sense of reenacting modern/colonial power, but they transgress such orders and suggest new futures.

For Jean and John Comaroff, "the ongoing re-evaluation of signs" is an essential element of African religious experimentation and creativity.[81] Religious signs and rituals may tap into assumptions of universality (such as the universality of modern/colonial demonization) in order to empower and shape particular realities. As Jean Comaroff writes, the utility of religion stretches "far beyond the domain of ritual itself, penetrating acutely into the experiential fabric of everyday life."[82] Often this has been accomplished through using and reappropriating the Christianity of the colonizers, be it through symbols, rituals, or biblical metaphors.[83] Comaroff calls it "wrest(ing) the message from the messenger."[84] Christianity provides a rich—and coded—ability to challenge the hegemony of modernity/coloniality.[85]

As previously noted, Meyer's work on Christianity among the Ewe persuasively demonstrates that among the long list of possible countersignifying symbols and rituals, "images of the Devil and demons are means by which to address the attractive and destructive aspects of Ewe's encounter with global economics, politics and culture."[86] The demonic can be recycled and rethought. In another context, Jared Sexton uses Lucifer "to think about supporting and sustaining forms of life independent of the trappings of sovereign power."[87] Similarly, O'Donnell argues that demons have "a deconstructive potential, one that works to undermine the structures of demonization that name them such."[88] None of this is an argument that the demonic is only decolonial, but that among the many things demons can be is counterhegemonic.

One of the primary reasons my interpretation of demons as doing decolonial work is functional is that, as Taussig proposes, rationality as an explanative order is central to colonial terror.[89] As such, rationality does not hold the same promise of creating new worlds, worlds anew from the one modernity/coloniality demands. Taussig writes, "If terror thrives on the production of epistemic murk and metamorphosis, it nevertheless requires the hermeneutic violence that creates feeble fictions in the guise of realism, objectivity, and the like, flattening contradiction and systematizing chaos."[90] So while there is an inherent risk in recoding and recycling the demonic—the risk is that of the replaying of racialized tropes of hypersexuality, evil, primitivism—there is a far greater risk in simply acceding to the modern/colonial definition of rationality which will never allow for the flourishing of Africa, Africans, or African sexuality. The interplay between the signified demonizations of domination and the countersignifying decolonial demons demonstrates the falsity of modern/colonial universality and its enduring power.

DECOLONIAL DEMONS

Sex with demons, then, imagines alternative sexualities in a language not translatable into "imperial theological language."[91] My goal here is not to arbitrate the viability of decolonial demons but to demonstrate their opposition to modernity/coloniality. While not expressly claimed by my interlocutors, this opposition is found compellingly in their deliverance rituals, sexual experiences, and narratives about demons.

I loathe to put too specific parameters around these new sexual worldings for two primary reasons. The first is that this book's rituals, sexual experiences, and narratives about demons tell a compelling story that need not be recast. The creativity and boundlessness of the scenes shared far outpace my limited ability to write about them. Secondly, the Pentecostal sexual worldings herein are always prone to more creativity, and to concretize them in the moment of this ethnographic encounter would be to miss out on the perpetual unfolding of worlds. And so, without specifically naming this new sexual world with categories and stipulations, I want to outline the variety of characteristics that make these new worlds powerful.

Sex with demons is extravagant. I borrow the word extravagant from Jack Halberstam, who himself borrows it from Peter Coviello, as a term that describes a creative ambivalence or libidinal illegibility or "the extravagances that flourish in the space of a not-yet-congealed sexual specificity."[92] None of my interlocutors viewed sex with demons as an identity. Similarly, no one really viewed sex with demons in binaries, even when publicly it was performed as "gayism or lesbianism." Instead, they merely described it in terms of excess. I read that excess as reaching beyond the human of modernity/coloniality which demands libidinal legibility. Instead, sex with demons is purposefully illegible, difficult to even describe, and impossible to completely differentiate the boundaries between the demonic and the human. Sex with demons, suspicious of any notion of stability, is extravagant. Or, sex with demons might fit into what Timothy Morton calls "unfathomable intimacies." That is to say that in sex with demons, pleasure is "not heteronormative, not genital, not geared to ideologies about where the body stops and starts."[93] Instead, freed of such modern/colonial constructs, sex with demons is capacious in every sense from who is involved to how it happens to what even constitutes a body.

Sex with demons is unproductive. As emphasized in pneumoeroticism and evidenced throughout the various scenes, these sexual relationships run contrary to the assumption that Pentecostals are obsessed with reproduction. This is not to completely disavow reproduction as a primary concern for many Pentecostals but to demonstrate that they imagine worldings entirely separate from the need for reproduction in cisheteropatriarchy. Because of the modern/colonial context we are reconsidering these worldings within, to eschew reproduction via sensuous relationships with the demonic is inherently dissident.

There is rooted in the choices of these sexual worldings—the gender-bending, the instability, the nonhuman actors—a disavowal of heteronormativity and its ordering of the (re)productive human. In their creativity, Pentecostals seem to agree with Althaus-Reid that "heterosexuality is ubiquitous and unremarkable."[94] Indeed, the productivity and reproductivity inherent in heterosexuality is unremarkable, monotonous, and unimaginative. Sex with demons is fantastic, ever-changing, and creative. Indeed, the regulatory ideal of sex with demons appears to be creativity and pleasure rather than reproduction. Creativity here should be defined by its refusal to be bound by productivity. In their search for pleasure, remember that almost all of my interlocutors noted the intense pleasure in sex with demons exceeding any human-cum-human relations. In prioritizing creativity and pleasure, binaries such as woman/man or homosexual/heterosexual, or perhaps even human/divine fall away, and we are left with nearly limitless sexual possibilities rather than orientations. Orientations make even less sense when considering how the demons themselves are capable of dramatic instantaneous changes from masturbation to animality to an old woman with a penis. If one can say anything about the scenes that have been retold herein, they are not unremarkable.

Sex with demons is not hierarchically ordered. Sex, like everything in modernity/coloniality, is hierarchical. Those hierarchies are built around categories like race, gender, or sexual orientation. For example, we've already explored how the "animacy hierarchy" defines human life over and against the animal, flowing from white, able-bodied humans down through animals to inanimate objects. But sex with demons refuses hierarchies largely by emphasizing fluidity rather than stable categories. Race, for example, is malleable with Mami Wata as a prime example. Occasionally Mami Wata is depicted as fair and white, Indian, or black. Gender shifts are normal with pronouns failing my interlocutors in capturing who they were sleeping with. Orientations are meaningless due to sex not being a strictly or exclusively human activity. This new thing is not beholden to the racialized cisheteropatriarchal order of modernity/coloniality. Instead, its vantage point emphasizes the expansive possibilities of being.

Perhaps the most obvious place where hierarchy is dismembered is in the relationality between demon and human. It is a complex relationality. Instead of defining sexuality by ideas of agency and sovereign subjects with bounded bodies, sexuality is tenuous, risky, and boundless. Sex is anything but a coherent act between bounded entities. Accordingly, the entities involved—humans and demons—are open-ended concatenations, interrelated life forms, or intimate co-presences.

Sex with demons is entropic. It demands that disorder, randomness, spontaneity, and uncertainty be embraced, not merely tolerated, and certainly not ordered by the impulses of modernity/coloniality. Crawley writes, "Disorder is undoneness."[95] He adds that Blackpentecostalism is primarily about the embrace of this undoneness not as a singular act but as a mode of being, something to be sustained. Undoneness as a mode of being aptly describes sex with demons, which should not be confused with a singular act. Instead, every story of sex with demons is about how life changes, expectations change, the very ways of walking and moving through this world change. This makes demons decolonial in the sense that decoloniality is "a program of complete disorder."[96] The world order only changes via this disorder, "where the darker side of human nature could be played out."[97] In embracing such disorder, sex with demons moves without expectation. Given its emphasis on undoneness, sex with demons allows life, knowledge, and history to unfold differently than modernity/coloniality.

In *Demonic Grounds*, Katherine McKittrick extends this argument for the disorderly by noting that the fields of mathematics, physics, and computer science use the term *demonic* to connote "a working system that cannot have a determined or knowable outcome."[98] The demonic is nonlinear and non-teleological. The future is unknown. McKittrick writes, "With this in mind, the demonic invites a slightly different conceptual pathway—while retaining its supernatural etymology—and acts to identify a system (social, geographic, technological) that can only unfold and produce an outcome if uncertainty, or (dis)organization, or something supernaturally demonic, is integral to the methodology."[99] Sex with demons is just such a conceptual pathway that does not seek resolution but revels in uncertainty, recursivity, and infinite permutations and combinations.

Sex with demons is not salvific. To be clear, demonic entropy flies in the face of salvation. That should be obvious in its disavowal of teleology. Sex with demons is pleasurable and perilous, one thing and then, in an instant, something else, something unexpected. It should also be obvious that sex with demons is not salvific in its embrace of excess, its refusal of hierarchies, and its unproductive nature. But perhaps most obvious of all, it is not salvific because sex with demons is cavorting with the very symbol of anti-salvation. And this is not some recovery project by which demons are used as a means to salvation; it is the embrace of the most baseless, monstrous elements of anti-salvation. By refusing the salvific, by embracing the monstrous and the demonic, sex with demons refuses the orders of modernity/coloniality.

Sex with demons is sensuous. To have sex with demons is to experiment with the senses, with sensorial overload, and with the body's capacity to feel. It is a sensuous experiment in living free of modernity/coloniality. Instead of seeking freedom in the linguistic or the rational, sex with demons reorders the sensorium, finds power in excessive sensuality, and demands multiple ways of being be taken seriously. The Pentecostal sensorium refuses the limitations of the five senses, demanding new ways to perceive the world(s). The world constructed through sex with demons is felt in ways imperceptible to the philosophy of the five senses. *Seductive Spirits* has attempted to articulate some of those senses, but they continue to exceed and escape categorization. Touch reaches beyond the immanent, eyes see things the untrained eye has no hope of noticing, voices are heard that are from beings visiting and melding with the human bodies from which they emanate. The (s)expanded and (s)expanding sensorium is, in a word, decolonial.

In this conclusion, I have sought to illuminate the potential of sex with demons to create new ways of being. In so doing, I offer this conclusion in the service of redirecting sex with demons into more innovative and subtle examinations of the decolonial possibilities of religion. The creativity and recursivity that Pentecostals demonstrate through sex with demons is always unfinished, always one story or one experience away from further transformation. As Greg Thomas has written, "The sexual logic of colonialism has proved most difficult to shake. Neither the colonizer, for certain, nor the colonized has crafted a satisfactory opposition to this erotics of racism and empire."[100] For Thomas, exorcism is the solution to "the demonic apparatus of colonialism, and its delineation of racial boundaries, disciplining of various sexual expressions, and diminishment of religious expressions."[101] Perhaps, though, as this conclusion contends, an exorcism of sorts is already happening in the ritual of deliverance, not at the moment of priestly or prophetic scripts and docility, not in the casting out, but in the intimate embrace of creative sexual worldings and performances that occur in the ritual.

Introduction

1. Due to the sensitivity of my research I will use pseudonyms throughout this book with the exception of citations from other scholars about churches peripheral to this study. Nobody has written extensively about the figures central to this book.

2. Birgit Meyer, *Translating the Devil: Religion and Modernity among the Ewe in Ghana* (Trenton: Africa World Press, 1999), xvi.

3. Paul Gifford, *African Christianity: Its Public Role* (London: Hurst and Co., 1998), 108.

4. The expedient wrapping of bodies is a move intended for modesty. Female (and only female) deliverees have their legs wrapped in cloth during deliverance to protect "their modesty."

5. Two notes are relevant here. First, masturbation is the focus of chapter 3. More importantly, it is worth acknowledging the slippage that occurs throughout *Seductive Spirits* between the terms *spirit* and *demon*. The slippage is not in error but mirrors the capacious Pentecostal umbrella category of otherworldly evil beings. In their religious lives, Pentecostal Ghanaians regularly encounter evil manifestations of an expansive cosmos ruled by Satan but represented on earth by demons, witchcraft, sorcery, magic, ancestors, and traditional deities. The Pentecostals throughout this book regularly shift between spirits and demons as if they are synonymous, and accordingly, *Seductive Spirits* also treats them as synonymous.

6. Here, again, we encounter some slippage between the terms *slain* and *removed*. The two terms indicate radically different outcomes for the offending demons, death or departure elsewhere. The Pentecostals in this text were cre-

ative, not consistent. And so, sometimes there seemed to be a performance of the demon's death, and sometimes it was discussed as if it flew off elsewhere. But this divergence is not altogether important. It will quickly become apparent that the central interest of deliverance-dominant Pentecostals is not what happens after someone is dispossessed but instead an obsession with the creative possibilities while the demon abides.

7. The extemporaneity of Pentecostal deliverance stands in sharp contrast with exorcisms of official Catholicism, which has very clearly delineated processes and procedures.

8. Cf. Jon Bialecki, "Quiet Deliverances," in *Practicing the Faith: The Ritual Life of Pentecostal-Charismatic Christians,* ed. Martin Lindhardt (New York: Berghahn Books, 2011), 247–276.

9. Pastors commonly inveigh against such leggings—dismissing them as a hybrid of Western (they only make sense in the cold) and demonic (sexually revealing) influences.

10. The virus was HIV. All of the prophets in this book claim to cure people of HIV. Deliverance is considered a way to immediately heal HIV. The prophets always promise discretion as they discuss somebody's HIV diagnosis in front of small and large crowds, but everyone knows what the "virus" is.

11. Stephen Hunt, "Managing the Demonic: Some Aspects of the Neo-Pentecostal Deliverance Ministry," *Journal of Contemporary Religion* 13.2 (1998): 223.

12. Hunt, "Managing the Demonic." 222.

13. Thomas Csordas, *The Sacred Self: A Cultural Phenomenology of Charismatic Healing* (Berkley: University of California Press, 1997), 32.

14. Sextify / seksˈtəˌfī/ verb: to give sexual testimony. See Monique Moultrie, *Passionate and Pious: Religious Media and Black Women's Sexuality* (Durham, NC: Duke University Press, 2017), 27.

15. Walter Stephens, *Demon Lovers: Witchcraft, Sex and the Crisis of Belief* (Chicago: University of Chicago Press, 2001). Cf. Armando Maggi, *Satan's Rhetoric: A Study of Renaissance Demonology* (Chicago: University of Chicago Press, 2001); Armando Maggi, *In the Company of Demons: Unnatural Beings, Love, and Identity in the Italian Renaissance* (Chicago: University of Chicago Press, 2006); Ioan P. Couliano, *Eros and Magic in the Renaissance* (Chicago: University of Chicago, 1987).

16. L. H. Stallings, *Funk the Erotic: Transaesthetics and Black Sexual Cultures* (Urbana: University of Illinois Press, 2016), 4.

17. Jessica Moberg, "Maintaining Sexual Purity: Ritualized, Embodied and Spatial Strategies among Neo-Charismatics in Stockholm," in *Annual Review of the Sociology of Religion: Volume 8 Pentecostals and the Body,* ed. Michael Wilkinson and Peter Althouse (Leiden: Brill, 2017), 240. Another example of a text that tends

NOTES TO THE INTRODUCTION

to take formal Pentecostal discourses at face value is Chammah J. Kaunda, *Genders, Sexualities, and Spiritualities in African Pentecostalism: "Your Body is a Temple of the Holy Spirit"* (New York: Palgrave Macmillan, 2020).

18. Nimi Wariboko, *Nigerian Pentecostalism* (Rochester, NY: University of Rochester Press, 2014), 115.

19. It is noteworthy that there is a growing literature that explores sexuality in West Africa, but it tends to focus on the figure of the prophet or pastor. See: Abimbola Adunni Adelakun, *Powerful Devices: Prayer and the Political Praxis of Spiritual Warfare* (New Brunswick, NJ: Rutgers University Press, 2023) and Ebenezer Obadare, *Pastoral Power, Clerical State: Pentecostalism, Gender, and Sexuality in Nigeria* (Notre Dame, IN: University of Notre Dame Press, 2022).

20. Wariboko, *Nigerian Pentecostalism*, 81.

21. James K. A. Smith, *Thinking in Tongues: Pentecostal Contributions to Christian Philosophy* (Grand Rapids, MI: William B. Eerdmans, 2010), xxi.

22. Smith, *Thinking in Tongues*, xviii.

23. Ashon Crawley, *Blackpentecostal Breath: The Aesthetics of Possibility* (Durham, NC: Duke University Press, 2016), 4.

24. Crawley, *Blackpentecostal Breath*, 86, 176.

25. Crawley, 2.

26. Crawley, 2–3.

27. Crawley, 26.

28. For example see: Bruce Lincoln, *Gods and Demons, Priests and Scholars: Critical Explorations in the History of Religions* (Chicago: University of Chicago Press, 2012); David Gordon White, *Daemons Are Forever: Contacts and Exchanges in the Eurasian Pandemonium* (Chicago: University of Chicago Press, 2021); S. Jonathon O'Donnell, *Passing Orders: Demonology and Sovereignty in American Spiritual Warfare* (New York: Fordham University Press, 2021). Also note the 2022 Conference at Trinity College Dublin entitled "Demons: God and Bad."

29. Lincoln, *Gods and Demons*, 31.

30. Lincoln, 42.

31. Gordon White, *Daemons Are Forever*, 1.

32. The 2010 Census stated that Ghana was 71.2 percent Christian. Approximately 28.3 percent of the total population was Pentecostal. In greater Accra, Pentecostals represent 44 percent of the population.

33. Opoku Onyinah, *Pentecostal Exorcism: Witchcraft and Demonology in Ghana* (Deo, 2012), 139. While West African Pentecostal practices may emphasize deliverance more than other locales, Ghanaian and Nigerian ministries are trendsetters for Pentecostal practice. Not only do the practices from West Africa get performed in diaspora, but they influence Pentecostal performance globally. While writing much of this book in Texas, I could easily find practitioners of each

of the deliverance practices in this book within a short drive of my house.

34. Onyinah, *Pentecostal Exorcism*, 2.

35. Birgit Meyer, "'Delivered from the Powers of Darkness': Confessions of Satanic Riches in Christian Ghana," *Africa* 65.2 (1995): 236.

36. Kwabena Asamoah-Gyadu, *African Charismatics: Current Developments within Independent Indigenous Pentecostalism in Ghana* (Leiden: Brill, 2005), 183.

37. Asamoah-Gyadu, *African Charismatics*, 186.

38. Kwofie often talked about Africa as being especially possessed due to the presence of traditional religions, thus why he references Africa specifically in this quote.

39. Dayna S. Kalleres, *City of Demons: Violence, Ritual, and Christian Power in Late Antiquity* (Berkeley: University of California Press, 2015), 1–3. In an interesting note of interpenetration between antiquity and the contemporary, one of Kalleres's sources in constructing the term *diabolization* is Birgit Meyer's work in Ghana.

40. O'Donnell, *Passing Orders*, 14.

41. Birgit Meyer, "'If You Are a Devil, You Are a Witch, and If You Are a Witch, You Are a Devil.' The Integration of 'Pagan' Ideas into the Conceptual Universe of Ewe Christians in Southeastern Ghana," *Journal of Religion in Africa* 22.2 (1992): 108.

42. Wariboko, *Nigerian Pentecostalism*, 4.

43. Nathanael Homewood, "The Supersensual Supernatural: Sexual Spirits in the History of Christianity," in *Religion: Super Religion*, ed. Jeffrey J. Kripal (New York: Macmillan Reference USA, 2016).

44. Abamfa Atiemo, "Deliverance in the Charismatic Churches in Ghana," *Trinity Journal of Church and Theology* 4.2 (1994–5): 47.

45. Atiemo, "Deliverance in the Charismatic Churches in Ghana,"47.

46. O'Donnell, *Passing Orders*, 24.

47. Michael T. Taussig, *The Devil and Commodity Fetishism in South America* (Chapel Hill, NC: University of North Carolina Press, 2010), 18.

48. Reprinted in Jonathan Z. Smith, *Map Is Not Territory: Studies in the History of Religions* (Chicago: University of Chicago Press, 1978), 172–189.

49. Kalleres, *City of Demons*, 1–3, 31.

50. Meyer, *Translating the Devil*, 211–212.

51. Meyer, 172.

52. In order to maintain anonymity, I will not provide citations for Kwofie's autobiography which only makes an appearance here and in chapter 1.

53. Sean McCloud, *American Possessions: Fighting Demons in the Contemporary United States* (Oxford: Oxford University Press, 2015), 38.

54. Jonathan R. Baer, "Redeemed Bodies: The Functions of Divine Healing in Incipient Pentecostalism," *Church History* 70.4 (Dec. 2001): 735.

55. Frank and Ida Mae Hammond, *Pigs in the Parlor* (Impact Books, 1973), 9.

56. Malachi Martin, *Hostage to the Devil: The Possession and Exorcism of Five Contemporary Americans* (New York: HarperOne, 1992), 155.

57. Bryan S. Turner, *The Body and Society* (Los Angeles: Sage, 1984).

58. Derek Prince, *They Shall Expel Demons: What You Need to Know about Demons–Your Invisible Enemies* (Chosen Books, 1998), 89.

59. Such a theology, explicitly embraced by the prophets in this text, may fly in the face of more traditional understandings of spirits in Ghana. See, for example, Kwasi Wiredu, "Introduction: Decolonizing African Philosophy and Religion," in *Decolonizing African Religions: A Short History of African Religions in Western Scholarship* by Okot P'Bitek (New York: Diasporic Africa Press, 2011), xxvii. Wiredu writes,

> Other aspects of the conceptual superimposition need to be noted. The beings I have, by implication, described as superhuman (but, note, not supernatural) are often called spirits. If the notion of spirits is understood in a quasi-physical sense, as they sometimes are, in narratives of ghostly apparitions even in Western thought, there is no problem of conceptual incongruity. But if the word "spirit" is construed, as so often happens, in a Cartesian sense to designate an immaterial substance, no such category can be fitted into the conceptual framework of Akan thought. The fundamental reason for this is to be found in the spatial connotation of the Akan concept of existence. Given the necessary spatiality of all existents, little reflection is required to see that the absolute ontological cleavage between the material and the immaterial will not exist in Akan metaphysics. Again, that Africans are constantly said to believe in spiritual entities in the immaterial sense can be ascribed to the conceptual imposition in the accounts of African thought during colonial times and their post-colonial aftermath.

60. Wariboko, *Nigerian Pentecostalism*, 121.

61. Anthony Pinn, *Embodiment and the New Shape of Black Theological Thought* (New York: New York University Press, 2010), 9.

62. As many before me have, I write *modernity/coloniality* throughout to demonstrate that coloniality is constitutive of and not derivative of modernity. The slash unites the concepts which are at their very core united. One cannot think of modernity without also confronting coloniality which made modernity possible for Western civilization.

63. Candy Gunther Brown, "Spiritual Property Rights to Bodily Practices:

Pentecostal Views of Yoga and Meditation as Inviting Demonization," in *Annual Review of the Sociology of Religion: Volume 8 Pentecostals and the Body*, ed. Michael Wilkinson and Peter Althouse (Leiden: Brill, 2017): 55.

64. Michael Wilkinson and Peter Althouse, *Annual Review of the Sociology of Religion: Volume 8: Pentecostals and the Body* (Leiden: Brill, 2017), 55. 2.

65. Wariboko, *Nigerian Pentecostalism*, 115.

66. Kristina Wirtz, "Spirit Materialities in Cuban Folk Religion," in *The Social Life of Spirits*, ed. Ruy Blanes and Diana Espirito Santo(Chicago: University of Chicago Press, 2014), 131.

67. For sense-ability see Robert S. Desjarlais, *Body and Emotion: The Aesthetics of Illness and Healing in the Nepal Himalayas* (Philadelphia: University of Pennsylvania Press, 1992). I borrow sense-knowledge from Pentecostal theologian E. W. Kenyon who dismissed the senses using this term. See E. W. Kenyon, *The Two Kinds of Knowledge* (Kenyon's Gospel Publishing Society, 1942).

68. Josh Brahinksy, "Pentecostal Body Logics: Cultivating a Modern Sensorium," *Cultural Anthropology* 27.2 (2012): 217.

69. Wariboko, *Nigerian Pentecostalism*, 261.

70. Joshua Brahinsky, "Crossing the Buffer: Ontological Anxiety among US Evangelicals and an Anthropological Theory of Mind," *Journal of the Royal Anthropological Institute*, 26.1 (2020): 45.

71. Mami Wata will be prominent in "Spousal Scenes," but for now it is worth noting that she is a spirit that emerges from the sea and is a mermaid, half human, half fish.

72. Hunt, "Managing the Demonic," 220–221. Obviously, there are a whole host of senses that are untouched by this book. That does not mean they are absent from the deliverance sensorium. For example, occasionally the olfactory sense was invoked. As my interlocutor Phillip told me, "Spirits are even here, if you are open they can enter you as you are walking around the world. Depends on where you pass. I once went to the beach, I sensed a spirit in the form of a smell. I began to cough and I realized the demon was there. So, spirits can possess people." For an additional example, Lincoln notes that frequently "foul smells index demonic presence and activity." See Lincoln, *Gods and Demons*, 35.

73. Asamoah-Gyadu, *African Charismatics*, 165.

74. Meyer, *Translating the Devil*, 171.

75. "For our struggle is not against enemies of blood and flesh, but against the rulers, against the authorities, against the cosmic powers of this present darkness, against the spiritual forces of evil in heavenly places" (Ephesians 6:12), NRSV.

76. Michael Wilkinson, "Pentecostalism, the Body and Embodiment," *Annual Review of the Sociology of Religion, Volume 8: Pentecostals and the Body* (Leiden, Brill, 2017), 22.

77. Simon Coleman, *The Globalisation of Charismatic Christianity* (Cambridge: Cambridge University Press, 2000), 25.

78. Crawley, *Blackpentecostal Breath*, 12.

79. Crawley, 13–14.

80. Crawley, 28.

81. Brahinsky, "Pentecostal Body Logics," 217.

82. While I emphasize that a specific Pentecostal culture has emerged that values the senses, I think local exploration of what senses are operative and how such senses operate in Pentecostal rituals remain underexplored. I do not assume that the senses elucidated herein will necessarily have the same purchase in Pentecostal cultures beyond Ghana.

C.f. Bruno Reinhardt's claim, "Pentecostalism in general has a global DNA." Or as A. Christian van Gorder writes, "It is a transnational phenomenon and much of African Pentecostalism seems interchangeable with messages and mannerisms that emanate from Tulsa, Los Angeles, or Dallas." See Bruno Reinhardt, "Soaking in Tapes: The Haptic Voice of Global Pentecostal Pedagogy in Ghana," *Journal of the Royal Anthropological Institute* 20.2 (2014): 320. Or see A. Christian van Gorder, "Beyond the Rivers of Africa: The Afrocentric Pentecostalism of Mensa Otabil," *Pneuma* 30 (2008): 34.

83. Louise Vinge, *The Five Senses: Studies in a Literary Tradition* (Lund: Liber Laromedel, 1975), 107.

84. Kathryn Geurts, *Culture and the Senses: Bodily Ways of Knowing in an African Community* (Berkley: University of California Press, 2003), 5. Emphasis in original.

85. Geurts, *Culture and the Senses,* 10.

86. Zakiyyah Iman Jackson, *Becoming Human: Matter and Meaning in an Antiblack World* (New York: New York University Press, 2020), 89.

87. Crawley, *Blackpentecostal Breath*, 114.

88. Crawley, 12.

89. Crawley, 179.

90. Janice Boddy, "Colonialism: Bodies under Colonialism," in *A Companion to the Anthropology of the Body and Embodiment*, ed. Frances E. Mascia-Lees (Oxford, UK: Wiley-Blackwell, 2011), 119.

91. Edward Sugden, ed. *Wesley's Standard Sermons, Version 2* (London: Epworth, 1964), 230–231.

92. Crawley, *Blackpentecostal Breath*, 114.

93. Walter Mignolo and Rolando Vazquez, "Decolonial Aesthesis: Colonial Wounds/Decolonial Healings," *Social Text,* July 15, 2013. https://socialtextjournal.org/periscope_article/decolonial-aesthesis-colonial-woundsdecolonial-healings/.

94. Gayatri Gopinath, *Unruly Visions: The Aesthetic Practices of Queer Diaspora* (Durham, NC: Duke University, 2018), 8.

95. Stallings, *Funk the Erotic*, 14.

96. Martyn Percy, "Sweet Rapture: Subliminal Eroticism in Contemporary Charismatic Worship," *Theology and Sexuality* 6 (1997): 71.

97. Harvey Cox, *Fire from Heaven: The Rise of Pentecostal Spirituality and the Reshaping of Religion in the Twenty-First Century* (Cambridge, MA: Da Capo Press, 1995), 9.

98. Cox writes, "the erotic and the spiritual energies of life, may not be as distinct, as some theologians would have us believe. Whenever I think of that little church I think of Lois and how, even though she never wore a trace of rouge or lipstick, when she prayed, eyes closed, her head tilted back and her hands raised, the way all the people in her church prayed, I thought she was the most beautiful girl I had ever seen." See Cox, *Fire from Heaven*, 10–13.

99. Percy, "Sweet Rapture," 84.

100. For the same phraseology in the American context see: Amy DeRogatis, *Saving Sex: Sexuality and Salvation in American Evangelicalism* (New York: Oxford University Press, 2015), 86–87.

101. Adewale Adelakun, "Understanding Sexuality from the Security Gospel Perspective: Mountain of Fire and Miracles Ministries as a Case Study," *Hervormde Teologiese Studies/Theological Studies* 73.3 (2017), 4–5.

102. Adelakun, "Understanding Sexuality from the Security Gospel Perspective," 5.

103. Hunt, "Managing the Demonic," 226.

104. Donna J. Haraway, *Staying with the Trouble: Making Kin in the Chthulucene* (Durham, NC: Duke University Press, 2016), 58.

105. Joseph Laycock, "Carnal Knowledge: The Epistemology of Sexual Trauma in Witches' Sabbaths, Satanic Ritual Abuse, and Alien Abduction Narratives," *Preternature: Critical and Historical Studies on the Preternatural* 1.1 (2012): 113.

106. Marcella Althaus-Reid, *The Queer God* (New York: Routledge, 2003), 124.

107. Althaus-Reid, *Queer God*, 125.

108. Althaus-Reid, 126.

109. S. Nyanzi, "Queering Queer Africa," in *Reclaiming Afrikan: Queer Perspectives on Sexual and Gender Identities* (Athlone: Modjaji Books, 2014), 65.

110. Keguro Macharia, *Frottage: Frictions of Intimacy across the Black Diaspora* (New York: New York University Press, 2019), 62–63.

111. Macharia, *Frottage*, 37.

112. The ancient Greek term for spirit (good, bad, or otherwise).

113. Joseph Quayesi-Amakye, *Prophetism in Ghana Today: A Study on Trends in Ghanaian Pentecostal Prophetism* (Scotts Valley, CA: CreateSpace, 2013), 3.

114. The prophets dominate in such a way that for the sake of simplicity, I will

not provide monikers for the ministries and will instead refer to them by the name of the senior prophet.

115. Aliyyah I. Abdur-Rahman, *Against the Closet: Black Political Longing and the Erotics of Race* (Durham and London: Duke University Press, 2012), 27.

116. Greg Thomas, *The Sexual Demon of Colonial Power: Pan-African Embodiment and Erotic Schemes of Empire* (Bloomington: Indiana University Press, 2007), 23.

117. Michael Jackson and Albert Piette (eds.), *What Is Existential Anthropology?* (New York: Berghahn Books, 2015), 12.

118. Wirtz, "Spirit Materialities in Cuban Folk Religion," 118

119. The unusual use of the prefixal *trans* and the hyphen here will make more sense in the context of chapter 6 where trans- possibilities play a significant role. The hyphen is a way of cracking open the term so that whatever the prefixal *trans* is attached to defines multiple or a range of ways of being rather than mediation between two monolithic poles.

120. Andre Corten and Ruth Marshall-Fratani (eds.), *Between Babel and Pentecost: Transnational Pentecostalism in Africa and Latin America* (Bloomington: Indiana University Press, 2001), 10–11.

Chapter 1

1. For example, Emmanuel has whipped at least three congregants with a belt, been rough with pregnant women, and I've seen him kick congregants. See Nathanael Homewood, "The Fantastic Fetus: The Fetus as a Super-Citizen in Ghanaian Pentecostalism," *Citizenship Studies Journal* 22.6 (2018): 618–632. In the thick description of some chapters herein it will become apparent that I think all sorts of deliverance events are violent.

2. Jesse Weaver Shipley, "Comedians, Pastors and the Miraculous Agency of Charisma in Ghana," *Cultural Anthropology* 24 (2009): 523–552.

3. The Black Stars are Ghana's popular national soccer team.

4. Stephen Hunt, "Managing the Demonic: Some Aspects of the Neo-Pentecostal Deliverance Ministry," *Journal of Contemporary Religion* 13.2 (1998): 216.

5. Ogbu Kalu, *African Pentecostalism: An Introduction* (Oxford: Oxford University Press, 2008), 71.

6. Michael W. Cuneo, *American Exorcism: Expelling Demons in the Land of Plenty* (New York: Broadway Books, 2001), 88–89.

7. I often purchased mine from a bookstand at a *tro tro* stop on Madina Road near the Accra Mall.

8. Birgit Meyer, "'Make a Complete Break with the Past': Memory and Postcolonial Modernity in Ghanaian Pentecostalist Discourse," *Journal of Religion in Africa* 28.3 (1998): 319.

9. Meyer, "Make a Complete Break," 324.

10. Jomo Kenyatta, *Facing Mount Kenya: The Tribal Life of the Gikuyu* (London: Mercury, 1961 [1938]), 153.

11. Opoku Onyinah, *Pentecostal Exorcism: Witchcraft and Demonology in Ghana* (Deo, 2012), 2.

12. Birgit Meyer, *Translating the Devil: Religion and Modernity among the Ewe in Ghana* (Trenton: Africa World Press, 1999), 169.

13. [Note" The Akan are the most populous people group in Ghana and their culture plays a significant role in the country both historically and contemporarily.]

14. Onyinah, *Pentecostal Exorcism*, 175.

15. Kwabena Asamoah-Gyadu, *African Charismatics: Current Developments within Independent Indigenous Pentecostalism in Ghana* (Leiden: Brill, 2005), 96–131.

16. For more on this subject see: Nathanael Homewood, "The Supersensual Supernatural: Sexual Spirits in the History of Christianity," in *Religion: Super Religion,* ed. Jeffrey J. Kripal (New York: Macmillan, 2016), 341–356.

17. Jennifer Wright Knust, *Unprotected Texts: The Bible's Surprising Contradictions about Sex and Desire* (New York: HarperOne, 2011), 158–61.

18. Heinrich Institoris and Jakob Sprenger *Malleus Maleficarum, Translated with an Introduction, Bibliography and Notes by the Rev. Montague Summers* (London: Pushkin Press, 1948), 30.

19. For most of Christianity, sexual spirits like Asmodeus are referred to as *incubus* and *succubus,* and Ghanaian Pentecostals mostly adhere to the standard stories and Christian theologies of *incubi* and *succubi.* An incubus is a male demon who most often sleeps with female humans. A succubus is a female spirit or demoness who most often beds human males. Debate continues as to whether they are unique gendered forms, or single spirits capable of bending gender to their capricious whims. The Latin names *incubus* and *succubus* mean "that which lies upon" and "that which lies down under."

20. Jeanne Rey, "Mermaids and Spirit Spouses: Rituals as Technologies of Gender in Transnational African Pentecostal Spaces," *Religion and Gender* 3.1 (2013): 70.

21. Part of the poem is quoted in the Preface to P'Bitek's *Decolonizing African Religions.* See: Okot P'Bitek, *Decolonizing African Religions: A Short History of African Religions in Western Scholarship* (New York: Diasporic Africa Press, 2011), vii-x.

22. Sean McCloud, *American Possessions: Fighting Demons in the Contemporary United States* (Oxford: Oxford University Press, 2015), 93–94.

23. McCloud, *American Possessions,* 93–94.

24. Wariboko cites an example where a prominent Nigerian pastor talked about kissing God. See: Nimi Wariboko, *Nigerian Pentecostalism* (Rochester, NY:

University of Rochester Press, 2014), 40. Percy cites the example of Carol Arnott of the Toronto Airport Church talking about how she was a special bride of Jesus; she was the one for whom Jesus was saving his first dance for. See: Martyn Percy, "Sweet Rapture: Subliminal Eroticism in Contemporary Charismatic Worship," *Theology and Sexuality* 6 (1997): 84–85.

25. See for example, Susan M. Vogel, *African Art, Western Eyes* (New Haven, CT: Yale University Press, 1997), 246–267.

26. Birgit Meyer, *Sensational Movies: Video, Vision, and Christianity in Ghana* (Berkley: University of California Press, 2015), 212.

27. Chimaraoke O. Izugbara, "Sexuality and the Supernatural in Africa" in *African Sexualities: A Reader*, ed. Sylvia Tamale (Cape Town: Pambazuka Press, 2011), 542.

28. Izugbara, "Sexuality and the Supernatural," 542.

29. Izugbara, 542.

30. Emmanuel Eni, *Delivered from the Powers of Darkness* (Kijabe: Kijabe Printing Press, 1987).

31. Asamoah-Gyadu, *African Charismatics,* 170–171.

32. Atiemo, "Deliverance in the Charismatic Churches in Ghana,"44.

33. Eni, *Delivered from the Powers of Darkness*, 11.

34. Asamoah-Gyadu, *African Charismatics,* 172.

35. Eni, *Delivered from the Powers of Darkness*, 16.

36. Eni, 16–17.

37. Eni, 30–31.

38. Meyer, "Delivered from the Powers of Darkness," 242–243.

39. Meyer, 243–244.

40. Meyer, 237.

41. Kalu Abosi, *Born Twice: From Demonism to Christianity* (1989).

42. Abosi, *Born Twice,* 1, 17, 47. Mami Wata has a great many spellings. When citing specific cases I maintain fidelity to their chosen spelling.

43. Abosi, *Born Twice,* 102

44. The city under the sea is filled with scientific inventions. Demons are ever creating new inventions with the intention to lure humans. As such, no goods in the world can be trusted for they might come from the underworld with evil intentions. See: Birgit Meyer, "Commodities and the Power of Prayer: Pentecostalist Attitudes towards Consumption in Contemporary Ghana," *Development and Change* 29.4 (1998).

45. Steve Brouwer, Paul Gifford, and Susan D. Rose, *Exporting the American Gospel: Global Christian Fundamentalism* (New York: Routledge, 1997), 169–170.

46. Onyinah, *Pentecostal Exorcism,* 162–163.

47. Victoria Eto, *How I Served Satan: How I Served Satan Until Jesus Christ Deliv-*

ered Me: A True Account of My Twenty One Experience as an Agent of Darkness and of My Deliverance by the Powerful Arm of God in Christ Jesus (Shallom Christian Ministries International, 1981), 1–4.

48. Throughout I use various spellings of Mami Wata as preferred by the various sources used. Upon her birth, Ogbanje spirits introduced her to Mami Wata. See: Misty Bastian, "Married in the Water: Spirit Kin and Other Afflictions of Modernity in Southeastern Nigeria," *Journal of Religion in Africa* 27.2 (1997). In this text Bastian defines ogbanje as "returning children," that is spirits who manifest as human children but eventually expire.

49. Eto, *How I Served Satan*, 1–2.

50. Asmodee bears a strong resemblance to Asmodeus who is the spirit of lust and referenced in the Book of Tobit.

51. Eto, *How I Served Satan*, 3–4.

52. Eto, 3–4.

53. Eto, 3–4.

54. Eto, 3–4.

55. Eto, 3–4.

56. Eto, 7.

57. Eto, 21–23.

58. Eto, 21.

59. Eto, 38.

60. Eto, 39.

61. Eto, 42.

62. Eto, 46.

63. Victoria Eto, *Exposition on Water Spirits* (Plummet Publishing, 2004), 16.

64. Eto, *Exposition on Water Spirits*, 1.

65. Eto, 17.

66. Eto, 17.

67. Eto, 16.

68. Eto, 17.

69. Meyer, "Delivered from the Powers of Darkness," 241–242.

70. Meyer, "Delivered from the Powers of Darkness," 241–242. Meyer is one of the only scholars I know who takes seriously the sexual implications of these deliverance tales and provides the following interpretation (see p. 246):

> The story of Diabolo also features such an appropriation of the reproductive organs. In the film, a man misuses the belly of an unsuspecting woman by impregnating her in the form of a snake. Here the snake becomes a phallus . . . as far as its sex is concerned the snake is thus ambivalent: it can take the place of the male penis as well as of the female belly in order to produce money instead

of a child. Diabolo has given away his fertility and is no longer able to beget children. As we have seen from his sexual intercourse with the third woman, even in human form he is able to sire only snakes. In the story of Diabolo the satanic money results from the perversion of human sexuality. The woman is impregnated by the snake, but instead of a child she gives birth to money and dies, whereas Diabolo profits. That the money comes out of her mouth instead of her vagina once again underlines the perversion of nature.

71. Paul Gifford, "The Complex Provenance of Some Elements of African Pentecostal Theology," in *Between Babel and Pentecost: Transnational Pentecostalism in Africa and Latin America,* ed. Andre Corten and Ruth Marshall-Fratani (Bloomington: Indiana University Press, 2001), 65.

72. Paul Gifford, "The 'New' Christianity in Africa: The Charismatic Explosion," in *Exporting the American Gospel: Global Christian Fundamentalism,* ed. Steve Brouwer, Paul Gifford, and Susan D. Rose (New York: Routledge, 1996), 170.

73. See Rosalind Hackett, "Discourses of Demonization in Africa and Beyond," *Diogenes* 50.3 (2003): 61–75. I find Hackett to be a more responsible curator of the varied influences as she not only names indigenous influences but explores their influence.

74. O'Donnell, *Passing Orders,* 27

75. McCloud, *American Possessions,* 21.

76. Onyinah, *Pentecostal Exorcism,* 144–145.

77. Onyinah, 159.

78. Gifford, "The Complex Provenance," 72.

79. Onyinah, *Pentecostal Exorcism,* 159. Cerullo is an American Pentecostal faith healer who had an extensive international reach through his crusades and corresponding Schools of Ministry. Benson Idahosa founded Church of God Mission International in Nigeria with an enormous influence on Pentecostalism throughout West Africa.

80. Gifford, "The Complex Provenance," 68.

81. Cuneo, *American Exorcism,* 92–93.

82. James Collins, *Exorcism and Deliverance Ministry in the Twentieth Century: An Analysis of the Practice and Theology of Exorcism in Modern Western Christianity* (Eugene: Wipf and Stock Publishers, 2009), 45.

83. Prince came ten years after the first significant crusade, that of Nigerian pastor Benson Idahosa.

84. Onyinah, *Pentecostal Exorcism,* 165.

85. Onyinah, 167.

86. Gifford, "The Complex Provenance," 69.

87. Atiemo, "Deliverance in the Charismatic Churches in Ghana,"43.

88. Collins, *Exorcism and Deliverance Ministry*, 51.

89. Cuneo, *American Exorcism*, 100.

90. Onyinah, *Pentecostal Exorcism*, 199.

91. Brouwer, Gifford, and Rose, *Exporting the American Gospel*, 170.

92. Cuneo, *American Exorcism*, 108. Cuneo writes that the Hammonds' cosmos is "a dangerous world, also, to be sure, with demons lurking in every crevice of daily life, brushing up against every bad habit, every thought and action, but (and here's the consoling part) the danger was capable of being contained, managed and finally conquered."

93. Hammond and Hammond, *Pigs in the Parlor*, 39.

94. Hackett, "Discourses of Demonization in Africa and Beyond," 200.

95. Gifford, "The Complex Provenance," 70.

96. Rebecca Brown, *He Came to Set the Captives Free* (New Kensington, PA: Whitaker House, 1986), 51.

97. Brown, *He Came to Set the Captives Free*, 58–63.

98. Brown, 64–65.

99. Rebecca Brown, *Prepare for War* (New Kensington, PA: Whitaker House, 1987), 108.

100. Brown, *Prepare for War*, 108.

101. Brown, 136–137.

102. Onyinah, *Pentecostal Exorcism*, 163.

103. Asamoah-Gyadu, *African Charismatics*, 169.

104. Cuneo, *American Exorcism*, xii–xiii.

105. Onyinah, *Pentecostal Exorcism*, 163.

106. Cuneo, *American Exorcism*, 10.

107. Gifford, "The Complex Provenance," 73.

108. Gifford, 73.

109. O'Donnell, *Passing Orders*, 45.

Chapter 2

1. Giorgio Agamben, *Nudities*, trans. David Kishik and Stefan Pedatella (Stanford, CA: Stanford University Press, 2011), 2.

2. Ashon Crawley, *Blackpentecostal Breath: The Aesthetics of Possibility* (Durham, NC: Duke University Press, 2016), , 4.

3. Marcella Althaus-Reid, *The Queer God* (New York: Routledge, 2003), 47.

4. Richard Kearney and Brian Treanor, *Carnal Hermeneutics* (New York: Fordham University Press, 2015), 2.

5. Kearney and Treanor, *Carnal Hermeneutics*, 2.

6. Richard Kearney, "The Wager of Carnal Hermeneutics," in *Carnal Herme-*

neutics, eds. Richard Kearny and Brian Treanor (New York: Fordham University Press, 2015), 40.

7. Althaus-Reid, *Queer God*, 34.

8. *Pneuma akatharton* appears twenty-one times in the New Testament in the context of demonic possession. See J. Reiling, "Unclean Spirits" in *Dictionary of Deities and Demons in the Bible,* edited by Karel van der Toorn, Bob Becking, and Pieter W. van der Horst (Grand Rapids, MI: William B. Eerdmans, 1999), 882. From here onward, I will often refer to deliverance-dominant Pentecostalism as pneumatic for its commitment to engage spirits good, bad, and otherwise.

9. Althaus-Reid, *Queer God*, 4.

10. Maggi, 12.

11. Georges Bataille, *Erotism: Death and Sensuality* (San Francisco: City Lights, 1986), 29.

12. Keguro Macharia, *Frottage: Frictions of Intimacy across the Black Diaspora* (New York: New York University Press, 2019), 2

13. L. H. Stallings, *Funk the Erotic: Transaesthetics and Black Sexual Cultures* (Urbana: University of Illinois Press, 2016), xii. I should also note that the use of Greek terms is not uncommon in Ghanaian deliverance Pentecostalism, especially among the clergy.

14. Georges Bataille, *The Tears of Eros* (San Francisco: City Lights, 1989), 70.

15. Marcella Althaus-Reid, *Indecent Theology* (New York: Routledge, 2002), 2–4.

16. Althaus-Reid, *Queer God,* 32.

17. Karl Eric Toepfer, *Theatre, Aristocracy, and Pornocracy: The Orgy Calculus* (New York: PAJ Publications, 1991), 9.

18. Toepfer, *Theatre, Aristocracy, and Pornocracy*, 9.

19. Macharia, *Frottage*, 85.

20. Judith Roof, "Orgy," in *Encyclopedia of Sex and Gender*, ed. Fedwa Malti-Douglas, vol. 3 (Detroit: Macmillan Reference USA, 2007), 1095–1096.

21. Michel Maffesoli, "Orgy: An Overview," in *Encyclopedia of Religion,* ed. Lindsay Jones (Detroit: Macmillan Reference USA, 2005), 6861.

22. Roof, "Orgy."

23. Stallings, *Funk the Erotic*, 153.

24. Lisa Blackman, *Immaterial Bodies: Affect, Embodiment, Mediation* (London: Sage, 2012), 13.

25. Macharia, *Frottage,* 67.

26. Althaus-Reid, *Queer God,* 30.

27. The spirits of this triad are often yoked together in Pentecostal discourse and performance. I maintain fidelity to these frequent categorizings of demons throughout *Seductive Spirits.*

28. Althaus-Reid, *Queer God*, 27.

29. Grant Wacker, *Heaven Below: Early Pentecostals and American Culture* (Cambridge, MA: Harvard University Press, 2001), 99.

30. Michael W. Cuneo, *American Exorcism: Expelling Demons in the Land of Plenty* (New York: Broadway Books, 2001), 81.

31. Birgit Meyer, "Magic, Mermaids and Modernity: The Attraction of Pentecostalism in Africa," *Etnofoor* 8.2 (1995): 51.

32. Sean McCloud, *American Possessions: Fighting Demons in the Contemporary United States* (Oxford: Oxford University Press, 2015), 86–87.

33. Althaus-Reid, *Queer God*, 28.

34. Procuring the name of the demon is a hotly contested issue among deliverance pastors and prophets. In some formulations naming the demon is an important and essential part of the process. Naming is tantamount to defeating the demon. To name something is to take authority over it. Others disagree and do not seek the name of the demon, concerned that such tarrying with the demonic leads to deception. Nonetheless, naming the demons was a fairly ubiquitous practice among the ministries I researched. Sometimes names are attributes—the spirit of masturbation or the demon of madness—but sometimes they can be very specific and personal, such as Maggie.

35. Depending on whom you talk to the number is either nine (counting each individual orifice) or seven (counting the eyes and ears as one each).

36. See: https://www.youtube.com/watch?v=61_rPgitFmc.

37. Abamfa Atiemo, "Deliverance in the Charismatic Churches in Ghana," *Trinity Journal of Church and Theology* 4.2 (1994–5):, 42.

38. Nimi Wariboko, *Nigerian Pentecostalism* (Rochester, NY: University of Rochester Press, 2014), 52.

39. Wariboko, 84.

40. Travis Warren Cooper, "Worship Rituals, Discipline and Pentecostal-Charismatic 'Technique Du Corps' in the American Midwest" in *Annual Review of the Sociology of Religion. Volume 8: Pentecostals and the Body* (Leiden: Brill, 2017), 77.

41. Blackman, *Immaterial Bodies*, 3.

42. Blackman, 1.

43. Florencia Tola, "The Materiality of 'Spiritual Presences' and the Notion of Person in and Amerindian Society," in *The Social Life of Spirits*, ed. Ruy Blanes and Diana Espirito Santo (Chicago: University of Chicago Press, 2014), 88.

44. Blackman, *Immaterial Bodies*, 57.

45. Blackman, 2.

46. Blackman, 145.

47. Blackman, 145.

48. Kristina Wirtz, "Spirit Materialities in Cuban Folk Religion," in *The Social Life of Spirits*, ed. Ruy Blanes and Diana Espirito Santo (Chicago: University of Chicago Press, 2014), 127.

49. This idea will be explored further in Chapter 3.

50. Tom Beaudoin, "Postmodern Practical Theology" in *Opening the Field of Practical Theology: An Introduction*, eds. Kathleen A. Cahalan and Gordon S. Mikoski (Lanham, MD: Rowman and Littlefield, 2014), 194.

51. Robert Reid-Pharr, *Black Gay Man: Essays* (New York: New York University Press, 2001), 85.

52. I have written about the cases of miracle babies elsewhere. I'd like to emphasize that unproductive does not have to be, for example, Marquis de Sade's dramatic stomping of pregnant bellies. That said, I have written about just such an act in the sense of Pentecostalism's (re)productivity. See: Nathanael Homewood, "The Fantastic Fetus: The Fetus as a Super-Citizen in Ghanaian Pentecostalism," *Citizenship Studies Journal* 22.6 (2018): 618–632.

53. Maffesoli, "Orgy: An Overview," 6861.

54. Toepfer, *Theatre, Aristocracy, and Pornocracy*, 9.

55. Toepfer, 9.

56. Bataille, *Erotism*, 69.

57. Althaus-Reid, *Queer God*, 28.

58. Bataille, *Erotism*, 9.

59. Bataille 16.

60. Toepfer, *Theatre, Aristocracy, and Pornocracy*, 10.

61. Althaus-Reid, *Queer God*, 29.

62. Althaus-Reid, *Queer God*, 19, 137.

63. Michel Foucault, *Discipline & Punish: The Birth of the Prison* (New York: Knopf Doubleday, 2012), 136.

64. Meyer, "Magic, Mermaids and Modernity," 63.

65. Birgit Meyer, *Translating the Devil: Religion and Modernity among the Ewe in Ghana* (Trenton: Africa World Press, 1999), 211.

66. Althaus-Reid, *Queer God*, 29.

Chapter 3

1. Thomas Laqueur, *Solitary Sex: A Cultural History of Masturbation* (New York: Zone Books, 2003), 103.

2. Laqueur, *Solitary Sex*, 103.

3. Laqueur, 97.

4. Laqueur, 97.

5. Laqueur, 112.

6. Laqueur, 126.

7. Laqueur, 151.

8. Laqueur, 158.

9. Laqueur, 153.

10. Laqueur, 158.

11. Laqueur, 13.

12. Bjorn Krondorfer, *Men and Masculinities in Christianity and Judaism: A Critical Reader* (London: SCM Press, 2009).

13. Derek Prince, *They Shall Expel Demons: What You Need to Know about Demons–Your Invisible Enemies* (Chosen Books, 1998), 41.

14. Prince, *They Shall Expel Demons*, 41.

15. Prince, 41.

16. Prince, 169–170.

17. Prince, 212.

18. Prince, 169–170.

19. Thomas Csordas, "Embodiment as a Paradigm for Anthropology," *Ethnos* 18.1 (1990): 5–47.

20. Thomas Csordas, *Body/Meaning/Healing* (New York: Palgrave Macmillan, 2002), 65.

21. Csordas, *Body/Meaning/Healing*, 66.

22. Csordas, *Body/Meaning/Healing*, 66. Also: Thomas Csordas, *The Sacred Self: A Cultural Phenomenology of Charismatic Healing* (Berkley: University of California Press, 1997), 173.

23. Csordas, *Body/Meaning/Healing*, 66.

24. See also http://www.peacefmonline.com/pages/local/religion/201203/97973.php. Accessed May 1, 2018.

25. In the interest of full disclosure, I did meet with Salifu Amoako on multiple occasions and attended his church many times, but neither he nor his church are used in this book outside of citations from Paul Gifford's work.

26. Paul Gifford, *Ghana's New Christianity: Pentecostalism in a Globalizing African Economy* (Bloomington: Indiana University Press, 2004), 100.

27. Birgit Meyer, *Translating the Devil: Religion and Modernity among the Ewe in Ghana* (Trenton: Africa World Press, 1999), 196.

28. Aisha M. Beliso-De Jesus, *Electric Santeria: Racial and Sexual Assemblages of Transnational Religion* (New York: Columbia University Press, 2015).

29. Zakiyyah Iman Jackson, *Becoming Human: Matter and Meaning in an Antiblack World* (New York: New York University Press, 2020), 150.

30. Janice Boddy, "Colonialism: Bodies under Colonialism," in *A Companion to the Anthropology of the Body and Embodiment*, ed. Frances E. Mascia-Lees (Oxford, UK: Wiley-Blackwell, 2011), 124. Here Boddy makes the case that individua-

tion is a core facet of Western culture and led to colonialists dismissing Sudanese women who believed in co-presences as irrational.

31. Marleen De Witte, "Touch," *Material Religion* 7.1 (2011): 151.

32. Kathryn Linn Geurts and Elvis Gershon Adikah, "Enduring and Endearing Feelings and the Transformation of Material Culture in West Africa," in *Sensible Objects: Colonialism, Museums and Material Culture,* ed. Elizabeth Edwards, Chris Gosden, and Ruth B. Phillips (New York: Berg, 2006).

33. This statement revealed his privilege, as my time frequenting the abodes of many of his followers exhibited the bathroom for many of his congregants is not exactly a place of privacy or pleasure-making

34. Michel Foucault, *The History of Sexuality: An Introduction Volume 1* (New York: Knopf Doubleday, 2012), 42.

35. Foucault, *The History of Sexuality,* 42.

36. Erica Frueh, *Erotic Faculties* (Berkley: University of California Press, 1996), 119.

37. It is common in Ghana to refer to one's penis as their manhood.

38. Juju is commonly defined as a kind of folk magic common in West Africa.

39. I am unsure of the origin of this specific prayer. Prophets plagiarize, or borrow liberally, from one another frequently, and I am not sure from where Ofori got this prayer.

40. Marleen De Witte, "Touched by the Spirit: Converting the Senses in a Ghanaian Charismatic Church," *Ethnos* 76.4 (2011): 507.

41. Marcella Althaus-Reid, *The Queer God* (New York: Routledge, 2003), 137–138.

Chapter 4

1. Charles Hirschkind, "The Ethics of Listening" *American Ethnologist* 28.3 (2001): 623–649.

2. David Daniels, "'Gotta Moan Sometime': A Sonic Exploration of Earwitnesses to Early Pentecostal Sound in North America," *Pneuma* 30.1 (2008): 26.

3. Linda van de Kamp, "Love Therapy: A Brazilian Pentecostal (Dis)Connection in Maputo," in *The Social Life of Connectivity in Africa,* ed. Mirjam de Bruijn and Rijk van Dijk (New York: Palgrave Macmillan, 2012), 215.

4. Martyn Percy, "Sweet Rapture: Subliminal Eroticism in Contemporary Charismatic Worship," *Theology and Sexuality* 6 (1997): 76.

5. Marleen de Witte, "Accra's Sounds and Sacred Spaces," *International Journal of Urban and Regional Research* 32.3 (2008): 702.

6. Daniel E. Albrecht, *Rites in the Spirit: A Ritual Approach to Pentecostal/Charismatic Spirituality* (Sheffield: Sheffield Academic Press, 1999), 148.

7. Carrie Noland, *Agency and Embodiment* (Cambridge, MA: Harvard University Press, 2009), 3–4.

8. Daniels, "'Gotta Moan Sometime,'" 12.

9. Daniels, 20.

10. Ashon Crawley, *Blackpentecostal Breath: The Aesthetics of Possibility* (Durham, NC: Duke University Press, 2016), 2.

11. Crawley, *Blackpentecostal Breath*, 140.

12. Crawley, 143.

13. De Witte, "Accra's Sounds and Sacred Spaces," 691.

14. Rijk van Dijk, "Contesting Silence: The Ban on Drumming and the Musical Politics of Pentecostalism in Ghana," *Ghana Studies* 4 (2001): 31–64.

15. De Witte, "Accra's Sounds and Sacred Spaces," 690.

16. Daniels, "'Gotta Moan Sometime,'" 6.

17. De Witte, "Accra's Sounds and Sacred Spaces," 700.

18. Robert S. Desjarlais, *Body and Emotion: The Aesthetics of Illness and Healing in the Nepal Himalayas* (Philadelphia: University of Pennsylvania Press, 1992), 29.

19. De Witte, "Accra's Sounds and Sacred Spaces," 700–702.

20. I wrestled with whether to introduce my own portmanteau, *kinesonic*, in this chapter. I largely struggled with the connotation of movement being designed that choreography carries. Designed seemed overdetermined in the face of Pentecostal spontaneity. Nonetheless, I decided to stick with Crawley's term because it accurately captures what I saw and how I think about the scenes in this chapter. What I do want to clarify, though, is that by choreography I mean the sequence of movements and not any kind of pastoral design(s). The movements are designed only in as much as they are a form of knowledge, communicating something beyond the scripts of modernity/coloniality.

21. Crawley, *Blackpentecostal Breath*, 93.

22. Crawley, 23.

23. Daniels, "'Gotta Moan Sometime,'" 12.

24. Daniels, 16.

25. Crawley, *Blackpentecostal Breath*, 136.

26. Crawley, 93.

27. Crawley, 109.

28. Crawley, 134.

29. Crawley, 137.

30. I have previously published the case of Morowa and Kifah. Nathanael J. Homewood, "Wrestling with Homosexuality: Kinesthesia as Resistance in Ghanaian Pentecostalism," in *Embodying Black Religions in Africa and Its Diasporas*, ed. Yolanda Covington-Ward and Jeanette S. Jouili, 253–272 (Durham, NC: Duke

University Press, 2021). Copyright 2021. All rights reserved. Republished by permission of the publisher, www.dukeupress.edu.

31. *Obroni* is a Twi word for a white person or foreigner.

32. Serena Owusua Dankwa, "It's a Silent Trade: Female Same-Sex Intimacies in Post-Colonial Ghana," *NORA: Nordic Journal of Women's Studies* 17.3 (2009): 195.

33. William Banks, "Queering Ghana: Sexuality, Community, and the Struggle for Cultural Belonging in an African Nation" (PhD diss., Wayne State University, 2013), 18.

34. Dankwa, "It's a Silent Trade," 196.

35. Birgit Meyer, "Visions of Blood, Sex and Money: Fantasy Spaces in Popular Ghanaian Cinema," *Visual Anthropology* 16.1 (2003): 15–41.

36. Dankwa, "It's a Silent Trade," 194.

37. Astrid Bochow, "Valentine's Day in Ghana: Youth, Sex and Secrets," in *Generations in Africa: Connections and Conflicts,* ed. Erdmute Alber, Sjaak van der Geest, and Susan Reynolds Whyte (Berlin: LIT Verlag, 2008), 353.

38. Adriaan van Klinken, "Gay Rights, the Devil and the End Times: Public Religion and the Enchantment of the Homosexuality Debate in Zambia," *Religion* 43.4 (2013), 519–520.

39. For ejaculation in church in a non-deliverance context see: Nathanael Homewood, "I Was on Fire: The Challenge of Counter-intimacies within Zimbabwean Christianity," in *Public Religion and the Politics of Homosexuality in Africa,* ed. Adriaan van Klinken and Ezra Chitando, 243–259 (New York: Routledge, 2016).

40. Nathanael Homewood, "Wrestling with Homosexuality: Kinesthesia as Affect and Resistance in Ghanaian Pentecostalism," in *Embodying Black Religions in Africa and Its Diasporas,* ed. Jeanette Jouili and Yolanda Covington-Ward (Durham, NC: Duke University Press, 2021), 253–272.

41. Julian Henriques, "The Vibrations of Affect and Their Propagation on a Night Out on Kingston's Dancehall Scene," *Body and Society* 16.1 (2010): 57–89.

42. Crawley, "'Gotta Moan Sometime,'" 136.

43. Katrien Pype, "Dancing for God or the Devil: Pentecostal Discourse on Popular Dance in Kinshasa," *Journal of Religion in Africa* 36.3–4 (2006): 296.

44. Pype, "Dancing for God or the Devil," 297–298.

45. Marcella Althaus-Reid, *The Queer God* (New York: Routledge, 2003), 18.

46. Althaus-Reid, *Queer God,* 18.

47. Michel Foucault, *Discipline & Punish: The Birth of the Prison* (New York: Knopf Doubleday Publishing Group, 2012), 136.

48. Althaus-Reid, *Queer God,* 52.

49. Crawley, *Blackpentecostal Breath*, 44.

50. Crawley, 137.

51. Nimi Wariboko, *Pentecostal Principle: Ethical Methodology in New Spirit* (Grand Rapids, MI: William B. Eerdmans, 2012), 23–25.

52. Victoria Eto, *Exposition on Water Spirits* (Plummet Publishing, 2004), 2–4.

53. Animal metaphors—for example, a hen and a cock, not a hen and a hen—are common and were shared by many of my informants.

Chapter 5

1. Jeanne Rey, "Mermaids and Spirit Spouses: Rituals as Technologies of Gender in Transnational African Pentecostal Spaces," *Religion and Gender* 3.1 (2013): 67–68.

2. Amira Mittermaier, *Dreams That Matter: Egyptian Landscapes of the Imagination* (Berkeley: University of California Press, 2011), 2. See also Katrien Pype, "Dreaming the Apocalypse: Mimesis and the Pentecostal Imagination in Kinshasa," *Paideuma* 57 (2011): 82.

3. See Mittermaier, *Dreams That Matter*, 10.

4. Chimaraoke O. Izugbara, "Sexuality and the Supernatural in Africa" in *African Sexualities: A Reader*, ed. Sylvia Tamale (Cape Town: Pambazuka Press, 2011), 545.

5. Tanya Luhrmann, "Metakinesis: How God Becomes Intimate in Contemporary U.S. Christianity," *American Anthropologist* 106.3 (2004): 518–528.

6. Luhrmann, "Metakinesis," 518.

7. Luhrmann, 518.

8. Luhrmann, 518.

9. Luhrmann, 519.

10. Luhrmann, 522.

11. Luhrmann, 522.

12. John Martin, "Metakinesis," in *What is Dance? Readings in Theory and Criticism*, ed. Roger Copeland and Marshall Cohen (Oxford: Oxford University Press, 1983), 23.

13. David Howes, ed. *The Sixth Sense Reader* (London: Bloomsbury Academic, 2009), 1.

14. Howes, *The Sixth Sense Reader*, 6.

15. Pamela Thurschwell, "The Erotics of Telepathy: The British SPR's Experiments in Intimacy" in *The Sixth Sense Reader*, ed. David Howes (London: Bloomsbury Academic, 2009), 183–208.

16. Thurschwell, "The Erotics of Telepathy," 198.

17. Thurschwell, 198.

18. Rey, "Mermaids and Spirit Spouses, 67–69.

19. Rey, 61.

20. The fear of Mami Wata can result in real tragedy. Izugbara tells the story of a bridegroom committing suicide prior to his traditional marriage ceremony. The reason for this dramatic decision was his spiritual spouse, "a 'mermaid' contracted inside the water before his birth," had given him a dire warning that he was not to marry a human. Izugbara, 544.

21. Opoku Onyinah, *Pentecostal Exorcism: Witchcraft and Demonology in Ghana* (Deo, 2012), 204.

22. Kwabena Asamoah-Gyadu, *African Charismatics: Current Developments within Independent Indigenous Pentecostalism in Ghana* (Leiden: Brill, 2005), 172.

23. Victoria Eto, *Exposition on Water Spirits* (Plummet Publishing, 2004), 18.

24. Paul Gifford, "Evil, Witchcraft, and Deliverance in the African Pentecostal Worldview," in *Pentecostal Theology in Africa*, ed. Clifton R. Clarke (Eugene: Pickwick Publications, 2014), 113.

25. Gifford, "Evil, Witchcraft, and Deliverance, "117.

26. Linda van de Kamp, "Converting the Spirit Spouse: The Violent Transformation of the Pentecostal Female Body in Maputo, Mozambique," *Ethnos: Journal of Anthropology* 76.4 (2011): 517.

27. Van de Kamp, "Converting the Spirit Spouse," 517.

28. Van de Kamp, 518.

29. Physical laws do not apply in this realm: "Snakes, fish, cats and birds talk; birds mutate into old women, humans into walls and materialize and dematerialize at will; a fetus talks from the womb; headless bodies and skeletons walk around; special spectacles reveal the inner lives of others; men menstruate and become pregnant; a woman instantly grows a penis whenever marriage is proposed; a husband discovers on a wedding night that his wife is a hermaphrodite and has the legs of a lion; organs are surreptitiously changed to witchcraft organs; the dead arise." See: Gifford, "Evil, Witchcraft, and Deliverance," 117.

30. Monique Moultrie, *Passionate and Pious: Religious Media and Black Women's Sexuality* (Durham, NC: Duke University Press, 2017), 23.

31. Birgit Meyer, "'Make a Complete Break with the Past': Memory and Postcolonial Modernity in Ghanaian Pentecostalist Discourse," *Journal of Religion in Africa* 28.3 (1998): 316–349.

32. Bruno Reinhardt, "Soaking in Tapes: The Haptic Voice of Global Pentecostal Pedagogy in Ghana," *Journal of the Royal Anthropological Institute* 20.2 (2014): 325–326.

33. Moultrie, *Passionate and Pious*, 34.

34. Moultrie, 27.

35. The prayers against spirit children are deeply rooted in Ghanain indigenous beliefs around childbirth. Early encounters between missionaries cite such

beliefs that when a child is born on earth, a mother mourns that child in the spiritual realm. See Kwasi Konadu, *On Our Way in This Part of the World: Biography of an African Community, Culture and Nation* (Durham, NC: Duke University Press, 2019), 63.

Chapter 6

1. Katrien Pype, "The Liveliness of Pentecostal/Charismatic Popular Culture in Africa," *Pentecostalism in Africa* 15 (2015): 358–360.

2. Michael Taussig, *Mimesis and Alterity: A Particular History of the Senses* (New York: Routledge, 1993), 2.

3. Birgit Meyer, "'Delivered from the Powers of Darkness': Confessions of Satanic Riches in Christian Ghana," *Africa* 65.2 (1995): 245.

4. Peter Horrobin, *Healing through Deliverance: The Biblical Basis* (Sovereign World, 1991), 101–102.

5. Madeline Manoukian writes of one particular phenomenon: animals, plants, and trees are believed to have spirits, but many are considered of little account because they have no power for evil. Those animals which have a powerful *sasa* (the bad, revengeful, hurtful element in a spirit; that part which must be "laid" or rendered innocuous) are designated as *sasa mmoa* (beasts with sasa): they include the elephant, the bongo, the duyker, the roan, the waterbuck, and certain others. When a hunter kills any of these, special funeral rites are held for the animal. Due to *sasa* these animals are not to be treated carelessly. Clearly this phenomenon does not apply in this case as we are not dealing with material animals. But the belief that animals or *sasa mmoa* could have a bad, revengeful, hurtful spirit persists. Madeline Manoukian, *Akan and Ga-Adangme Peoples: Western Africa* (New York: Routledge, 2017), 57.

6. John Parker, "Northern Gothic: Witches, Ghosts and Werewolves in the Savanna Hinterland of the Gold Coast, 1900s–1950s," *Africa* 76.3 (2006): 354.

7. Parker, "Northern Gothic," 358.

8. Parker, 366.

9. To be clear, this requires an interesting theological elasticity for Pentecostals. In most Christian traditions, animals are presumed to possess a prelapsarian innocence through creation. This innocence is not presumed in Pentecostalism for they could always already be a demon.

10. Hans Werner Debrunner, *Witchcraft in Ghana: A Study on the Belief in Destructive Witches and Its Effect on the Akan Tribes* (Accra: Presbyterian Book Depot, 1961), 48–52.

11. Onyinah, Opoku Onyinah, *Pentecostal Exorcism: Witchcraft and Demonology in Ghana* (Deo, 2012), 204.

12. Debrunner, *Witchcraft in Ghana*, 48–52.

13. Debrunner, 60.

14. Debrunner, 48–52.

15. Zakiyyah Iman Jackson, *Becoming Human: Matter and Meaning in an Anti-black World* (New York: New York University Press, 2020), 14.

16. Achille Mbembe, *On the Postcolony* (Berkeley: University of California Press, 2001), 2.

17. Gregory Delaplace, "What the Invisible Looks Like: Ghosts, Perceptual Faith, and Mongolian Regimes of Communication," in *The Social Life of Spirits*, ed. Ruy Blanes and Diana Espirito Santo (Chicago: University of Chicago Press, 2014), 54.

18. Delaplace, "What the Invisible Looks Like," 54.

19. Kristina Wirtz, "Spirit Materialities in Cuban Folk Religion," in *The Social Life of Spirits*, ed. Ruy Blanes and Diana Espirito Santo(Chicago: University of Chicago Press, 2014), 152.

20. Victoria Eto, *Exposition on Water Spirits* (Plummet Publishing, 2004), 38–39.

21. Eto, *Exposition on Water Spirits*, 18–19.

22. Eto, 18–19.

23. Paul Gifford, *Ghana's New Christianity: Pentecostalism in a Globalizing African Economy* (Bloomington: Indiana University Press, 2004), 100.

24. Gifford, *Ghana's New Christianity*, 100.

25. Gifford, 97.

26. Gifford, 98.

27. Jackson, *Becoming Human*, 53.

28. Mel Y. Chen, *Animacies: Biopolitics, Racial Mattering, and Queer Affect* (Durham, NC: Duke University Press, 2012).

29. Chen, *Animacies*, 11, 55.

30. Chen, 90.

31. Chen, 234.

32. Chen, 90.

33. Chen, 136.

34. Christina Elizabeth Sharpe, *In the Wake: On Blackness and Being* (Durham, NC: Duke University Press, 2016), 30.

35. Chen, *Animacies,* 13.

36. Chen, 128.

37. Chen, 128.

38. Chen, 129.

39. Chen, 129.

40. Chen, 104.

41. Jackson, *Becoming Human*, 31–32.

42. Sandra—like some others in this book—was not interviewed. The incredible crush of people at Emmanuel's deliverance services and the speed with which he moved from person to person made contact with many people utterly impossible.

43. Winthrop Jordan, Christopher Leslie Brown, and Peter H. Wood, *White over Black: American Attitudes toward the Negro, 1550–1812* (Chapel Hill: University of North Carolina Press, 2012), 32, 227, 230–232, 237. See also Keguro Macharia, *Frottage: Frictions of Intimacy across the Black Diaspora* (New York: New York University Press, 2019), 14–16.

44. Paul Christopher Johnson, "Possession's Native Land," *Ethnos* 84.4 (2019): 661–662.

45. Revelation 22:1 states: "Then the angel showed me the river of the water of life, bright as crystal, flowing from the throne of God and of the Lamb" (NRSV).

46. Exodus 22:19 states: "Whoever lies with an animal shall be put to death" (NRSV).

47. Jackson, *Becoming Human*, 101.

Conclusion

1. Dorothy Hodgson, "Embodying the Contradictions of Modernity: Gender and Spirit Possession among the Maasai in Tanzania," in *Gendered Encounters: Challenging Cultural Boundaries and Social Hierarchies in Africa*, ed. Maria Grosz-Ngate and Omari H. Kokole (New York: Routledge, 1998).

2. Birgit Meyer, "Modernity and Enchantment: The Image of the Devil in Popular African Christianity," in *Conversion to Modernities: The Globalization of Christianity*, ed. Peter van der Veer (New York: Routledge, 1996), 220. And Meyer, "'Make a Complete Break with the Past': Memory and Postcolonial Modernity in Ghanaian Pentecostalist Discourse," *Journal of Religion in Africa* 28.3 (1998): 340.

3. Paul Gifford, "The Complex Provenance of Some Elements of African Pentecostal Theology," in *Between Babel and Pentecost: Transnational Pentecostalism in Africa and Latin America,* ed. Andre Corten and Ruth Marshall-Fratani (Bloomington: Indiana University Press, 2001), 73.

4. Martin Lindhardt, *Power in Powerlessness: A Study of Pentecostal Life Worlds in Urban Chile* (Leiden: Brill, 2012), 194.

5. Birgit Meyer, "Magic, Mermaids and Modernity: The Attraction of Pentecostalism in Africa," *Etnofoor* 8.2 (1995): 64.

6. Meyer, "Magic, Mermaids and Modernity," 64.

7. Meyer, 64.

8. Greg Thomas, *The Sexual Demon of Colonial Power: Pan-African Embodiment and Erotic Schemes of Empire* (Bloomington: Indiana University Press, 2007), 154.

9. Walter D. Mignolo, "Foreword," in *Decolonizing Sexualities: Transnational*

Perspectives, Critical Interventions, ed. Sandeep Bakshi, Suhraiya Jivraj, and Silvia Posocco (Oxford: Counterpress, 2016), xii.

10. Meyer, for example, notes that Pentecostalism has often been connected to modernity.

11. Marcella Althaus-Reid, *Indecent Theology* (New York: Routledge, 2002), 103. Fanon writes similarly that Christianity "wages war on embryonic heresies and instincts, and on evil as yet unborn." See Frantz Fanon, *The Wretched of the Earth* (New York: Grove Press, 1963), 42.

12. Aliyyah I. Abdur-Rahman, *Against the Closet: Black Political Longing and the Erotics of Race* (Durham and London: Duke University Press, 2012), 3–6.

13. Meyer, "Magic, Mermaids and Modernity," 51.

14. Marcella Althaus-Reid, *The Queer God* (New York: Routledge, 2003), 52.

15. Althaus-Reid, *Queer God*, 135.

16. Bruce Lincoln, *Gods and Demons, Priests and Scholars: Critical Explorations in the History of Religions* (Chicago: University of Chicago Press, 2012), 39.

17. Charles Long, *Significations: Signs, Symbols, and Images in the Interpretation of Religions* (Aurora, CO: Davies Group, 1999), 4.

18. Long, *Significations*, 1.

19. There are many reasons to avoid reproducing genealogies. Genealogies or histories (especially histories of sexuality) have assumed a universality while averting their "gaze from its dark other." See Abdul R. JanMohamed, "Sexuality on/of the Racial Border," in *Discourses of Sexuality: From Aristotle to AIDS*, ed. Domna C. Stanton (Ann Arbor: University of Michigan Press, 1992), 116.

20. Georg W. F. Hegel, *Lectures on the Philosophy of World History*, ed. Johannes Hoffmeister, trans. H. B. Nisbet (Cambridge: Cambridge University Press, 1975), 99.

21. Jonathon O'Donnell, *Passing Orders: Demonology and Sovereignty in American Spiritual Warfare* (New York: Fordham University Press, 2021), 63.

22. David Brakke, "Ethiopian Demons: Male Sexuality, the Black-Skinned Other, and the Monastic Self," *Journal of the History of Sexuality* 10.3 and 4 (July/October 2001): 503.

23. Brakke, 507.

24. Abdul JanMohamed, *Manichean Aesthetics: The Politics of Literature in Colonial Africa* (Amherst: The University of Massachusetts Press, 1983), 269.

25. Brakke, "Ethiopian Demons," 506–513.

26. Brakke, 509–510.

27. Brakke, 527.

28. Brakke, 515.

29. Paul Christopher Johnson, "Possession's Native Land," *Ethnos* 84.4 (2019): 660.

30. Thomas, *The Sexual Demon of Colonial Power*, 7.

31. JanMohamed, *Manichean Aesthetics*, 36.

32. Johnson, "Possession's Native Land," 660.

33. Johnson, 661.

34. Johnson, 660–663.

35. Paul Christopher Johnson, *Spirited Things: The Work of "Possession" in Afro-Atlantic Religions* (Chicago: University of Chicago Press, 2014), 1.

36. For example, consider how the first verse of Rudyard Kipling's "The White Man's Burden," which stands as a celebratory hymn of coloniality, refers to the Other as "Half devil and half child."

37. Johnson, *Spirited Things*, 12.

38. Paul Christopher Johnson, "An Atlantic Genealogy of 'Spirit Possession,'" *Comparative Studies in Society and History* 53.2 (2011).

39. Thomas, *The Sexual Demon of Colonial Power*, 160.

40. Fanon, *The Wretched of the Earth*, 38, 41, and 45.

41. Fanon, 41.

42. Fanon, 41. In his footnotes, Fanon states, "We have demonstrated the mechanism of this Manichean world in Black Skin, White Masks." For such evidence see: Frantz Fanon, *Black Skin, White Masks* (New York: Grove Press, 2008), 27. There Fanon writes, "Apparently for her, Black and White represent the two poles of this world, poles in perpetual conflict: a genuinely Manichaean notion of the world. There, we've said it—Black or White, that is the question."

43. Fanon, *The Wretched of the Earth*, 40.

44. JanMohamed, *Manichean Aesthetics*, 4.

45. JanMohamed, 41.

46. JanMohamed, "Sexuality on/of the Racial Border," 106.

47. Homi K. Bhabha, *The Location of Culture* (New York: Routledge, 1994).

48. Althaus-Reid, *Queer God*, 38.

49. Keguro Macharia, *Frottage: Frictions of Intimacy across the Black Diaspora* (New York: New York University Press, 2019), 99.

50. Althaus-Reid, *Queer God*, 9.

51. Mignolo, "Foreword," xiv. Man in this case was (and still is) the Christian and White heterosexual from the West.

52. Thomas, *The Sexual Demon of Colonial Power*, 3.

53. JanMohamed, "Sexuality on/of the Racial Border," 106.

54. Fanon, *The Wretched of the Earth*, 41.

55. Jack Halberstam, *Wild Things: The Disorder of Desire* (Durham, NC: Duke University Press, 2020), 8.

56. Thomas, *The Sexual Demon of Colonial Power*, 7.

57. Michael T. Taussig, *The Devil and Commodity Fetishism in South America* (Chapel Hill, NC: University of North Carolina Press, 2010), 42.

58. Richard Brent Turner uses the term *self-signification* for what herein is referred to as countersignification. He defines it as "the counter-conception to the hegemonic discourse of an oppressive majority community." See Richard Brent Turner, *Islam in the African-American Experience*, 2nd ed. (Bloomington Indiana University Press, 2003), 3.

59. Turner, *Islam in the African-American Experience*, 3.

60. Long, *Significations*, 125–137.

61. L. H. Stallings, *Funk the Erotic: Transaesthetics and Black Sexual Cultures* (Urbana: University of Illinois Press, 2016), xii.

62. O'Donnell, *Passing Orders*, 8–9.

63. Althaus-Reid, *Queer God*, 134.

64. Katherine McKittrick, *Demonic Grounds: Black Women and the Cartographies of Struggle* (London: University of Minnesota Press, 2006), xxv.

65. In the interest of full disclosure, I never met Mensa Otabil nor does ICGC figure anywhere else into this book. I did attend a service and spend a few days at ICGC headquarters trying to find a recording I'd been made aware of by an interlocutor about Otabil and demons. However, the tape was never found, and everybody I asked doubted it ever existed, a conclusion I myself came to considering Otabil's recalcitrance around demons

66. A. Christian van Gorder, "Beyond the Rivers of Africa: The Afrocentric Pentecostalism of Mensa Otabil," *Pneuma* 30 (2008): 36.

67. Mensa Otabil, *Beyond the Rivers of Ethiopia* (Dallas, TX: Pneuma, 1992), 2.

68. Otabil, *Beyond the Rivers of Ethiopia*, 18.

69. Otabil, 15.

70. Otabil, 64.

71. Long, *Significations*, 74.

72. Van Gorder, "Beyond the Rivers of Africa," 35.

73. Fanon, *The Wretched of the Earth*, 55–58.

74. Fanon, 57. Fanon writes, "There are no limits—for in reality your purpose in coming together is to allow the accumulated libido, the hampered aggressivity, to dissolve as in a volcanic eruption. Symbolic killings, fantastic rides, imaginary mass murders—all must be brought out. The evil humors are undammed, and flow away with a din as of molten lava."

75. Fanon, 58.

76. Fanon, 56.

77. Fanon, *Black Skin*, xii.

78. JanMohamed, *Manichean Aesthetics*, 46.

79. Paul Stoller, *Embodying Colonial Memories: Spirit Possession, Power, and the Hauka in West Africa* (New York: Routledge, 1995), 90.

80. Raquel Romberg, "Ritual Piracy or Creolization with an Attitude," *NWIG: New West Indian Guide* 79.3/4 (2005): 175–218.

81. Jean Comaroff and John Comaroff, *Modernity and Its Malcontents: Ritual and Power in Postcolonial Africa* (Chicago: University of Chicago Press, 1993), xxii.

82. Jean Comaroff, *Body of Power, Spirit of Resistance: The Culture and History of a South African People* (Chicago: University of Chicago Press, 1985), 11.

83. Cf. JanMohamed, *Manichean Aesthetics*, 45–46.

84. Comaroff, *Body of Power*, 196.

85. Comaroff, *Body of Power*, 2.

86. Birgit Meyer, *Translating the Devil: Religion and Modernity among the Ewe in Ghana* (Trenton: Africa World Press, 1999), xxii.

87. Jared Sexton, *Black Men, Black Feminism: Lucifer's Nocturne* (New York: Palgrave Macmillan, 2017), 19. Cf. O'Donnell, *Passing Orders*, 153.

88. O'Donnell, 154.

89. Michael Taussig, *Shamanism, Colonialism, and the Wild Man: A Study in Terror and Healing* (Chicago: University of Chicago Press, 1987), 100.

90. Taussig, *Shamanism*, 100.

91. Althaus-Reid, *Queer God*, 134.

92. Halberstam, *Wild Things*, 27, 59.

93. Timothy Morton, "Guest Column: Queer Ecology," *Publications of the Modern Language Association of America* 125.2 (2010): 280.

94. Althaus-Reid, *Queer God*, 81.

95. Ashon Crawley, *Blackpentecostal Breath: The Aesthetics of Possibility* (Durham, NC: Duke University Press, 2016), 107–115.

96. Fanon, *The Wretched of the Earth*, 36.

97. Fanon, 41.

98. McKittrick, *Demonic Grounds*, xxiv.

99. McKittrick, xxiv.

100. Thomas, *The Sexual Demon of Colonial Power*, 160.

101. Thomas, 155.

Abdur-Rahman, Aliyyah I. *Against the Closet: Black Political Longing and the Erotics of Race*. Durham and London: Duke University Press, 2012.

Abosi, Kalu. *Born Twice: From Demonism to Christianity*. 1989.

Adelakun, Abimbola Adunni. *Powerful Devices: Prayer and the Political Praxis of Spiritual Warfare*. New Brunswick, NJ: Rutgers University Press, 2023.

Adelakun, Adewale. "Understanding Sexuality from the Security Gospel Perspective: Mountain of Fire and Miracles Ministries as a Case Study." *Hervormde Teologiese Studies/Theological Studies* 73.3 (2017): 1–6.

Agamben, Giorgio. *Nudities*. Translated by David Kishik and Stefan Pedatella. Stanford, CA: Stanford University Press, 2011.

Albrecht, Daniel E. *Rites in the Spirit: A Ritual Approach to Pentecostal/Charismatic Spirituality* (Journal of Pentecostal Theology Supplement Series 17). Sheffield: Sheffield Academic Press, 1999.

Althaus-Reid, Marcella. *Indecent Theology*. New York: Routledge, 2002.

Althaus-Reid, Marcella. *The Queer God*. New York: Routledge, 2003.

Asamoah-Gyadu, Kwabena. *African Charismatics: Current Developments within Independent Indigenous Pentecostalism in Ghana*. Leiden: Brill, 2005.

Atiemo, Abamfa. "Deliverance in the Charismatic Churches in Ghana." *Trinity Journal of Church and Theology* 4.2 (1994–5): 39–49.

Baer, Jonathan R. "Redeemed Bodies: The Functions of Divine Healing in Incipient Pentecostalism." *Church History* 70.4 (Dec. 2001): 735–771.

Banks, William. "Queering Ghana: Sexuality, Community, and the Struggle for Cultural Belonging in an African Nation." PhD diss., Wayne State University, 2013.

Bastian, Misty. "Married in the Water: Spirit Kin and Other Afflictions of Modernity in Southeastern Nigeria." *Journal of Religion in Africa* 27.2 (1997): 116–134.

Bataille, Georges. *Erotism: Death and Sensuality*. San Francisco: City Lights, 1986.

Bataille, Georges. *The Tears of Eros*. San Francisco: City Lights, 1989.

Beaudoin, Tom. "Postmodern Practical Theology." In *Opening the Field of Practical Theology: An Introduction*, edited by Kathleen A. Cahalan and Gordon S. Mikoski, 187–202. Lanham, MD: Rowman and Littlefield, 2014.

Beliso-De Jesus, Aisha M. *Electric Santeria: Racial and Sexual Assemblages of Transnational Religion*. New York: Columbia University Press, 2015.

Bhabha, Homi K. *The Location of Culture*. New York: Routledge, 1994.

Bialecki, Jon. "Quiet Deliverances." In *Practicing the Faith: The Ritual Life of Pentecostal-Charismatic Christians,* edited by Martin Lindhardt, 247–276. New York: Berghahn Books, 2011.

Blackman, Lisa. *Immaterial Bodies: Affect, Embodiment, Mediation*. London: Sage, 2012.

Boddy, Janice. "Colonialism: Bodies under Colonialism." In *A Companion to the Anthropology of the Body and Embodiment*, edited by Frances E. Mascia-Lees, 119–136. Oxford, UK: Wiley-Blackwell, 2011.

Bochow, Astrid. "Valentine's Day in Ghana: Youth, Sex and Secrets." In *Generations in Africa: Connections and Conflicts,* edited by Erdmute Alber, Sjaak van der Geest, and Susan Reynolds Whyte, 333–336. Berlin: LIT Verlag, 2008.

Brahinksy, Josh. "Pentecostal Body Logics: Cultivating a Modern Sensorium." *Cultural Anthropology,* 27.2 (2012): 215–238.

Brahinsky, Joshua. "Crossing the Buffer: Ontological Anxiety among US Evangelicals and an Anthropological Theory of Mind." *Journal of the Royal Anthropological Institute* 26.1 (2020): 45–60.

Brakke, David. "Ethiopian Demons: Male Sexuality, the Black-Skinned Other, and the Monastic Self." *Journal of the History of Sexuality* 10.3/4 (2001): 501–535.

Brouwer, Steve, Paul Gifford, and Susan D. Rose. *Exporting the American Gospel: Global Christian Fundamentalism*. New York: Routledge, 1996.

Brown, Candy Gunther. "Spiritual Property Rights to Bodily Practices: Pentecostal Views of Yoga and Meditation as Inviting Demonization." In *Annual Review of the Sociology of Religion. Volume 8: Pentecostals and the Body*, edited by Michael Wilkinson and Peter Althouse, 55–76. Leiden: Brill, 2017.

Brown, Rebecca. *He Came to Set the Captives Free*. New Kensington, PA: Whitaker House, 1986.

Brown, Rebecca. *Prepare for War*. New Kensington, PA: Whitaker House, 1987.

Chen, Mel Y. *Animacies: Biopolitics, Racial Mattering and Queer Affect*. Durham, NC: Duke University Press, 2012.

Coleman, Simon. *The Globalisation of Charismatic Christianity*. Cambridge: Cambridge University Press, 2000.

Collins, James. *Exorcism and Deliverance Ministry in the Twentieth Century: An Analysis of the Practice and Theology of Exorcism in Modern Western Christianity*. Eugene: Wipf and Stock Publishers, 2009.

Comaroff, Jean. *Body of Power, Spirit of Resistance: The Culture and History of a South African People*. Chicago: University of Chicago Press, 1985.

Comaroff, Jean and John Comaroff. *Modernity and Its Malcontents: Ritual and Power in Postcolonial Africa*. Chicago: University of Chicago Press, 1993.

Cooper, Travis Warren. "Worship Rituals, Discipline and Pentecostal-Charismatic 'Technique Du Corps' in the American Midwest." In *Annual Review of the Sociology of Religion. Volume 8: Pentecostals and the Body*, edited by Michael Wilkinson and Peter Althouse, 77–101. Leiden: Brill, 2017.

Corten, Andre, and Ruth Marshall-Fratani, eds. *Between Babel and Pentecost: Transnational Pentecostalism in Africa and Latin America*. Bloomington: Indiana University Press, 2001.

Couliano, Ioan P. *Eros and Magic in the Renaissance*. Chicago: University of Chicago Press, 1987.

Cox, Harvey. *Fire from Heaven: The Rise of Pentecostal Spirituality and the Reshaping of Religion in the Twenty-First Century*. Cambridge, MA: Da Capo Press, 1995.

Crawley, Ashon. *Blackpentecostal Breath: The Aesthetics of Possibility*. Durham, NC: Duke University Press, 2016.

Csordas, Thomas. "Embodiment as a Paradigm for Anthropology." *Ethnos* 18.1 (1990): 5–47.

Csordas, Thomas. *The Sacred Self: A Cultural Phenomenology of Charismatic Healing*. Berkley: University of California Press, 1997.

Csordas, Thomas. *Body/Meaning/Healing*. New York: Palgrave Macmillan, 2002.

Cuneo, Michael W. *American Exorcism: Expelling Demons in the Land of Plenty*. New York: Broadway Books, 2001.

Daniels, David. "'Gotta Moan Sometime': A Sonic Exploration of Earwitnesses to Early Pentecostal Sound in North America." *Pneuma* 30.1 (2008): 5–32.

Dankwa, Serena Owusua. "It's a Silent Trade: Female Same-Sex Intimacies in Post-Colonial Ghana." *NORA: Nordic Journal of Women's Studies* 17.3 (2009): 192–205.

Debrunner, Hans Werner. *Witchcraft in Ghana: A Study on the Belief in Destructive Witches and Its Effect on the Akan Tribes*. Accra: Presbyterian Book Depot, 1961.

Delaplace, Gregory. "What the Invisible Looks Like: Ghosts, Perceptual Faith, and Mongolian Regimes of Communication." In *The Social Life of Spirits*, edited by Ruy Blanes and Diana Espirito Santo, 52–68. Chicago: University of Chicago Press, 2014.

DeRogatis, Amy. *Saving Sex: Sexuality and Salvation in American Evangelicalism*. New York: Oxford University Press, 2015.

Desjarlais, Robert S. *Body and Emotion: The Aesthetics of Illness and Healing in the Nepal Himalayas*. Philadelphia: University of Pennsylvania Press, 1992.

De Witte, Marleen. "Accra's Sounds and Sacred Spaces." *International Journal of Urban and Regional Research* 32.3 (2008): 690–709.

De Witte, Marleen. "Touch." *Material Religion* 7.1 (2011): 148–155.

De Witte, Marleen. "Touched by the Spirit: Converting the Senses in a Ghanaian Charismatic Church." *Ethnos* 76.4 (2011): 489–509.

Eni, Emmanuel. *Delivered from the Powers of Darkness*. Kijabe: Kijabe Printing Press, 1987.

Eto, Victoria. *How I Served Satan: How I Served Satan Until Jesus Christ Delivered Me: A True Account of My Twenty One Experience as an Agent of Darkness and of My Deliverance by the Powerful Arm of God in Christ Jesus*. Shallom Christian Ministries International, 1981.

Eto, Victoria. *Exposition on Water Spirits*. Plummet Publishing, 2004.

Fanon, Frantz. *The Wretched of the Earth*. New York: Grove Press, 1963.

Fanon, Frantz. *Black Skin, White Masks*. New York: Grove Press, 2008.

Foucault, Michel. *Discipline & Punish: The Birth of the Prison*. New York: Knopf Doubleday, 2012.

Foucault, Michel. *The History of Sexuality: An Introduction, Volume 1*. New York: Knopf Doubleday, 2012.

Frueh, Erica. *Erotic Faculties*. Berkley: University of California Press, 1996.

Gifford, Paul. "The 'New' Christianity in Africa: The Charismatic Explosion." In *Exporting the American Gospel: Global Christian Fundamentalism*, edited by Steve Brouwer, Paul Gifford, and Susan D. Rose, 151–178. New York: Routledge, 1996.

Gifford, Paul. *African Christianity: Its Public Role*. London: Hurst and Co., 1998.

Gifford, Paul. "The Complex Provenance of Some Elements of African Pentecostal Theology," In *Between Babel and Pentecost: Transnational Pentecostalism in Africa and Latin America*, edited by Andre Corten and Ruth Marshall-Fratani, 62–79 (Bloomington: Indiana University Press, 2001).

Gifford, Paul. *Ghana's New Christianity: Pentecostalism in a Globalizing African Economy*. Bloomington: Indiana University Press, 2004.

Gifford, Paul. "Evil, Witchcraft, and Deliverance in the African Pentecostal Worldview." In *Pentecostal Theology in Africa*, edited by Clifton R. Clarke, 94–113. Eugene, OR: Pickwick Publications, 2014.

Geurts, Kathryn. *Culture and the Senses: Bodily Ways of Knowing in an African Community*. Berkley: University of California Press, 2003.

Geurts, Kathryn Linn, and Elvis Gershon Adikah. "Enduring and Endearing Feelings and the Transformation of Material Culture in West Africa." In *Sen-*

sible Objects: Colonialism, Museums and Material Culture, edited by Elizabeth Edwards, Chris Gosden, and Ruth B. Phillips, 35–70. New York: Berg, 2006.

Gopinath, Gayatri. *Unruly Visions: The Aesthetic Practices of Queer Diaspora.* Durham, NC: Duke University, 2018.

Hackett, Rosalind. "Discourses of Demonization in Africa and Beyond." *Diogenes* 50.3 (2003): 61–75.

Halberstam, Jack. *Wild Things: The Disorder of Desire.* Durham, NC: Duke University Press, 2020.

Hammond, Frank and Ida Mae. *Pigs in the Parlor.* Impact Books, 1973.

Haraway, Donna J. *Staying with the Trouble: Making Kin in the Chthulucene.* Durham, NC: Duke University Press, 2016.

Hegel, Georg W. F. *Lectures on the Philosophy of World History.* Edited by Johannes Hoffmeister, translated by H. B. Nisbet. Cambridge: Cambridge University Press, 1975.

Henriques, Julian. "The Vibrations of Affect and Their Propagation on a Night Out on Kingston's Dancehall Scene." *Body and Society* 16.1 (2010): 57–89.

Hirschkind, Charles. "The Ethics of Listening." *American Ethnologist* 28.3 (2001): 623–649.

Hodgson, Dorothy. "Embodying the Contradictions of Modernity: Gender and Spirit Possession among the Maasai in Tanzania." In *Gendered Encounters: Challenging Cultural Boundaries and Social Hierarchies in Africa,* edited by Maria Grosz-Ngate and Omari H. Kokole, 111–129. New York: Routledge, 1998.

Homewood, Nathanael. "The Supersensual Supernatural: Sexual Spirits in the History of Christianity." In *Religion: Super Religion,* edited by Jeffrey J. Kripal, 341–356. Detroit: Macmillan Reference USA, 2016.

Homewood, Nathanael. "I Was on Fire: The Challenge of Counter-intimacies within Zimbabwean Christianity." In *Public Religion and the Politics of Homosexuality in Africa,* edited by Adriaan van Klinken and Ezra Chitando, 243–259. New York: Routledge, 2016.

Homewood, Nathanael. "The Fantastic Fetus: The Fetus as a Super-Citizen in Ghanaian Pentecostalism." *Citizenship Studies Journal* 22.6 (2018): 618–632.

Homewood, Nathanael. "Wrestling with Homosexuality: Kinesthesia as Affect and Resistance in Ghanaian Pentecostalism." In *Embodying Black Religions in Africa and Its Diasporas,* edited by Jeanette Jouili and Yolanda Covington-Ward, 253–272. Durham, NC: Duke University Press, 2021.

Horrobin, Peter. *Healing through Deliverance: The Biblical Basis.* Sovereign World, 1991.

Howes, David. *The Sixth Sense Reader.* London: Bloomsbury Academic, 2009.

Hunt, Stephen. "Managing the Demonic: Some Aspects of the Neo-Pentecostal Deliverance Ministry." *Journal of Contemporary Religion* 13.2 (1998): 215–230.

Institoris, Heinrich and Jakob Sprenger. *Malleus Maleficarum, Translated with an Introduction, Bibliography and Notes by the Rev. Montague Summers.* London: Pushkin Press, 1948.

Izugbara, Chimaraoke O. "Sexuality and the Supernatural in Africa." In *African Sexualities: A Reader,* edited by Sylvia Tamale, 533–558. Cape Town: Pambazuka Press, 2011.

Jackson , Michael and Albert Piette. *What Is Existential Anthropology?* New York: Berghahn Books, 2015.

Jackson, Zakiyyah Iman. *Becoming Human: Matter and Meaning in an Antiblack World.* New York: New York University Press, 2020.

JanMohamed, Abdul R. "Sexuality on/of the Racial Border." In *Discourses of Sexuality: From Aristotle to AIDS,* edited by Domna C. Stanton, 94–117. Ann Arbor: University of Michigan Press, 1992.

JanMohamed, Abdul. *Manichean Aesthetics: The Politics of Literature in Colonial Africa.* Amherst: University of Massachusetts Press, 1983.

Johnson, Paul Christopher. "Possession's Native Land." *Ethnos* 84.4 (2019): 660–677.

Johnson, Paul Christopher. *Spirited Things: The Work of "Possession" in Afro-Atlantic Religions.* Chicago: University of Chicago Press, 2014.

Johnson, Paul Christopher. "An Atlantic Genealogy of 'Spirit Possession.'" *Comparative Studies in Society and History* 53.2 (2011): 393–425.

Jordan, Winthrop, Christopher Leslie Brown, and Peter H. Wood. *White over Black: American Attitudes toward the Negro, 1550–1812.* Chapel Hill: University of North Carolina Press, 2012.

Kalleres, Dayna S. *City of Demons: Violence, Ritual, and Christian Power in Late Antiquity.* Berkeley: University of California Press, 2015.

Kalu, Ogbu. *African Pentecostalism: An Introduction.* Oxford: Oxford University Press, 2008.

Kaunda, Chammah J. *Genders, Sexualities, and Spiritualities in African Pentecostalism: '"Your Body is a Temple of the Holy Spirit."* New York: Palgrave Macmillan, 2020.

Kearney, Richard, and Brian Treanor. *Carnal Hermeneutics.* New York: Fordham University Press, 2015.

Kearney, Richard. "The Wager of Carnal Hermeneutics." In *Carnal Hermeneutics,* edited by Richard Kearny and Brian Treanor, 15–56. New York: Fordham University Press, 2015.

Kenyatta, Jomo. *Facing Mount Kenya: The Tribal Life of the Gikuyu.* London: Mercury, 1961 [1938].

Kenyon, E.W. *The Two Kinds of Knowledge.* Kenyon's Gospel Publishing Society, 1942.

Knust, Jennifer Wright. *Unprotected Texts: The Bible's Surprising Contradictions about Sex and Desire.* New York: HarperOne, 2011.

Konadu, Kwasi. *On Our Way in This Part of the World: Biography of an African Community, Culture and Nation.* Durham, NC: Duke University Press, 2019.

Krondorfer, Bjorn. *Men and Masculinities in Christianity and Judaism: A Critical Reader.* London: SCM Press, 2009.

Laqueur, Thomas. *Solitary Sex: A Cultural History of Masturbation.* New York: Zone Books, 2003.

Laycock, Joseph. "Carnal Knowledge: The Epistemology of Sexual Trauma in Witches' Sabbaths, Satanic Ritual Abuse, and Alien Abduction Narratives." *Preternature: Critical and Historical Studies on the Preternatural* 1.1 (2012): 100–129.

Lincoln, Bruce. *Gods and Demons, Priests and Scholars: Critical Explorations in the History of Religions.* Chicago: University of Chicago Press, 2012.

Lindhardt, Martin Lindhart, *Power in Powerlessness: A Study of Pentecostal Life Worlds in Urban Chile.* Leiden: Brill, 2012.

Long, Charles. *Significations: Signs, Symbols, and Images in the Interpretation of Religions.* Aurora, CO: Davies Group, 1999.

Luhrmann, Tanya. "Metakinesis: How God Becomes Intimate in Contemporary U.S. Christianity." *American Anthropologist* 106.3 (2004): 518–528.

McCloud, Sean. *American Possessions: Fighting Demons in the Contemporary United States.* Oxford: Oxford University Press, 2015.

McKittrick, Katherine. *Demonic Grounds: Black Women and the Cartographies of Struggle.* Minneapolis: University of Minnesota Press, 2006.

Macharia, Keguro. *Frottage: Frictions of Intimacy across the Black Diaspora.* New York: New York University Press, 2019.

Maffesoli, Michel. "Orgy: An Overview." In *Encyclopedia of Religion,* edited by Lindsay Jones, 6861. Detroit: Macmillan Reference USA, 2005.

Maggi, Armando. *Satan's Rhetoric: A Study of Renaissance Demonology.* Chicago: University of Chicago Press, 2001.

Maggi, Armondo. *In the Company of Demons: Unnatural Beings, Love, and Identity in the Italian Renaissance.* Chicago: University of Chicago Press, 2006.

Manoukian, Madeline. *Akan and Ga-Adangme Peoples: Western Africa.* New York: Routledge, 2017.

Martin, John. "Metakinesis." In *What Is Dance? Readings in Theory and Criticism,* edited by Roger Copeland and Marshall Cohen, 23–24. Oxford: Oxford University Press, 1983.

Martin, Malachi. *Hostage to the Devil: The Possession and Exorcism of Five Contemporary Americans.* New York: HarperOne, 1992.

Mbembe, Achille. *On the Postcolony.* Berkeley: University of California Press, 2001.

Meyer, Birgit. "'If You Are a Devil, You Are a Witch, and If You Are a Witch, You Are a Devil.' The Integration of 'Pagan' Ideas into the Conceptual Universe of Ewe Christians in Southeastern Ghana." *Journal of Religion in Africa* 22.2 (1992): 98–132.

Meyer, Birgit. "'Delivered from the Powers of Darkness': Confessions of Satanic Riches in Christian Ghana." *Africa* 65.2 (1995): 236–255.

Meyer, Birgit. "Magic, Mermaids and Modernity: The Attraction of Pentecostalism in Africa." *Etnofoor* 8.2 (1995): 47–67.

Meyer, Birgit. "Modernity and Enchantment: The Image of the Devil in Popular African Christianity." In *Conversion to Modernities: The Globalization of Christianity*, edited by Peter van der Veer, 199–230. New York: Routledge, 1996.

Meyer, Birgit. "'Make a Complete Break with the Past': Memory and Postcolonial Modernity in Ghanaian Pentecostalist Discourse." *Journal of Religion in Africa* 28.3 (1998): 316–349.

Meyer, Birgit. "Commodities and the Power of Prayer: Pentecostalist Attitudes towards Consumption in Contemporary Ghana." *Development and Change* 29.4 (1998): 751–776.

Meyer, Birgit. *Translating the Devil: Religion and Modernity among the Ewe in Ghana.* Trenton: Africa World Press, 1999.

Meyer, Birgit. "Visions of Blood, Sex and Money: Fantasy Spaces in Popular Ghanaian Cinema." *Visual Anthropology* 16.1 (2003): 15–41.

Meyer, Birgit. *Sensational Movies: Video, Vision, and Christianity in Ghana.* Berkley: University of California Press, 2015.

Mignolo, Walter D. "Foreword." In *Decolonizing Sexualities: Transnational Perspectives, Critical Interventions*, edited by Sandeep Bakshi, Suhraiya Jivraj, and Silvia Posocco, vii–xxii. Oxford: Counterpress, 2016.

Mignolo, Walter, and Rolando Vazquez. "Decolonial Aesthesis: Colonial Wounds/ Decolonial Healings." *Social Text*, July 15, 2013. https://socialtextjournal.org/periscope_article/decolonial-aesthesis-colonial-woundsdecolonial-healings/.

Mittermaier, Amira. *Dreams That Matter: Egyptian Landscapes of the Imagination.* Berkeley: University of California Press, 2011.

Moberg, Jessica. "Maintaining Sexual Purity: Ritualized, Embodied and Spatial Strategies among Neo-Charismatics in Stockholm." In *Annual Review of the Sociology of Religion. Volume 8: Pentecostals and the Body*, edited by Michael Wilkinson and Peter Althouse, 239–255. Leiden: Brill, 2017.

Morton, Timothy. "Guest Column: Queer Ecology." *Publications of the Modern Language Association of America* 125.2 (2010): 273–282.

Moultrie, Monique. *Passionate and Pious: Religious Media and Black Women's Sexuality.* Durham, NC: Duke University Press, 2017.

Noland, Carrie. *Agency and Embodiment*. Cambridge, MA: Harvard University Press, 2009.

Nyanzi, S. "Queering Queer Africa." In *Reclaiming Afrikan: Queer Perspectives on Sexual and Gender Identities*, curated by Zethu Matebeni, 61–66. Athlone: Modjaji Books, 2014.

Obadare, Ebenezer. *Pastoral Power, Clerical State: Pentecostalism, Gender, and Sexuality in Nigeria*. Notre Dame, IN: University of Notre Dame Press, 2022.

O'Donnell, S. Jonathon. *Passing Orders: Demonology and Sovereignty in American Spiritual Warfare*. New York: Fordham University Press, 2021.

Onyinah, Opoku. *Pentecostal Exorcism: Witchcraft and Demonology in Ghana*. Dorchester, UK: Deo, 2012.

Otabil, Mensa. *Beyond the Rivers of Ethiopia*. Dallas, TX: Pneuma, 1992.

P'Bitek, Okot. *Decolonizing African Religions: A Short History of African Religions in Western Scholarship*. New York: Diasporic Africa Press, 2011.

Parker, John. "Northern Gothic: Witches, Ghosts and Werewolves in the Savanna Hinterland of the Gold Coast, 1900s-1950s." *Africa* 76.3 (2006): 352–380.

Percy, Martyn. "Sweet Rapture: Subliminal Eroticism in Contemporary Charismatic Worship." *Theology and Sexuality* 6 (1997): 71–106.

Pinn, Anthony. *Embodiment and the New Shape of Black Theological Thought*. New York: New York University Press, 2010.

Prince, Derek. *They Shall Expel Demons: What You Need to Know about Demons–Your Invisible Enemies*. Chosen Books, 1998.

Pype, Katrien. "Dancing for God or the Devil: Pentecostal Discourse on Popular Dance in Kinshasa." *Journal of Religion in Africa* 36.3/4 (2006): 296–318.

Pype, Katrien. "Dreaming the Apocalypse: Mimesis and the Pentecostal Imagination in Kinshasa." *Paideuma* 57 (2011): 81–96.

Pype, Katrien. "The Liveliness of Pentecostal/Charismatic Popular Culture in Africa." *Pentecostalism in Africa* 15 (2015): 345–378.

Quayesi-Amakye, Joseph. *Prophetism in Ghana Today: A Study on Trends in Ghanaian Pentecostal Prophetism*. Scotts Valley, CA: CreateSpace, 2013.

Reid-Pharr, Robert. *Black Gay Man: Essays*. New York: New York University Press, 2001.

Reiling, J. "Unclean Spirits." In *Dictionary of Deities and Demons in the Bible*, edited by Karel van der Toorn, Bob Becking, and Pieter W. van der Horst, 882. Grand Rapids, MI: William B. Eerdmans, 1999.

Reinhardt, Bruno. "Soaking in Tapes: The Haptic Voice of Global Pentecostal Pedagogy in Ghana." *Journal of the Royal Anthropological Institute* 20.2 (2014): 315–336.

Rey, Jeanne. "Mermaids and Spirit Spouses: Rituals as Technologies of Gender in Transnational African Pentecostal Spaces." *Religion and Gender* 3.1 (2013): 60–75.

Romberg, Raquel. "Ritual Piracy or Creolization with an Attitude." *NWIG: New West Indian Guide* 79.3/4 (2005): 175–218.

Roof, Judith. "Orgy." *Encyclopedia of Sex and Gender, Vol. 3*, edited by Fedwa Malti-Douglas, 1095–1096. Detroit: Macmillan Reference USA, 2007.

Sexton, Jared. *Black Men, Black Feminism: Lucifer's Nocturne*. New York: Palgrave Macmillan, 2017.

Sharpe, Christina Elizabeth. *In the Wake: On Blackness and Being*. Durham, NC: Duke University Press, 2016.

Shipley, Jesse Weaver. "Comedians, Pastors and the Miraculous Agency of Charisma in Ghana." *Cultural Anthropology* 24 (2009): 523–552.

Smith, James K. A. *Thinking in Tongues: Pentecostal Contributions to Christian Philosophy*. Grand Rapids, MI: William B. Eerdmans, 2010.

Smith, Jonathan Z. *Map Is Not Territory: Studies in the History of Religions*. Chicago: University of Chicago Press, 1978.

Stallings, L. H. *Funk the Erotic: Transaesthetics and Black Sexual Cultures*. Urbana: University of Illinois Press, 2016.

Stephens, Walter. *Demon Lovers: Witchcraft, Sex and the Crisis of Belief*. Chicago: University of Chicago Press, 2001.

Stoller, Paul. *Embodying Colonial Memories: Spirit Possession, Power, and the Hauka in West Africa*. New York: Routledge, 1995.

Sugden, Edward. *Wesley's Standard Sermons, Version 2*. London: Epworth, 1964.

Taussig, Michael. *Shamanism, Colonialism, and the Wild Man: A Study in Terror and Healing*. Chicago: University of Chicago Press, 1987.

Taussig, Michael. *Mimesis and Alterity: A Particular History of the Senses*. New York: Routledge, 1993.

Taussig, Michael T. *The Devil and Commodity Fetishism in South America*. Chapel Hill, NC: University of North Carolina Press, 2010.

Thomas, Greg. *The Sexual Demon of Colonial Power: Pan-African Embodiment and Erotic Schemes of Empire*. Bloomington: Indiana University Press, 2007.

Thurschwell, Pamela. "The Erotics of Telepathy: The British SPR's Experiments in Intimacy." In *The Sixth Sense Reader*, edited by David Howes, 183–208. London: Bloomsbury Academic, 2009.

Toepfer, Karl Eric. *Theatre, Aristocracy, and Pornocracy: The Orgy Calculus*. New York: PAJ Publications, 1991.

Tola, Florencia. "The Materiality of 'Spiritual Presences' and the Notion of Person in and Amerindian Society." In *The Social Life of Spirits*, edited by Ruy Blanes and Diana Espirito Santo, 69–92. Chicago: University of Chicago Press, 2014.

Turner, Bryan S. *The Body and Society*. Los Angeles: Sage, 1984.

Turner, Richard Brent. *Islam in the African-American Experience*, 2nd ed. Bloomington: Indiana University Press, 2003.

Van de Kamp, Linda. "Love Therapy: A Brazilian Pentecostal (Dis)Connection in Maputo." *The Social Life of Connectivity in Africa*, edited by Mirjam de Bruijn and Rijk van Dijk, 203–225. New York: Palgrave Macmillan, 2012.

Van de Kamp, Linda. "Converting the Spirit Spouse: The Violent Transformation of the Pentecostal Female Body in Maputo, Mozambique." *Ethnos: Journal of Anthropology* 76.4 (2011): 510–533.

van Dijk, Rijk. "Contesting Silence: The Ban on Drumming and the Musical Politics of Pentecostalism in Ghana." *Ghana Studies* 4 (2001): 31–64.

Van Gorder, A. Christian. "Beyond the Rivers of Africa: The Afrocentric Pentecostalism of Mensa Otabil." *Pneuma* 30 (2008): 33–54.

Van Klinken, Adriaan. "Gay Rights, the Devil and the End Times: Public Religion and the Enchantment of the Homosexuality Debate in Zambia." *Religion* 43.4 (2013), 519–540.

Vinge, Louise. *The Five Senses: Studies in a Literary Tradition*. Lund: Liber Laromedel, 1975.

Vogel, Susan M. *African Art, Western Eyes*. New Haven, CT: Yale University Press, 1997.

Wacker, Grant. *Heaven Below: Early Pentecostals and American Culture*. Cambridge, MA: Harvard University Press, 2001.

Wariboko, Nimi. *Pentecostal Principle: Ethical Methodology in New Spirit*. Grand Rapids, MI: William B. Eerdmans, 2012.

Wariboko, Nimi. *Nigerian Pentecostalism*. Rochester, NY: University of Rochester Press, 2014.

White, David Gordon. *Daemons Are Forever: Contacts and Exchanges in the Eurasian Pandemonium*. Chicago: University of Chicago Press, 2021.

Wilkinson, Michael. "Pentecostalism, the Body and Embodiment." In *Annual Review of the Sociology of Religion. Volume 8: Pentecostals and the Body*, edited by Michael Wilkinson and Peter Althouse, 15–35. Leiden: Brill, 2017.

Wilkinson, Michael, and Peter Althouse. *Annual Review of the Sociology of Religion. Volume 8: Pentecostals and the Body*. Leiden: Brill, 2017.

Wiredu, Kwasi. "Introduction: Decolonizing African Philosophy and Religion." In *Decolonizing African Religions: A Short History of African Religions in Western Scholarship* by Okot P'Bitek, xi–xxxvii. New York: Diasporic Africa Press, 2011.

Wirtz, Kristina. "Spirit Materialities in Cuban Folk Religion." In *The Social Life of Spirits*, edited by Ruy Blanes and Diana Espirito Santo, 126–156. Chicago: University of Chicago Press, 2014.

Endnotes are indicated by "n" followed by the endnote number.

SP SPIRITUAL PHENOMENA
TANYA LUHRMANN and ANN TAVES, Series Editors

Spiritual Phenomena features investigations of events, experiences, and objects, both unusual and everyday, that people characterize as spiritual, paranormal, magical, occult and/or supernatural. Working from the presupposition that the status of such phenomena is contested, it seeks to understand how such determinations are made in a variety of historical and cultural contexts. Books in this series explore how such phenomena are identified, experienced, and understood; the role that spontaneity and cultivation play in the process; and the similarities and differences in the way phenomena are appraised and categorized across time and cultures. The editors encourage work that is ethnographic, historical, or psychological, and, in particular, work that uses more than one method to understand these complex phenomena, ranging from the qualitative to quantitative surveys and laboratory-based experiments.

Hugh Turpin, *Unholy Catholic Ireland: Religious Hypocrisy, Secular Morality, and Irish Irreligion*

Alicia Puglionesi, *Common Phantoms: An American History of Psychic Science*

Yoram Bilu, *With Us More Than Ever: Making the Absent Rebbe Present in Messianic Chabad*

David J. Halperin, *Intimate Alien: The Hidden Story of the UFO*

J. Bradley Wigger, *Invisible Companions: Encounters with Imaginary Friends, Gods, Ancestors, and Angels*

Kelly Bulkeley, *Lucrecia the Dreamer, Prophecy, Cognitive Science, and the Spanish Inquisition*

The authorized representative in the EU for product safety and compliance is:
Mare Nostrum Group
B.V Doelen 72
4831 GR Breda
The Netherlands

www.ingramcontent.com/pod-product-compliance
Lightning Source LLC
Chambersburg PA
CBHW030338270326
41926CB00009B/876

* 9 7 8 1 5 0 3 6 3 8 0 6 8 *